Voice of Carlo

*The Autobiography of
William Farrell*

VOICE OF REBELLION
CARLOW 1798

The Autobiography of
WILLIAM FARRELL

Introduction by
Patrick Bergin

Edited by Roger McHugh

WOLFHOUND PRESS
& in US and Canada
Irish American Book Company

This edition 1998
Published by
WOLFHOUND PRESS Ltd
68 Mountjoy Square
Dublin 1
Tel: (353-1) 874 0354
Fax: (353-1) 872 0207

Published in US and Canada by
The Irish American Book Company
6309 Monarch Park Place
Niwot, Colorado 80503
USA

First Published, Dublin 1949 as *Carlow in '98*

Copyright © 1949, 1998

All rights reserved. No part of this book may be reproduced or utilised in any form or by any means digital, electronic or mechanical including photography, filming, recording, photocopying, or by any information storage and retrieval system or shall not, by way of trade or otherwise, be lent, resold or otherwise circulated in any form of binding or cover other than that in which it is published without the prior permission of the publisher.

 Wolfhound Press receives financial assistance from The Arts Council/An Chomhairle Ealaíon, Dublin, Ireland.

British Library cataloguing in Publication data
A catalogue record for this book is available from the British Library.

ISBN 0 86327 687 3

Cover Design: Wolfhound Press/ Reprolink
Cover Photograph: Bill Doyle
Printed in Scotland by Caledonian Book Manufacturing

151

struggles of the man that was dying before me and Endeavoured to pray as well as I could but In a little time some One came behind me and called me by my name — I turned round and perceived it was Mr Robert Rochfort, Brother to the Colonel — Now Farrell, said he you have only a few minutes to live and I would recommend It to you to give whatever Information Is In your power In order to put a stop to this Unfortunate rebellion you were Engaged In It is the only atonement you can make to your Country for all the blood that has been spilled and you should do it to the Utmost Extent In your power as it may be a Means of stopping it altogether preventing more bloodshed and restoring peace — I wish It was In my power to stop it Sir said I — When I was at liberty I done my best to stop it and would do it again if I could but I could give no Information now that would be of the least use — That is very strange said he turning away — I immediately turned round and resumed my position as before and In a Minute or two he came back and called me again — Now Farrell said he from the deep manner you were Implicated In this business you must of course have a very Extensive Knowledge of Men concerned In it and the Gentlemen have taken your case Into consideration and wish to shew you all the Lenity they can and they have now commissioned me to tell you that If you give Information against these Men so as they may be brought to justice you shall have your life — Don't be led away with the foolish notion that it would be any discredit to you to give Information against them it would be the very reverse you would serve your Country by helping to restore peace and you would serve the wretched people themselves because the sooner rebellion was put down the sooner bloodshed would cease and if you were apprehensive of any danger from them you should be protected at the Castle Or sent abroad to any place you wished — It is not In my power Sir, to give Information against them — Impossible! said he

Facsimile page of original manuscript, reproduced by courtesy of Mrs. Alice Kane Smith

CONTENTS

Introduction by Patrick Bergin ix
Preface by Roger McHugh xiii
Chapter One — Green Years 1
Chapter Two — Background of Revolt 14
Chapter Three — United Irishmen All 27
Chapter Four — Preparations and Premonitions 41
Chapter Five — Men and Shadows 54
Chapter Six — Treachery and Terror 64
Chapter Seven — Eve of the Rising 76
Chapter Eight — Woe to the Conquered 88
Chapter Nine — Jail Journal 102
Chapter Ten — The Executions 113
Chapter Eleven — Interrogation and Intercession 131
Chapter Twelve — Lottery of Death 148
Chapter Thirteen — Suspense 166
Chapter Fourteen — Court-Martial 180
Chapter Fifteen — The Gallows' Steps 197
Chapter Sixteen — Discords of Liberty 205
Chapter Seventeen — Last Glances 223

Introduction by Patrick Bergin

Dear Reader,

The book that you are now holding is an exact copy of *Carlow in '98*, a work that lived on our bookshelf at home for as long as I can remember.

My father, Senator Paddy Bergin, constantly referred to it and encouraged us to read it. He had been a county councillor in Carlow and deeply involved with the politics of both the town and county. His father before him, my grandfather, was the railway signalman for the town and lived in a house called *Blue Bell* which is still there.

My mother's family were Galbally and Granny Galbally's maiden name was Wall. She was related to Mick Wall, mentioned in chapter nine. He was one of the many men tortured and dragged through the town. He did not inform and his brave last words, not recorded here but as remembered by my Gran, were: 'I shall leave only one widow.'

There were many stories, including those from Farrell's autobiography, told in our house in my childhood, and many of the names and places in those stories exist to this day. So for sentimental reasons *Carlow in '98: The Autobiography of William Farrell* has a treasured place in my heart.

As the '98 bicentenary approached and numerous memorial events were being planned from Antrim to Wexford and here too in Carlow, I kept an eye out for the republication of this book but to my great surprise discovered that it was not to be. Most of the focus was to be on Wexford, Vinegar Hill and related happenings. I mentioned the book to government ministers and their secretaries; I asked ambassadors; I questioned historians as to whether they had read *Carlow in '98*. For the most part I found total ignorance not only of the book but of the relevance and extent of the events in Carlow. 'What happened in Carlow?' was the surprised reply. So, I felt it my duty to do something about the situation. I contacted Seamus Cashman, the publisher at Wolfhound Press, who immediately saw the importance of this document and account of events, and I am thankful that he agreed to reprint the book.

Probably the single most important aspect of the book is the fact that it is an eyewitness account of the events of 1798. It is written by a man who was there and who lived through the build-up and aftermath of the horror. It is written with passion but also with care and clarity and concern for accuracy, in a style that will remind many of the great writers of the eighteenth and nineteenth centuries. There are wonderfully detailed descriptions of an Irish county town of the time, accounts of social events such as handball competitions and May Day celebrations, and of course vivid character descriptions making many of the people come alive again. Most graphic of all are the writer's accounts of events themselves, recreating all the shock and horror of the terrible conflict with its tortures and hangings. These eyewitness accounts make this book crucial to our understanding, showing readers these events through the eyes of one who was there.

I urge you to read this extraordinary book. It is a largely ignored and unknown classic of Irish historical literature. May it awaken interest and understanding and encourage reconciliation and peace.

With regards to the memory of my father, the people of Carlow, and the spirit of William Farrell —

I remain yours sincerely,

Patrick Connolly Bergin

To the Memory

of

THEO DILLON

the Editor's small part in this
book is dedicated

PREFACE

THIS ACCOUNT of the rising of 1798 in Carlow was written by William Farrell, an eyewitness of its bloody events. He gives us its background, an Irish country town in the eighteenth century, shows us its inhabitants at school or trade, spending their leisure hours hurling and playing handball, celebrating May Day or attending volunteer parades. The greater part of his record concerns his own relations with the United Irishmen and his sufferings during the scenes of terror and of slaughter which followed the suppression of the rising. These scenes were etched into his mind by fear and remorse. Farrell himself experienced a lottery of death in which men's lives were staked on the chance of a song, the fashion of a haircut, the favour of a jailer or the mood of a militiaman. He describes such things with a simplicity which is starkly graphic. Reading his account one stands beside the brothers Maher as they are scourged to death or sees Michael Heydon walking to the scaffold " as unconcerned as if he was going to some place of amusement " or hears Michael Wall cry out to his torturers to put an end to his sufferings by killing him ; and so one understands the fate of the rank and file of the insurrectionary movement of that time, the tremendous odds against which they struggled, their simple heroism, their defeat and despair. The fate of such men is not often recorded in history, though it lives on in the tradition of such places as Carlow. But here at least it is inscribed permanently for all to read.

That is one reason why I think Farrell's book will live. Another reason is the skill with which his narrative is unfolded. He was a man of considerable literary talents, improved by his taste in reading and by his early exercises in composition. Pope, Swift, Goldsmith were his favourite authors and his graphic writing probably owes much to them. The greatest literary influence he experienced was Homer, in Pope's translation, which he read during his formative years, and something of the truth and force which he praises in Homer's " description of the different scenes in the council or in the field " is to be found in his own account of similar events. When he is narrating Farrell is at his best. In expressing opinions, which he does only occasionally, he is inclined to rant and to grow tedious. His arguments against England and against the United Irish system are somewhat overdone and are often mutually contradictory; they lead him to maintain, for instance, that the examples of France and of America were a shining light to oppressed nations but that only a nation of heroes like the French could hope to win freedom. His sense of defeat and of the deterioration of his country after the Union is partly responsible and there is discernible in his attitude a certain uneasiness about his defection from the United Irishmen which, I think, leads him to minimize the chances of successful revolution in Ireland at that time. Yet there is some weight to his suggestions for the material improvement of Ireland and to his criticism of the laxity of the revolutionary organization. Incidentally, his suggestion about drilling with pitchforks rather than with pikes in order to " keep o' the windy side of the law " was advanced by John Mitchel about fifty years later in the columns of the *United Irishman*. Farrell's blows to right and left, at any rate, do not throw him off balance in describing what he saw and heard.

Many of his portraits of the figures of that time come alive in his lines. Here, for example, is Major Dennis, who interrogated him :

" He was a man about five feet eight inches high, broad and strong made, very much in flesh all over, but particularly prominent in the belly, remarkably full in the face, which was as red as scarlet and he might be about forty years of age. He was particularly attentive to every article of his dress. He always had the very finest and highest coloured scarlet cloth in his coat, white Marseilles waistcoat, blue pantaloons and cocked hat and feather and though he might be near sixteen stone weight, still he showed a great deal of action and strength. . . . He was leaning back in awful majesty in his chair, with his arms folded, his hat on and the side cock foremost, his large swollen face and coat so exactly of a colour that there was scarcely a shade of difference between them."

This is a portrait which might be envied by any novelist. But the character which emerges most alive from the book is that of the author himself.

William Farrell wrote his account between 1832 and 1845, when he was an old man employed as gate-keeper of a public institution in Carlow. His manuscript consists of 187 parchment pages bound roughly between tattered leather covers. The handwriting is fairly close but distinct and the manuscript is in excellent condition. Farrell's express wish was that it should not be published until after his death. At one time it was preserved by the late Professor Robert Donovan of my own university and it is now the property of Mrs. Alice Kane Smith of Carlow, through whose courtesy this edition appears. I have chosen to present it in this form, as a human document of general interest, rather than in a scholarly annotated edition of the original text. But only such alterations as were necessary to make the narrative clear to the reader have been made and these were comparatively slight; the division of the account into titled chapters, the recasting of a few sentences, better punctuation, one or two changes in spelling. The author's occasional grammatical errors are on the whole preserved, for they fit in with his own account of himself and rather emphasize than diminish the worth of his general achievement, an achievement which belongs to history and, I think, to literature.

Men repay their debt to their country in various ways and not always as they have designed. If Farrell had fought for the cause which he believed lost before the attempt to assert it in arms in Carlow was made, there is little doubt that he would have perished beside men of unflinching determination such as Michael Heydon. Where the rank and influence of Sir Edward Crosbie could not save his own neck it is certain that Farrell would not have escaped the gallows. The miracle is that under the circumstances he escaped at all. He was twenty-six years old when that happened. He was sixty when he began this account and seventy-three when he finished it. The most terrible irony overhangs his last lines for, full of hope for the future of his country as they are, they were written as the most devastating of our famines began. Yet, though the work of this obscure Irishman may point to conclusions other than those he intended, his debt was amply paid.

ROGER McHUGH.

University College,
Dublin.

CHAPTER ONE

GREEN YEARS

I was born in the beginning of the year 1772, just at the time when the Penal Laws, after having robbed and destroyed the country, stood still for want of more work or for want of opposition. In fact, if gratification could find its way into hell, there could be hardly a more gratifying spectacle to infernal malice than to see one portion of Adam's race succeed so well in making the other so supremely miserable. The robbery did not stop with the temporal property of the hapless sufferers. No, it was too subtle, too refined to stop there. The managers knew well that as long as the mind is free and enlightened it is not so easy to keep the body enslaved, so they seized on their mental property (by far the most valuable part) and robbed them of their education, their knowledge and even of their very language. So deeply did their successful oppressors sink them in barbarism, that they lost all notions of their origin or that their ancestors ever swayed the sceptre of royalty in the country and actually thought they were fitted by nature and designed for abject slavery and that their ruthless oppressors were almost sprung from the heathen gods. Nothing in fact could exceed the lowly submission on the one side or the boundless, insulting, consequential pride on the other.

It is mentioned by Doctor Curry in one of his works (I believe it is his history of the civil wars) that there were twenty-four families of the O'Farrell's robbed of their estates in the County Longford and sent wanderers on the world, wherever chance or Providence might direct, to be hewers of wood and drawers of water, without knowing "One spot of all the world their own," a sad, sad change to the descendants of the Kings of Annaly. It certainly was extraordinary to see so many of one name having estates to lose in one county.

My grandfather, Ambrose Farrell, without map, chart or compass steered his way into Dublin, where he kept a respectable shop as a merchant tailor. My grandmother was receiving her education at a boarding-school in Dublin at the time and was of one of the first families of the County Westmeath. I know the name but forbear to mention it, as they might think themselves lessened by one so humble as I am claiming kindred; but if it went by antiquity, I think a Milesian ought to be as good.

However it happened that my grandfather and she became acquainted is more than I can tell but, be it as it may, they not only got acquainted but actually got married. The match, in my opinion, was not a very suitable one for my grandfather, for the young women of rank have high ideas of polished society and an extensive knowledge of English and French books, music, drawing, etc. Yet they are totally ignorant of that circle in which a man in business moves and are no more fit to struggle in it for their bread than cage-birds would be to struggle with the wild ones. A man should chose a wife in the same circle of life he has been reared in himself; not but there is a vast difference in the dispositions of people reared even in the same circle, but where there is a family well known for honesty, virtue and abilities, there will be hardly any disappointment in chosing there.

After my grandfather's marriage, he continued his business for some years in Dublin and, as he was a very ingenious man in fitting up drapery in gentlemen's houses, he was frequently employed in that way. Among the many calls he had to attend to, there was one from a wealthy gentleman of this county, who was fitting up his house in great splendour; and, when he did come, he took such a liking to the country that he resolved to settle in it and accordingly took a farm and removed his family from Dublin.

This, I think, was a most unfortunate move for my

grandfather, for to know how to manage a farm properly a man would require to be brought up to it as he would to any other business; and, even with those who are regularly bred to it, there are many bad managers who are hard set to pay rent and live; but to a man that knows nothing at all of it it must be certain ruin. Just so did it happen with my grandfather; he was broke out of his farm and left to struggle with the world as well as he could. When my father grew up to man's estate, he got married. My mother's name was Smith and my maternal grandmother's name was Howe. Her family was of English descent and by intermarriages were partly Catholics and partly Protestants, but they were some of the good old sort of Protestants, kind-hearted and generous; and though they were of a very warlike temper, if opposed or thwarted, yet if you took them courteously they would if possible outdo you in courtesy. In short, if any good blood ever came to this country from England, the Smiths and Howes had as good a claim to it, I believe, as any others.

When my father, John Farrell, and my mother were married, he had with respect to property little or nothing to begin the world with, but he had what was better; he had industry and perseverance, skill and most profound judgment in any thing he undertook, honesty to a scruple, besides great bodily strength and activity; and with these qualities he set out in the world. A man commencing in such a manner to acquire a competence for a family has extraordinary obstacles to contend with and they are greatest, of course, at the beginning. The first five pounds a man makes on the clear is a labour of Hercules; it is, in fact, a victory. The next ten are made with less trouble and the next twenty with less trouble still and so on, till everything comes quite easy at last.

This was the case with my father. There was no toil too great for him, no obstacle so great but he overcame, so much had he the welfare of his family at heart. And, when he came to be in easy circumstances, it was always a gratification to him to do any kindness in his power to his neighbours; and so great was his prudence and foresight that he always kept clear of contentions with them and his correctness and integrity in his dealings were such that—

> His word would pass for more than he was worth.

The character drawn by Pope of his father would suit him as exactly as if he was the person it was done for, particularly the following couplet:

> No courts he saw, no suits would ever try;
> Nor dared an oath, nor hazarded a lie . . .

I was his eldest son living and though of a very delicate frame was uncommonly active and possessed of more strength than would be imagined from my appearance, and of a very passionate temper. As soon as I was able to use a hornbook, I was sent to a schoolmistress, a kind, affectionate, old woman, who had the happy art of making the difficulties attending the first labour of the child as light as possible. The sour, morose temper of some teachers makes a child hate learning but this good woman's plan was to make a child love it and she was always successful. She watched every difficulty and helped the child over it, till by degrees it became familiar to him. She had abundance of pleasant observations and kind tales to suit the child's temper, as occasion required, so that instead of being a place of pain and sorrow, her school was a scene of pleasure and delight to her little scholars. It was a particular custom of hers, when she got a new scholar, to teach him the first day how he should behave when he went home in the evening.

"Now, my child," she would say, "when you go home, you must ask your father or mother's blessing, whichever you happen to meet first, it is no matter which, either will do, or if they are both together it is the same thing. Now, go down on your knees, like a good child, and hold up your hand till I learn you how to ask it: 'Pray, father (or mother), pray to God to bless me and make me God's true and faithful servant to my life's end. Amen.'—and I will go home with you myself the first time, until you come used to it and then you can do it by yourself and you must be very careful and do whatever your father and mother bids you and say your prayers night and morning and then God Almighty will love you and bless you and let nobody do you any harm. All your school-fellows here do the same and if any of them were bold I have a little bird that goes to every house and hears everything that's said or done in it and tells it to me and then you know I should be very angry and should beat them with the rod but I don't like that; no, no, I don't like using the rod at all."

It is surprising what an effect her kind discourses had on her little audience, particularly the story of the little bird, and what pains would be taken not to say or do anything amiss for fear it should hear us. And, as all loved the kind old woman and as she managed to make us love learning, it was surprising how fast we advanced in it. Oh, happy days of real happiness and innocence, how few and fleeting were you!

As soon as I could spell well, which was too soon in one sense, I was taken from my kind, good tutoress and sent to a master who was the most famous in the neighbourhood for writing and arithmetic; but the day I left her and went to him was the day that commenced my sorrows in this world and lost the happiness I never since found. He was a man who had been in the Army and his school was conducted exactly on military principles. Everything was to be done by the way of no thanks and by the force of the switch or cat-o'-nine-tails. There was a roll called every morning at a certain hour precisely and any boy not present was marked with an *a* before his name to denote absence. There would be no use in giving an excuse if he came in five minutes afterwards, no matter how fair or well grounded it might be, or how good his conduct might be; for, if once marked down, there it stood against him till Saturday evening, when the whole week's arrears were cleared off in the following manner: for being absent once, no punishment; twice absent, two severe slaps on the hands of a heavy flat rule; thrice absent, three slaps; and four times absent, strip and get the cats.

The first week I commenced I was a very good boy (as I thought); I had all my lessons well and gave the master no trouble but on the contrary got some praise from him, which was not easy to do. But I never dreamed of what was to come on on Saturday evening. However, it arrived at last and when lessons were all over and I imagined we were going to be dismissed as usual, I was informed by some of the boys that we could not go till the roll was called.

" What roll ? " said I.

" Oh, sure the roll is called every Saturday evening."

"And what is that for ? "

" Oh, sure everyone absent twice or three times will be slapped and every one absent four times will be whipped."

I stared with astonishment and could hardly believe it.

" Oh, my boy, you'll see it immediately; how often were you absent ? "

" I don't know ; sure I wasn't told in the beginning and sure they would not punish one the first week, when they did not tell me the rules."

" Oh, no matter for that, my boy, you'll get it as well as the rest and you'll remember it the better next time."

" I will not get it, nor I won't let them give it to me ; it was their fault they didn't tell me or I'd be early enough."

" Oh, here they are ! Here they are ! We'll soon see now ! "

The master just walked upstairs with the roll book and cat-o'-nine-tails which he layed down very deliberately and commenced calling the roll and ordering the boys that were to be whipped at one side and those to be slapped on the other. Excuses, cries and lamentations were all in vain. He commenced to work and whipped severely and, to expedite the business, ordered a turnkey-looking fellow to go over and slap the others. I was the first he came to and ordered me to hold out my hand.

" For what ? " said I.

" Till you are slapped ; you are absent three times and you are to get three slaps for not being here to answer your name at seven o'clock in the morning."

"And sure I wasn't told that and I have no right to be slapped; I'd be here early enough if I was told."

"No matter for that; you were absent and you must be slapped."

"I will not."

"Come, hold out your hand this minute!"

"My hand is sore" (which was really the case) "and I won't hold it out."

Here one of the boys said, "it's better for you hold out your hand and he'll only hit you easy, for the master won't see him."

"Yes," said he taking up the word, "I'll only hit you easy and I'll stand between you and the master."

On this assurance I held out my hand but I no sooner done so than the savage gave me a blow that I almost thought knocked my hand off. The pain and agony shot to my very heart and I screeched most terribly. But my cries were only like "whispers in a storm." There was such uproar with those whippings that I was not heard. It was a thousand pities there was not some good man by that would have knocked the scoundrel down. As soon as I recovered a little, he ordered me to hold out the other hand. I told him plainly I would not.

"You must, sir; hold it out immediately."

"I will not hold it out."

Here he made me another promise he would not hit hard and was sorry he hurted me so much, but as soon as I held it out he gave me just the same sauce and then slapped the other hand again. Crying was no use, though I cried nearly all the way home and told the usage I got and that I would never go to that school again, that I would go back to the good old woman. This would not at all be allowed, but I was promised in order to pacify me that the master should be spoke to about it and that I should not be used so again. This indeed was the very case, for I took very good care never to be in his power.

The punishment was frequent almost every day and besides what the master gave he had a method of making the boys punish each other. It was this; there was a spelling class formed every evening; the first boy was asked to spell a word and if he missed it it went on to the second, etc., and if it even went to the last boy and that he spelled it he should slap every boy that missed it on the hand with a wooden ruler and then stand at the top of the class himself. This was the cause of bitterness and ill-will amongst them, sometimes threats and ill words and very often pitched battles or boxing matches. To what baneful courses will wrong discipline or bad example drive those who are naturally kind-hearted! What a difference this was to the kindness and good nature not only taught by my good old schoolmistress, but of which she set the example herself!

I continued in this school till I was nearly twelve years of age and from the severity of it I contracted a confirmed hatred to tyrants and tyranny. As the master's religion was of the Church of England, he compelled every boy to have the New Testament for a school-book and the Catholic clergy at that time made no objection to it. But I would beg of all men of common sense or who have the least respect for the sacred writings never to let them into the hands of schoolboys again.

The master, indeed, was really the best teacher of writing and as much of arithmetic as was necessary for a person in business, and there is no doubt whatever he taught was hardly ever forgot, as he made every boy remember it by the force of severity. At the early age I was taken from school I could not be expected to know very much. I could read and write and cipher as well as any other boy of my age, and that was but middling. The only thing I was to call good at was spelling and at that I was capital. I was passionately fond of tales and romances. I read the *Seven Champions of Christendom*, the fairy tales and *Arabian Nights' Entertainments* with delight. But of all the works of fiction that came within my reach there was none fitted my taste so exquisitely as *Jack the Giant Killer*; there was not a tyrant he subdued with the aid of his invisible cloak, shoes of swiftness and sword of sharpness but I shouted for joy and cried, "Sweet fellow Jack!"

Much as I hated and detested persecution I seemed like one born for it, for before I was twelve years of age I was taken out of this school of persecution and bound apprentice. This was only out of the frying pan into the fire. For the trade I was bound to was a most difficult trade to learn and the master a man of such a passionate temper that, if you did not take his meaning at once, it was so much the worse for yourself. I happened to be of a very inquisitive disposition and always wished to know the sense and meaning of what I was going about. It was better for me at times that I let it alone. For a man that did not know it himself would not like to acknowledge his ignorance, and a man that did, perhaps, would not wish to tell. And for both reasons I sometimes got insulted or even abuse for being so impertinent as to enquire. This very badly agreed with my temper and I sometimes gave as good as I got. But my master, who was skilled in the ways of the world, had an indirect way of accomplishing a matter, if he found the other failed. He was a man that had no great knowledge of books nor did not want to have it. He considered it all lost time and an idle habit to be minding them at all. He fixed his whole attention on turning his business to most advantage in making his boys use every expedition in doing as much work as was possible in the day and in doing the same himself, and at this no man could surpass him. He certainly did not spare himself no more than the boys, but there was this difference: he had the hope of gain to sweeten his labour; the boys had none, not even the smallest encouragement in that way. His mode of teaching was exactly on the plan of my old schoolmaster, by harshness and severity. I was cut off from information of every kind, except what belonged to the little circle of the trade that travelling journeymen saw on the road from one town to another; the different kind of employers they worked for, the wages they earned, who the best workmen were and in what points of the trade they surpassed others, their stories (sometimes exaggerated, sometimes lies and sometimes truth, and sometimes a mixture of lies and truth); this and the attention and application necessary to learn to work well generally occupied the whole of a boy's time and is nearly the stock of information he received at any trade during his seven years' servitude; at least it was so with me for, though I lived in the midst of a populous town, I was allowed no more intercourse with mankind than if I was in a monastery. I had a regular hour for being up in the morning to work and the same at night for giving over and going to bed, after the painful task of the day was over. And the master had the ingenious knack of persuading us that the more work we did the better for ourselves, for he would never allow himself to be under any obligation or that he had any gain by it, on the contrary that he had more loss of time instructing us than we were worth to him, so completely skilled was he in English policy to " Clap the padlock on the mind." Though I was very credulous in some things still I did not relish this doctrine, for, let it disguise itself as it would, " still Slavery thou wert a bitter draught " and it was against my will I took it.

I longed during the whole week for Sunday, when I might have some relaxation, as I delighted in exercise and liberty. But in this my wary master disappointed me as much as possible; some excuse, some invention was used to keep me within and he was as fertile at invention in these cases as a man that learned the seven Sciences. However, when I did get out at last, I knew no bounds; every exercise was nearly alike to me, hurling, leaping, football or handball, but the latter was my favourite and, though I had but a part of one day in the week to practise, and confined all the rest, still I was nearly as expert at them as most boys of my age and generally went through more bodily fatigue on that day than I did in the rest of the week, but it never done me any injury, on the contrary I always considered it did me service.

Alas, alas, what a change have I lived to witness in the course of about forty or fifty years; no assemblage now of boys or young men to be seen going through the exercises I delighted in so much; and, if I was to judge from appearances, neither strength nor action nor spirit in them to qualify them for such sports, a set of degenerate weakly looking creatures, broken down with trouble and affliction, with spindleshanks and puny frames tied up in suspenders, so that it is one in ten of them but you will see with a humpy back or a humpy shoulder. What dandy tailor or other enemy to mankind invented them? But to return, I was compelled to drudge on through my servitude or more properly speaking my slavery and, though I dragged my chain at every step, still as I proceeded I gained so much knowledge of a business I disliked that I was accounted tolerably clever at it—I wished for some relaxation but had no time to get it in any way, except by reading, and I had no books that would at all answer my taste, and to read one that did not would be the worst penance of all on me.

However, kind fortune at length threw one in my way; it contained the three first books of Homer's Iliad in prose and, though I might have heard the name of Homer mentioned, still I had not the remotest idea of what kind of man he was; but before I read these half through, I was quite enchanted with them. There was not a scene he so beautifully described but I fancied I was looking on and wondered how I could be so long in the world without meeting his works or how those that read them could be so insensible to their merits as not to proclaim them to every one. For my part, there was not one that I thought had books or a taste for reading but I was asking about Homer's works or if they could direct me where I could get them. At last to my great joy and surprise I met them where I least expected. There was an old man that used to frequent the shop. He was an Irish scholar and could read and write the language. I happened to ask him one day if he ever heard of the Iliads. He told me he did and had them too, the whole twenty-four.

"Twenty-four!" said I, in amazement.

"Yes," said he, "and they are all in verse."

Here my amazement increased and I begged to know if he would have the goodness to lend them to me.

"Indeed I would," said the good old man; "lend them to you with pleasure, if I had them here, but they are in Clonmel and it would be too far to bring them, except they were in my own care, for I would not like to trust them with any one for fear they would be injured; but I will be going there shortly and I will bring them to you myself."

My curiosity was raised to such a pitch by hearing of twenty-four books, and in verse too, that I entreated him, in every way I could, not to delay. The good old man had a kind Irish heart which yielded so much to me that he actually sent for it a distance of forty miles and had it brought to me. I thought every day a year till it came, so great was my anxiety to see so wonderful a work. And when it did come I not only read but I, if possible, devoured it.

Many and many a cold frosty night did I spend over it after my work of the day and in an upper room, unknown to the family. The cold of the night did not prevent me. No, though I would be nearly as cold as ice at it, still I would not give over as long as I could keep an eye open and it was sleep alone drove me to bed. His description of the different scenes in the Council or in the field were so beautiful and given with so much truth and force, that I almost fancied I was present, looking on and hearing what passed. It was, in fact, the reading of this great work that first enabled me to form some judgment of what good writing or good speaking ought to be. The groundwork of it was truth (which I always panted after and loved); it was on this foundation the mighty Homer stood and without it all his other extraordinary decorations would have been useless—not that we are to suppose Homer himself was present to hear the speeches or see the great actions performed by his heroes, but that in composing and relating them he makes them speak and act exactly as such men should do according to their station, their temper, their ability and the situation they were placed in. After reading it attentively, it was very difficult to please me in books.

None but first-rate authors would answer my taste, such as Pope his great translator, Swift, Goldsmith or such as them. The others in general seemed defective to me and I could not bear to peruse a limping, stumbling work. From being a great lover of poetry I began to make some attempt at it myself, but this I found at first to be a labour of Hercules. However, by perseverance I strove to get over the first difficulties, which are always the greatest, and in time I came on to put a few lines together, containing some little share of sense as well as sound but this was only for my own amusement, as I was so shy of being accounted a poet that it was very few I would let know it.

CHAPTER TWO

BACKGROUND OF REVOLT

THERE was nothing very particular or worth relating took place with me, my occupations being nearly all of a piece, viz. endeavouring to acquire a still greater knowledge of my business, improving myself with books and writing, and the athletic exercises I have mentioned of which I was very fond, until that dreadful curse of Ireland, the system of " United Irishmen " was introduced ; and oh, with what deep regret do I look back at the state of the country at that period and at the present. We had, to be sure, a great deal of poverty on one hand in the country at the time but, if we had, we had also a great deal of wealth on the other. Working tradesmen and labourers in general had but a small allowance for their labour but provisions and all other necessaries were cheap in proportion, while the generality of employers of every description were comfortable and wealthy and able to keep them constantly at work. They were enabled to do this by the higher orders always spending their fortunes at home and by their being always satisfied with and always encouraging home manufacture and always making it a point of honour to allow their tradesmen such prices for their work as enable to live. And as for the very poor that were compelled to ask alms, they were relieved plentifully in the towns, while those who led a roving life and frequented fairs and markets were able, many of them, to hoard up money and give fortunes with their daughters. There was no such thing known as men, willing and able to work, obliged to starve for want of it ; and, if anything was wanting to show the easy circumstances of the people, it would be found in the numbers in every town and in every part of the country that could afford time to practise all the manly athletic exercises so well known to Irishmen as hurling, football, cudgelling, tennis or handball, leaping, wrestling, vaulting, throwing the sledge or bar or grinding-stone; and at every outlet of Carlow there were fields like commons, free to every one that chose to amuse themselves, and one of the best ball-courts in Ireland within and it was really astonishing to what a pitch of perfection men arrived at these sports and as every place eagerly wished for the name of having the best men, neither time or pains were spared to obtain a mastery in them though it generally took seven, eight or ten years of constant practice for the purpose; and let no one imagine it was all lost time either, for one of the surest passports to a good wife and fortune was to be famous at any of these. Such a person, provided his character was good, would be preferred, and justly, to a drone that would have property.

Tim Corcoran was our best hurler and all the Castle Hill boys were trained by him in a field called at that time the Tobacco Meadows and free to every one that chose to amuse themselves in it; and though he was a man that had gained laurels in many a hard contested field, he had always the rare talent of gaining the applause of his opponents as well as his friends and was never known, when engaged in that dangerous exercise, to hurt any man or do anything dishonourable. I shall just relate an anecdote that will perhaps serve to illustrate his character. He was one day engaged in a very great match in which the celebrated Tom Grimes was at the opposite side. Grimes was a man of such great strength and action that he was allowed to be an overmatch at jostling for any man in the country. However, in the course of the play Corcoran gave him a fall; Grimes took fire at finding his honour hurt and made several attempts to retaliate which Corcoran carefully avoided, but at length, seeing his resentment continue, he took an opportunity of addressing him as follows: " Mr. Grimes, I hope you are not angry with me for what has happened. It was only by merest chance, for though I did throw you, I would not at all pretend to be so good a man as you and I hope you won't have any ill will to me for it."

Grimes was mollified; in an instant the wound his honour received was healed up and he generously exclaimed, " Give me your hand, Corcoran, there is not a man in the Green shall hurt you to-day." He carried the same good temper everywhere and the softest boy was as safe in practising with him as the hardiest veteran and so dexterous did his pupils become under his tuition that there was no part of the town or neighbourhood a match at hurling for the Castle Hill boys.

Our handball players were of the very best description that could be found in Ireland and might be divided into three classes; first rate, second rate and third rate. Of the first-rate players there were about ten or a dozen so nearly equal that take any two or four of them that chance would put together and you could rarely fail of having a good match. Mr. Jack Bagot, a gentleman from Rufflin (or, as it is now politely called, Rutland) about three miles distant from town, might be placed foremost. Then there was Joe Dowling and his brother Jim, Paddy Foley—one of the sweetest players I ever saw standing in a court—every blow from him right or left like clock-work and no matter how hard the ace was or if it even went against him, he was always good-humoured and came out laughing. Tom Nowlan comes next, a powerful player; he and Foley once played single-hand and it was literally a dead match; there was but one ace between them and that gave the game to Nowlan, but it was his superior strength won it and not any want of skill or bottom on Foley's part.

The other first-rate players I do not at present recollect, but I have one in store that not only surpassed all the first-rate players but surpassed any other man, I am confident, that was in existence. This was the famous Jack Fogarty. His friends in town were wealthy and respectable and kept the two mills, the Castle Mill and Town Mill, and carried on the baking business extensively. Fogarty was a fine person of a man, about five feet ten inches, straight and strong made, a weighty long arm, a kind and pleasing countenance, aquiline nose, sandy hair, and skin as white as snow. His people lived quite convenient to the ball-court, which was kept at the time by Bob Rankin, a man known far and near for his superior skill in that exercise. Young Fogarty delighted in the play and old Rankin delighted in instructing him until at length he acquired such a mastery of the game that his play was exactly like "sleight of hand." His temper, too, differed as much as his play from that of any other man. He was always cool, always steady, always undaunted; and no matter how great, how important or how difficult the match was that he was engaged in, he walked into the court as careless and with as much composure as if he was going to take his tea, and during the course of the game, if he was hindered of a ball by a looker-on (as often happens) it never made the least alteration in him or drew an angry word from him. It was in his blows alone he was sharp and severe; for, indeed, he never gave a soft one and always in low play skimming the very line; but his favourite blow, the blow by which he beat all the men that came before him was this; when the ball hopped to his liking, he drew his arm and his whole body till he got it on an exact line with his hip and then brought himself to such a balance that he could cover any part of the wall he pleased in a twinkling and neither the players nor even the sharpest looker-on could tell, till it left his hand, for what part he designed it. For, if he drew his right hand and set himself to send the ball to the left, his opponents set themselves to run there after it; and when he got them in this position, he shot it suddenly straight into the right, so swift and sharp to the line that they could never recover themselves to have the least chance of taking it, and this wonderful feat he could perform with right or left hand but he invariably sent it where it was not at all expected and so swift and so close to the line that it could never be taken after him. By this method of disappointing his opponents, he always kept them in a state of fear and uncertainty, always bustling, always running, while he himself was always at his ease, always his own master and theirs and always so careless that he obtained the appellation of " lazy Jack " ; for in fact no man could take a run out of him, for if a ball went any way contrary he would not distress himself to run a single yard after it but walk away and leave it there and when questioned about his easy manner of taking balls a friend would say, " Why, Jack, the balls wait for you."

" No," he would reply, " they don't wait for me, no more than for any one else, but when I strike out a ball to a man I watch him and the moment he draws his arm I know the very spot he will send it to and J am there before it, waiting."

But no one could gain any knowledge of the kind by watching himself, and I often wondered that of all the great players we had in town at the time and that saw his method no one ever could learn to give his master-blow, or even to attempt it. But as every town or village that has a ball-court or old walls or a gable-end has some players they fancy the finest in the world (but who if they went into a regular court with proper lines and proper rules would be only like lumber in the way of good players) I shall say a few words more about Fogarty that will show more clearly and beyond all dispute the man he was. When he was just in his prime, there was a grand procession of the different trades in Dublin called " the Franchise " but generally pronounced " the Fringes." This was considered so curious a sight that people from all parts of Ireland went to see it. Among the rest Fogarty and some of the Carlow people went. There was at that time a wealthy man, in business in Dublin, of the name of Kearns, who was so great a ball-player that there was no man in Dublin to equal him. Fogarty met him in his own favourite court. They both engaged in a double match and to the surprise of all the Dublin people, Fogarty won it. They played again and again but it was still the same thing. Fogarty won as long as he chose to play. At length Kearns gave up the match and walking up to Fogarty said, " Young man, perhaps you would play a game single-handed ? " " With all my heart," was the reply. The match went on. Fogarty was victorious. They went on again but it was all the same thing; as long as he chose to play, Fogarty still won. " Well," said Kearns, as the last game was over, " you are the greatest player in the world." Such an acknowledgment, coming from such a man as Kearns, fully acquits me of any exaggeration in what I have said of this extraordinary man, so I conclude recommending to every young man that is a lover of this manly exercise to endeavour to learn Fogarty's blow as I have described it and, if any one should be so fortunate as to get master of it, he will find that he will have little more to do than laugh at any man that plays against him.

At leaping, which was greatly practised everywhere at the time, my brother, Tom Farrell, took the sway. There was scarcely a meeting anywhere without a leaping-match and every part of the town and country had its brag men; but at every meeting Tom was best of the best men. His favourite was the three standing leaps, which are the most difficult, as they must be given from the force and spring of the body alone, without any run to assist, and though many could do them well, still no one he ever met at the time at any meeting could cover the same length of ground. People in general, when they go to measure leaps, generally do it by stepping, but this is a very uncertain way, for they can make the steps long or short, according as they wish to favour their friend, and will very gravely tell you he leaped twelve, thirteen or fourteen yards (a thing never done since Fionn Macoul's time). Besides, by this way of measuring, the ground a man stands on is brought in, which should not be done, at least it was not customary with us to do it, but we always measured from a man's toes where he set off to his heels where he stopped ; now, by measuring according to this rule, my brother's three leaps were thirty-six the length of my foot with my shoe on and my shoe being eleven inches long made the leaps exactly eleven measured yards from his toes where he stood to his heels where he stopped ; and this he did on ground exactly level, without the least rise one way or the other, and he did it too without falling, as we never allowed a man to come down on his breech or at full length on his back. Nothing would do with us but a fair upright leap and this he always did. Any one that chooses to beat Tom Farrell's leap in this manner may try it as soon as he pleases but I know I could never meet the man would do it.

Cock-fighting was also very much practised at that time, but has now fallen into disuse and I am very glad of it; there was too much low scheming and cheating connected with it, there was too much time lost with it; it brought young people into the lowest and worst company. If a man lost his money on a match, it was certain loss to him. If he won, it was not certain gain, for a crowd of schemers surrounded him and the whole or more generally went for drink besides various other things that make me very glad to hear no more of cock-fighting.

There was one amusement I delighted in very much and which I am sorry is now no more; it was the humours of a May day. It was observed, I believe, nearly the same way through all parts of the kingdom. For a month at least before it arrived, May day was spoken of with rapture, particularly by young lads and lasses that had no objection to a sweetheart. It came at last and they were out in groups in every direction from sunrise, making merry with syllabub-cakes, dancing, courting etc., but in no way that could offend modesty; but there was one ceremony that deserves particular notice, as nothing tends more to show the innocence and credulity of the times. The young woman that had a variety of suitors and that was uncertain of the sincerity of her favourite, sought out carefully for a snail without a shell. Having obtained the prize, she brought it home carefully and placed it between two pewter plates with some salt on the bottom one. The salt made the snail twist and turn at a great rate and she fancied he was all the time writing her sweetheart's name. When he had been there long enough to perform the task assigned him, the plates were removed and the bottom one examined with the most scrutinising attention, to know whether the snail had doomed her to good or ill fortune for the remainder of life. The snail hardly ever failed of bringing good news, for no matter what the characters were that he made, she would insist on it being the name she wished for and no other and, if any old crony was present (and they were never wanting) that was skilled in the occult sciences, she knew her business too well to contradict the matter and then, if she went a step farther and communicated the news to the young man, it would very probably bring on the match, as she might readily insinuate it would not be lucky on his part to refuse; but let the matter go as it would, the snail got the highest praise for his profound learning and wisdom. A certain poet I have met with somewhere, in writing on the subject of the humours of a May day, touches that point in the following humorous manner, viz.:

> The Milk-maids had their tasks all done,
> And home returnéd full of fun,
> One of them with a flowing pail,
> Another with a fav'rite snail,
> In joyful hope it would discover,
> The Man that was to be her lover,
> Although she knew it long agone,
> But two heads wiser are than one,
> And if the Snail of doubts could cure her,
> 'Twould make the matter still the surer.
> The Snail when laid between two plates
> Mysteriously consults the fates
> Then writes the Name we understand
> Of him that is to have her hand
> But in what language new or old
> No Mortal yet could e'er unfold.
> But that's no matter—be it Greek,
> High Dutch or Hebrew it must speak
> For she translates it in a minute
> And when she does the deuce is in it
> If she don't make it plainly show
> The very name she wants to know,
> Then stares with wonder and surprise
> How snails can be so mighty wise
> And to her cronies all relates
> The Story of the Snail and plates;

> Says they were Druid's Secretaries
> And answered all mysterious queries
> And that they were (in days of yore)
> The *Droughtyeen* call'd by men of lore,
> Of sev'ral other wonders speaks
> Then throws him to the ducks or drakes,
> Hard fate alas upon the ground
> To fling a scholar so profound,
> One that to wisest men was known
> And knew all fortunes—but his own.
> Thus having finished the romance
> They all prepare to join the dance.

But to return to my subject; every one, as I said, that could afford it were out " Maying," as it was called, but there was one person in particular that deserves to occupy a conspicuous niche in the Temple of Fame and that was the celebrated Catty Flood. Her husband, Paddy Flood, as he was then plainly called, was an attorney. Catty was a widow and possessed of an extensive brewery. Paddy thought Catty and the brewery would answer him very well and Catty had no objection. To make a long story short, they were married, but if they were Catty didn't give up all her right and title to command. She was a tall, strong, resolute woman, right well able to take her own part, so that the civiller a poor man would be with her, the better for himself; of course she was man of the house as well as Paddy. They had a large dairy of cows, generally from eighteen to twenty, and every May morning regular Catty went out Maying to one of her own fields after collecting all the boys and girls she could and there gave them the milk of four cows made into syllabub, with plenty of cakes and crackers; but every one that went in should dance, they would have no business there if they didn't, while she played the fiddle herself and danced away as merry as the best of them. To give her character in a few words, she was the prince of good fellows and her maiden name was Hogan. The remainder of the day was spent in bringing home maypoles and putting them up, midst music and dancing and bonfires. There were factions in every quarter of the town at the time and every gentleman they had influence on they went to him for a maypole and were never refused. I remember five maypoles up in the town together; one in the quarries, one in the Closh, one in the Potatoe-Market, one in Burrin Street and one on the Castle Hill. The Quarry Boys and Closh Boys generally went to old Mr. Burton of Burton Hall, the King of the County Carlow, for their maypoles, the other factions to Garryhunden and Clogrenan. Their friends at home, in the meantime, were preparing themselves to form a long dance to go out to meet them; the girls all dressed in white, with every other finery they had or could borrow, the boys (their partners) all with white stockings, white waistcoats and white shirts, all clean out of the fold, and as they wore no coats to hide their finery they made a remarkable gay nice appearance; and to set off all, their hats were trimmed either with white tape or white paper and cockades of ribbon, if they could get them. Then there were three or four of the most active humoursome fellows they could get with their faces blackened, artificial humps on their backs, and disguised every way as much as possible, with long wattles in their hands and bladders tied on the ends of them; these were called bladder-men and their duty was to clear the way by frightening the children, kissing the old women and girls, and rising fun and humour every way they could. When all was ready, the whole party set out, the best dancer of the young men carrying a garland and the best dancer of the young women his partner; and when they met the maypole they turned about and danced before it to the place where it was to be put up, where there was a large bonfire and hundreds of their friends shouting and huzzaing for them, and this merriment they kept up till a late hour at night and sometimes the whole night, and all the expense of it out of their own pockets, besides their loss of time.

We had also the Old Irish Volunteers; scarce a town or village in Ireland but had a Corps, but in Carlow in particular there was one of the handsomest dressed Corps and best appointed in every respect that could be found. There were three regular Companies in it; the Grenadier Company; the Light Infantry and the Battalion, and clothed at their own expense. There was scarcely any man, even in the most trifling business, but could afford to buy his own clothing and not only that but could afford his time to go to drills and parades and at times to go a long distance to reviews and pay all expenses himself. Could that be done now? No, in the whole town of Carlow there couldn't be half a Corps raised like the old one. And how was it done then? Why, we had our own Parliament, which (let it get what blame it may) yet always took care of the main point, to keep plenty of employment for the people. We had nothing used in the country but Irish manufacture and if any merchant in Dublin brought over English goods, the Liberty boys assembled, took him out of his house or wherever they could catch him, brought him prisoner to the Weavers' Square, stripped him naked and after daubing him all over with warm tar, shook a bag of feathers on him, then marched him with a straw rope round his neck through the city, amidst the shouts of the people, and neither Lord Mayor or police or army ever interfered to hinder them. The manufacture of the country was considered good enough for any man in it and no other would be allowed to be used. There was no such thing heard as people enquiring for English cloth or English leather, nor no Englishmen would think of telling them they didn't know how to clean their own shoes if he didn't send them blacking. On this account, workmen of every description had plenty to do and though the wages in general was very low, still, as I said before, everything they wanted to buy was low in proportion and though working men rarely could save money, still they could live and rear families too and at any rate were always sure of having work to do.

The case differed materially with master-tradesmen or those who could carry on any kind of dealing on their own account; their profits were good and there was a great deal of wealth among them and that in good gold and silver. I do not think there was any such thing known as banknotes in them days (I mean in general use) and as for compounding and laying mean schemes, to deceive a neighbour and then swindle and rob him of his property was never so much as dreamed of. Character was of some value in those days for if a man suffered it to be stained he might just as well quit society at once; illgotten wealth would be no use to him, as every one would despise and insult him; the very beggars would scarcely take a charity from him; his children would be shunned and avoided and it would be disgraceful to have a connection with them. Is that the case now? No, no, no, it is no disgrace at all to be a mean scoundrel provided the wretch makes money by it. If he does, he may laugh at the man he has deceived, aye, and at all men of honour, well knowing that if one of them dare lay the horsewhip on his tender hide, the law that gave him room and thereby encouraged him to be a rogue will protect him for doing what it gave him leave to do and will punish any one that dare say *Bah* to him.

In the short space of about forty years, from being a nation of honest, industrious and wealthy tradesmen and dealers of every description, headed by honourable noblemen and gentlemen, we have become a nation of swindlers, bankrupts and beggars. A nation possessing a soil and climate, producing every necessary of life as abundantly as any other spot on the globe, and every province, every county, every town in it producing its thousands of human beings in a state of starvation, men able and willing to labour for their bread and no one to give them employment, and at the very same time thousands upon thousands of acres of land lying waste and uncultivated—what do our rulers mean? Do they mean to thin the human race, to murder them by famine? There is not a doubt of it. There is no use in mincing the matter or in calling things by any other than their right names; thousands upon thousands have died of starvation in Ireland these thirty years past and thousands are little better than dying of it this moment, though it is the month of October, the plentiful end of the year 1842, but how they will be next spring and summer when provisions are always dear and scarce God alone who gives plenty to the birds only knows. Perhaps their cry has reached the Throne of Mercy and, if it has, those who have lived sumptuously may well tremble. Pharaoh was a mighty man at thinning the human race or, at least wishing to do it but he was only a bungler at the work; he only put double or treble labour on them but as a man would feed a horse well that he wanted much work from, so Pharaoh fed the Israelites; but as labour and food were conducive to health, he missed his aim, for they increased and multiplied. But rulers of the present times take a far different course from Pharaoh for thinning the human race, for they neither ask the people to do double work or treble work; no, they very cleverly ask them to do nothing at all, but let the land lie waste and let them die of hunger for want of employment; but if Pharaoh was drowned in the sea for attempting, merely for planning and attempting the indirect murder of the Israelites, what is to be the fate of those who not only planned and attempted, but who have actually put the plan in execution and have swept off silently tens of thousands of the human race!

I do not say but there was distress and a great deal of distress in the country forty or fifty years ago; for the tradesmen and labourers had plenty to do, still their wages only allowed them barely to exist and those who were rendered incapable of working by sickness or old age and who were too high spirited to ask alms (of which there were great numbers) were in the very deepest distress. Besides all this, there was a regular scarcity every year for a month or two or three, between the old provisions being out and the new coming in, which bore heavily even on the working classes, but there was one thing which I gladly mention for the honour of my countrymen on these trying occasions, that the kindness and hospitality of Irishmen to each other was never known to fail. Had it not been for this, thousands would have inevitably perished every year, but by this means, by always standing together and assisting each other, they uniformly struggled over every difficulty.

CHAPTER THREE

UNITED IRISHMEN ALL

In this state the country was, until as I said before, that heavy curse of Ireland, the system of " United Irishmen " was introduced. If anything was wanting to show the unsuspecting innocence and simplicity of the people and their total ignorance of the plans of wily statesmen, nothing could show it clearer than their allowing themselves to be prevailed on to take the oath of that society. I do not recollect the whole of it at present and I heartily wish I had never known it; but I recollect as much of it as is sufficient for my present purpose. It began as follows:
" I A. B. do swear that I will persevere in endeavouring to form a brotherhood of affection among Irishmen of all religious persuasions."

So far it was very good, but would be much better if men could be taught to have an affection for each other without taking an oath at all. However, this was only the gilding on the pill. It was only a hoodwinker to prevent the people of seeing the dangerous part that was to follow:
"And that neither hopes, fears, rewards or punishments, shall cause me to inform of or give evidence against any member or members of said society, either collectively or individually."

Now where is the man living that could undertake to say safely, and that beforehand, what effect " hopes, fears, rewards or punishments " would have on him? Or if we did hear a man aver it on his bare word that he would brave the tortures of the rack sooner than violate an unlawful oath or even a lawful one, would we not be very apt to set him down a very great braggadocio or a very rash man? But to swear beforehand that he would be invincible, that no torture should subdue him, would in my opinion be the height of ignorance or folly or madness.

I know very well that the innocent ignorant people (and myself among the number) never dreamed of racks or tortures and that the taking an oath of love and affection to their countrymen could never deserve punishment, but can I say so much for the person or persons who framed it? I cannot and I have no hesitation in pronouncing them either a set of mad enthusiasts or a set of the greatest villains on earth; and of the two I am most inclined to place them in the latter class, for of all plans that ever was laid, none that I could hear of ever succeeded so effectually in spilling the blood of Ireland by wholesale as this very " Brotherhood of affection " did in the end and that, too, without causing any blame to the government of cruelty but throwing all the blame on the unhappy people, who neither planned it nor knew how to plan it. It was a system that was wholly unnecessary and, as time proved, had no chance on earth of success. England was in her full pride and power, both by sea and land at the time and her councils were led and ruled by one of the most able destroyers of the human race that ever appeared; he ruled the distant empire of India with as much ease as he would a county in Scotland or Wales, although the Native Kings and Princes and Nabobs were from the beginning ready armed and made the most desperate resistance; and if they could not succeed in opposing the policy and force of England, what man in his senses could imagine that the people of Ireland (as ignorant and unlettered at the time as the very Indians) could have a chance of anything but destruction, by rising up against their ready armed and disciplined rulers and, with nothing but sticks in their hands, to think of encountering the artillery and musketry and bayonets of England.

To be sure, the French revolution had taken place at the time and had been successful and some people imagined that what was done in one country might be done in another, but in this they were sadly mistaken. There was no nation on earth fit to conquer oppression and establish liberty for themselves by force but France alone. If any one should ask the reason why, I answer, because all nations in the Old World felt oppression as well as France and disliked it, of course, as much as France, but not one of them dare face certain death to put it down and obtain liberty, but France. The authors of the United Irish system seemed well aware of this, for from the very commencement they kept France steadily in view. They knew very well they dare not attempt a revolution without foreign aid and actually sent delegates to France to apply for it, and when they knew this, what occasion had they to endanger the people's lives by drawing them into a sworn combination or conspiracy to assist the French in liberating themselves? Does any one ever think of swearing a hungry man to eat roast beef particularly if the taking of the cattle led him into danger and when this person proposing it knew very well he would eat it as eagerly without taking any oath at all? Just so with the people of Ireland or any other country suffering under oppression. Let not rulers deceive themselves; all they want is an opportunity to shake it off. Let us suppose for a moment that the Emperor of Hayti wanted to free the slaves in Jamaica, would he have any occasion to swear them beforehand to assist him in making them happy? The idea is ridiculous. But our wise leaders could not advance one step without having the people first sworn; not, to be sure, that they would eat roast beef but that they would assist the people that would come to get it for them, and though these words were not in the oath, it was the very sense they attached to it. They took very good care to put no words in the oath that the law could take hold of. If they did, the people would get alarmed and wouldn't take it at all but it led them on. It made a beginning and they had but one step more to take (the getting of things called arms) to put them completely in its power.

It is really astonishing how no writer of ability stepped forward to sound the alarm and put people on their guard. A Swift or an O'Leary would have done it, but we had neither, though I must own that it was carried on with such secrecy and spread with such rapidity that it would be very difficult to do it for the general impression was that the words " I will persevere in endeavouring to form a brotherhood of affection among Irishmen of all religious persuasions " implied that they were bound by the oath to exert themselves in gaining over as many as they could and swearing them in to the Society, and on this account it spread in every direction like wild-fire.

A very few weeks were sufficient to spread it through such a town as Carlow, for numbers of persons actually carried prayer books in their pockets, not for the purpose of devotion, but for the purpose of swearing in the people, and the more they increased in numbers, the greater facility there was in getting more members; for the first alarm being worn off, it was made a complete joke of at last. It became the fashion and people would laugh as heartily at what was going forward as they would at any other piece of amusement. Alas, alas, they little knew it was their own death warrants they were signing, the fatal day they became United Irishmen. What a pity it was to draw people so simple and so unsuspecting into such a snare and how great must the guilt of the person or persons be that planned it, if they done it purposely. They are long since perhaps swept into an endless eternity as well as those they ruined and what good has it done them? What have they gained by the ruin they caused others? was it worth their while for the little time they had to be in this world to employ it doing so much mischief? would they do it over again if they could come back? No, surely they would not!

Oh, my friends and fellow-countrymen (or whoever you are that reads this story), never be drawn in to join any society that requires an oath. If any man should ask you to do it, on pretence of being a friend, be quite certain he is your deadly enemy. Seize the villain instantly and drag him to justice. Will swearing make a bad man good, a vicious man virtuous, a rogue honest, or a coward brave? Woeful experience will tell you if you are caught in their snare that it will not. Many and many a time have I advised the neighbouring people of the Queen's County against the Whitefeet System and showed them the consequences that would follow. I advised them at the risk of gaining their ill will, for I saw plainly the advice was unpalatable, but I did not care for that; I could not remain neutral and see my countrymen plunge in ruin without endeavouring all in my power to prevent it by imparting to them the benefit of my dear-bought experience. Some of them would not be stopped, but the dreadful examples that were made in Maryboro brought them to their senses and I had the gratification of receiving the most unfeigned thanks of some that escaped for the pains I took in warning them of the danger.

When the United system was unfortunately introduced into Carlow, I was happy and comfortable. I was after serving my time to a respectable trade and though I was only in the line of a working journeyman, still it was for my brother-in-law and sister (to whom I served my apprenticeship) I worked, which gave me some little consequence above the generality of working men. They were some of the wealthiest and most respectable people in the town at the time and with them I was accustomed to as good a table and as respectable company as any other tradesman, I believe, in it and I always had a taste and could afford to keep myself dressed suitable to my station in life.

Alas, alas, how little did I dream of the hard, hard road that was before me! Parents, whoever you are, no matter how high or how low your station in life, rear up your children in the love and in the fear of God, let that be your first great object, teach them to seek first His kingdom and you have His own word pledged for it that all things else will be given to them. Do not depend too much on your own worldly wisdom for planning out their course. It may deceive you. It has deceived thousands. Pray fervently to the Almighty, who gave them to you to direct and protect both them and yourselves. Give alms to the poor, to obtain their prayers for them, and when they come hungry to your door seeking for food, let your children be the bearers of your relief to them, that they may not only obtain their prayers, but learn imperceptibly to have compassion for the misfortunes and woes of others. Do not imagine that giving them great wealth or great learning will be a security to them through life. Either or both, if misapplied, may be a curse instead of a blessing, for if a man is enslaved and swayed by bad passions, they only give him more power to do more mischief, to the ruin of himself as well as to the ruin of others, and I have no hesitation in affirming that the man reared on a mountain, without knowing a letter in the book, but who knows and practises his duty to God and his neighbour is by a hundred degrees more safe and more happy even in this life ; to say nothing at all about the next.

There were five brothers and three sisters of us and we had as good a prospect in the beginning of being comfortably settled as many of our neighbours. We were scattered over the four quarters of the world ; one died in the East Indies, one in Jamaica and one in East Florida. The remainder (with the exception of one brother still living in America) died at home, and as for myself, though I never travelled fifty miles from where I am at present, it was my lot (glory be to my good God whose ways are inscrutable) to go through such scenes of danger, affliction and distress as I would not take all the wealth on earth to face again. I have lived (thanks again be to my good God) to see all my best friends dead and gone, all their property gone, even my trade, that was one of the best in Ireland, gone to ruin ; youth and strength, everything gone from me but one which I always prized above all, my character. This, thank God, in every vicissitude and danger of life I always kept unsullied and though I was reduced to the deepest distress and want, yet. He who feeds the birds was pleased in His mercy to open a door for me, where in a retired but humble situation I can, in the sixty-fifth year of my age, spend a vacant hour in writing a history of times gone by.

But to return ; when the United system had been some time on foot in our town, I was applied to by different friends (as they thought themselves) to join it and I was rallied a good deal on my singularity in not being like everybody. All this had no effect on me, for light as people in general made of it, I was resolved to examine it to the bottom, if possible, before I would have anything to do with it. I remembered very well the stories of the White Boys, particularly the sad fate of Father Sheehy and others who suffered in Clonmel, and I was fully resolved never to have anything to do with any system that could possibly bring me in contact with laws whose touch was destruction. My answer invariably was to every person that importuned me on the subject, that I should be first satisfied there was nothing in it that the law could make criminal, before I joined it. In vain did they tell me that the first men in the kingdom and the wisest men had joined it; that it was not only harmless, but laudable; that surely there could be no harm in swearing to form a "Brotherhood of affection" among Irishmen; that numbers of Protestants in town were foremost in it; and that it was strange obstinacy in me to be making objections to it. Was I wiser than all the world now that every one was joining it?

"Every one may do as they please," said I, "and so will I, and I will never join it, or any other society, till I am fully satisfied on the points I mention."

Just as if it was planned by some masterhand in villainy, a circumstance occurred that swept away all difficulties on the subject. There were some persons taken up and imprisoned in Ulster or, as it is called, by way of giving consequence to it above the other provinces, *the North*, as if there was any thing sweeter or more grateful in the sound of the cold " black North " than in East or West or South; yet one of the sharp sour-scheming pack will never be heard to say he is from Ulster. No, every jackanapes of them, with the assumed consequence and important strut of a Bashaw, would inform you, " I am from the North," or, as if it was still more consequential, " I am a Northern "; and what made the thing more grievous was that the people of the East or the Easterns (the lovely place where the sun rises) always gave these swindlers, sharpers and pickpockets precedence of themselves, and what was the consequence? Why, that they supplanted them in every calling of life, put them out of their places, and at length became their masters! And it was little matter; they well deserved it, when they were so mean as to think themselves inferior to such a pack, to the sweepings of every poorhouse and Charter-house and foundling-house in bleak Ulster, that they should treat them with contempt and assume a mastery over them. Not that I mean to say that all the people of Ulster are men of this description—far from it—I know very well there are no men in Ireland showed more spirit (or I believe so much) as the Catholics of Ulster, in resisting oppressors and persecutors who endeavoured to root them out of a province so favoured by Government in order to prevent them of sharing in the various favours bestowed on it. To their praise I say it that they nobly fought it out with them and maintained their ground, and that on their own dunghill and against superior numbers with superior arms. But it is the adventurers who flew from Ulster I allude to, who always assumed a consequence over the Catholics of this country that was never allowed them at home, and I am more disgusted with my own countrymen for suffering it and not treating it with the contempt it deserved, as the brave Catholics of Ulster did under all their disadvantages.

But as I was saying, there were some persons taken up and imprisoned in Ulster on a charge of being United Irishmen, and when they were brought to trial they not only did not deny it but they publicly avowed it before judge and jury. Their test oath was scrutinised and sifted according to all the forms of law, and it was triumphantly declared there was nothing in it that the law could make criminal and they were publicly acquitted in the face of the country.

A more effectual step could not have been taken to propagate the system, to give wings to it, to make it fly like wild-fire through the country and blindfold those writers or speakers that were capable of sounding the alarm and putting the people on their guard. For my part, as soon as I heard it I no longer hesitated in joining it. I took care, however, to apply to a person I could confide in, as I still had some doubts and was resolved, though I done so, to take no active part or make myself in any way conspicuous but pass on as civilly as possible among my neighbours. At the same time I gave the person that swore me in a particular charge not to mention it to any one as I did not wish it should be known. The precaution was quite vain, as the joke was too good a one to be kept secret; for in fact the swearing in a member at the time was considered no more than a joke and besides they had so much difficulty in getting my assent to join them that it made the joke doubly good, and it was not more than two or three days after when I found by the jeers and laughter of my acquaintance that every one of them knew it. I let them jeer on, but one thing I was fully determined, that I would never go one step farther in the business on any account whatever. Alas, alas, how little does a man know, when he takes one wrong step, how far it may lead him. I know it by sad experience, and I can safely say that from the very day I unfortunately joined that society to the present (which is now close upon forty years) it has been nearly an uninterrupted scene of danger, distress and affliction to me.

I continued my resolution of keeping strictly on the reserve for some time when one morning, as I came in to the shop to my usual employment, I was told by Patrick Bergan, a young man, an apprentice, that there was a person called in great haste to warn me to attend a meeting at a certain time and place, that there was a great delegate in town from " the North," that there was only twelve of the most intelligent persons in town selected to meet him, and that I was one of them. It was very flattering, certainly, to a young lad (particularly if he was ambitious) to be pointed out as a wise man on such an occasion, but it had a different effect on me, for I saw danger in it in an instant and I replied in an angry tone, " They must hold their meeting without me, then, for I won't attend it."

"You won't?" said he with astonishment. "Why, how can you help it?"

"The easiest thing in the world," said I; "by not going to it."

"Oh, but," said he, "when you are chosen to attend, I think it's paying you a very great compliment and I know if I was called on and could go like you I'd do it in a moment and if you don't go you will only be remarked."

"I don't care a single straw," said I, "for any one's remark. I was determined from the beginning to have nothing further to do with it and no one shall put me out of my course. Besides, how can I tell who this fellow from the North is? And do you think I will put myself in the power of one I don't know who may be a spy or an informer, for anything I can tell, so that go I won't and that ends it."

"Well," said Bergan, "he bid me tell you that no excuse would be taken and that go you should, and he will be here presently again, as he is only gone to warn a few others."

I became very angry at this and used some words I don't wish to repeat. I knew the messenger well; he had been bred to a trade that was not very profitable, besides he was not over and above industrious and would rather a good deal be employed at something else that would support him in ease and idleness, and on this account the business he was on matched him to a hair. I was expecting him every moment and was fully prepared to meet him. He dashed into the shop at last, nearly out of breath, and with a look of importance and wonder, said, "Well, you're to be ready for the meeting, mind, at such an hour to-day and at such a place."

"What meeting?" said I, very coolly, or rather, very sourly, or a mixture of both.

"What meeting?" said he. "Why didn't he tell you" (pointing to the apprentice) "there is a delegate in town from the north, and there's only twelve of the most intelligent men in town chose to meet him, and you're one of them; so be ready. I am wore off my legs going through the town and I haven't a moment to stay. I must be off to warn the rest."

"Oh, I can't attend it," said I, in the same tone I used at first, only a little more careless.

"You what?" said he; "you can't attend, is it? Then, how well a man from the north can travel so many miles to attend and to serve us and how well I can leave my business going through the town to warn you all and nothing for it but killing and fatiguing myself!"

"I don't want to hinder you or the man from the north or any other man to do what you please, and I'll take the same liberty for myself and do what I please."

"So you won't come then to the meeting?"

"No."

"Then I tell you you *must* come!" said he, with all the authority of one that had me in his power.

"And I tell you I must not, nor will not, either," said I.

"Well, remember that!" said he, pointing his finger and shaking his head in a most threatening manner; "remember that!" as he went off.

As soon as he was gone I looked over with astonishment at Bergan (who had been in the business before me and who frequently urged me to join so good a society) and said, "There's for us! Did you hear that? There's a pretty specimen of brotherly affection! Is that the brotherly affection you were boasting so much of?"

Bergan, who was sorry for two reasons, first, for my refusing to go, and secondly, for the behaviour or misbehaviour of the person, was a little puzzled how to act, but he endeavoured to settle the matter by laying the blame equally on both sides. "He certainly had not a right to behave in such a manner," said he; "but he was only vexed at your refusal, and you know you could go if you liked, there was nothing to prevent you."

"But when I did not like," said I, "was I to be browbeat and bullied? But I must know from Peter Ivers if such conduct is allowed; and if it is, I fear it augurs badly for the business."

As Ivers was a man that afterwards made such a very conspicuous figure on the theatre of Ireland, it may not perhaps be uninteresting to say something respecting him.

His father, who lived in the middle of the persecution of the Penal Laws and who, like every one of his class, had not much favour to expect from men in power, and who scorned to stoop to them to look for it, nobly bore up against the adversity that surrounded him, and depended on his own exertions alone (the best dependence ever a man had) to buffet the storms of the world. He was a man of an enthusiastic and highly independent spirit, that was not to be easily daunted by difficulties, and though I could never learn that he was able to acquire much wealth, still in all difficulties he invariably maintained an unsullied character, and no man living could ever say that he lost a shilling unfairly by Jemmy Ivers. In his person he was of rather a low stature but very broad and strong made, a very plain homely countenance, but something animated, kind and inviting in it. He had as good a share of learning (which was a very rare commodity in them times) as any man in his station, was very communicative, was a logician by nature but quite cheerful and friendly as long as he had his way; but if any one opposed him or showed a disposition to sack him on any point, he would find he would be just as wise to let it alone. Upon the whole, he was a cheerful, entertaining companion and every one liked his company.

As he loved learning and well knew the superiority it gives a man, it is quite natural to expect he did not neglect the education of his only son, Peter, who was his very image in mind and person. He sent him, when very young, to the best English school that was in town, the master of which was a Mr. Banks. In this school was taught reading, writing, the whole course of arithmetic and book-keeping, no more, but in writing in particular he excelled, not in the fashionable pot-hooks and hangers that are done nowadays, but in a handsome legible copper-plate hand that could be read as easily as print. It was at this school I first became acquainted with Ivers and though it was a school where boys were very apt to quarrel and fight at times, still Ivers and I never quarrelled. We always had a liking for the company of each other and the friendship that commenced there lasted through life.

It may be considered strange how a person educated at such a limited school could obtain a sufficiency of learning to qualify him for the important station he afterwards held in society. I shall endeavour to explain it. Our parish priest, the Revd. Mr. Gernon, died and was succeeded by the Revd. Mr. Staunton, who was sent to us from Graignemana. The Revd. Mr. Staunton was a most zealous and exemplary clergyman, and as soon as he was settled in the parish, he set about reforming every abuse that came within his reach (and they were many) such as bull-beating, cock-fighting, manfighting, gambling and everything of that description. He also formed a religious society and choir to sing in the chapel (a thing before unknown to us) which he taught himself, and besides that he assembled a select number of boys in the vestry-room, where he became their schoolmaster, where he spared no pains to seek our genius and to improve it. Of all the boys that were under his care, Ivers was the shining star, and became so expert a logician that he was at last fully a match on many points for Mr. Staunton himself. No wonder he should take so important a lead among people that knew little or nothing.

As soon as the United system was introduced, he embraced it eagerly. He had the example of France before him, where the people by a successful revolution had shaken off tyranny and oppression and where numbers from obscurity and poverty had been raised to high rank and affluence. These matters made a weighty impression on our hero, who under a plain appearance and humble exterior was really ambitious. Accordingly, he bent the whole force of his genius to increase and organise the United Irishmen, and such an ascendancy did he gain over every one, that everything he said was law. He was, in fact, the O'Connell of the day. As soon as the grave, the steady, the deep solid rock of sense, the Revd. Mr. Staunton heard of it, he sent for him and used all his endeavours to dissuade him from the course he was taking. The kind, the good, the charitable curate, the Revd. William Fitzgerald, who had been in France during the Revolution and who narrowly escaped with his life out of it, also endeavoured, with all the force of his eloquence, to stop his career; but all was in vain, for Ivers was as good (or thought he was as good) a logician as either of them and contended the point inch by inch, and unfortunately for himself and his country, remained immovable in his opinion, for, with all his shining abilities, he wanted one ingredient that totally unfitted him for being a first-rate leader in so important a business (and he wouldn't be second if possible to any man)—he never had that length of foresight nor depth of judgement so absolutely necessary to guide and guard a man in weighty and difficult and dangerous affairs; but these are things that often are not known till it is too late, but at that time the generality of people could see no fault in Ivers and, if they even did, it would be useless (perhaps dangerous) to express it.

As soon as I received the ill treatment I mentioned from his messenger, I made it my business, as soon as possible, to see him and, after repeating the story, asked him if that was the treatment those were to receive who joined the Society, or was that the kind of " Brotherly Affection " that was to be diffused among the people. He expressed the greatest concern for what happened, said that the man's conduct was grossly improper; " and," said he, " I will make it my business to see him and give him a severe lecture for it and I believe my best way is not to employ him any more, for I see plainly he is not fit to do such business."

CHAPTER FOUR

PREPARATIONS AND PREMONITIONS

EVERYTHING now went on swimmingly; the people were as merry as crickets, for every man that unfortunately joined it, as soon as he got the signs and passwords, thought there was some magic in it that would make him happy the remainder of his day, and even my own first apprehensions began to vanish. In about a fortnight from the dispute I had as related, my friend Bergan informed me one evening (oh, I remember it well; it was a Sunday evening, above all evenings in the year) that Peter Ivers had given him a message for me.

"A message?" said I, with astonishment, "ah, what message can it be? To attend a meeting, I suppose. And sure you know my determination on that point already and that I never will attend one, so it is quite useless for you to give me any message."

"Why, you mistake the matter entirely," said he: "for he does not want you to take any part in any meeting, he merely wishes to show you how things are going on and surely that can do you no harm and then if you don't like it you needn't go any more."

I now began to hesitate and he urged the matter more and more till at length, whether it was "pride, folly or fate," I unfortunately gave way and went to the meeting. When I was there for some time, I was startled by Ivers proposing to me to take some situation. I told him I could not do it; that, from the particular nature of my employment in having to attend a shop where there was such extensive business carried on, that I could not possibly spare time to attend to anything else. Ivers made quite light of the matter and said, "Oh, man, there is no such difficulty at all in the matter, I'll take care to make it quite easy to you."

"Why," said I, "wouldn't I have to attend meetings, and that is a thing I could not do; so you had better appoint some one else that will answer better."

"That is just as you please," said he; "for, if any pressing occasion came on, I would do your business myself, so that you need never leave the shop, if you don't like."

I found it was vain to be making objections, for if I made a hunderd Ivers would answer them with the greatest ease, so the election went on and before I left the room I was chosen a member of the baronial committee. During the interval between this time and the baronial meeting, I had various doubts as to how I should proceed or whether I would or would not attend, but when the time came I actually did go and when I once broke the ice I had no farther hesitation about it and attended every meeting as regular as any one else. After being at several meetings, and the committees for the different baronies being formed, it was considered full time to form a county committee and the mode of forming it was by sending forward three persons from each baronial committee, who were to be chosen by ballot.

For this purpose there was a certain day appointed for the election and various were the consultations and conjectures as to who the fortunate persons would be. Every one knew that Ivers would be the first man chosen, but who the other two would be was the query. Before the day arrived, Ivers gave me a whisper to know if I was elected would I stand it. I told him I could not, that my business would not allow it—that it gave me as much as I could do to attend baronial meetings and that I could not do any more. He said it would make no difference in that respect, that baronial and county meetings would not be held the one day, and that if my business did happen to interfere, he would excuse me and act in my place.

Things remained so till the day of election arrived. The three members when elected were to go forward to form the county committee; one as delegate, one as treasurer and one as secretary. As soon as they had met and had everything arranged, they proceeded at once to the election of a delegate. Ivers had it with a triumphant majority and great acclamation. The next was the treasurer and for this Mick Heydon was elected and I was chosen as secretary. Though much caution I used before I embarked deeply in the affair, still, when I was once appointed to office, I attended it with the greatest diligence. I was never absent either from baronial or county meetings, but there was one rule I invariably followed at every one of them, and that was to observe the disposition of every one present as closely as I could and not to appear conspicuous myself, as I had a strong notion (which time has proved to be correct) that where a considerable number of persons assembled on such an occasion, there was great danger of some of them being untrue, if a time arrived of putting them to too close a test, and if that did happen to be the case, that they should have as little to say against me as possible.

The organisation of the people had proceeded to a great length. They had officers, sergeants, corporals and privates, as regular as an army, and so far it did not create any apparent alarm. It was still nearly what it was in the beginning; not much more than a laugh for each other and for the people in general, for there was no talk at all as yet of getting what they called arms, as if a piece of rusty iron on the end of a stick deserved the name of arms and was fit to face gun and bayonet and cannon. To be sure, the battle of Jemappe was won by pikes but if it was, it was Frenchmen that used them and Dumourier (I think) that commanded.

But was our simple, ignorant, unlettered countrymen fit to do such an action? No, nor no other nation on earth at the time but Frenchmen alone. I may be asked, haven't we as brave men in Ireland as in any part of the world? I answer we have many, but to have a whole nation of heroes (and nothing else would do for a revolution) that would rush on like a whirlwind against disciplined armies and, though they were swept down like grass at the muzzles of their guns, would still despise danger and death and mount over heaps of slain, till they were higher than the cannon, and stopped their effect, and then actually seize the cannon and turn them on their enemies; and this not in one or two or ten or twenty battles, but every day a battle was wanting, and think it glorious to live or die in it, I never heard of any nation producing them but France alone. I do not pretend to say what overstrained oppression on one side (the side of wealth and power) and the spread of intelligence and consequent dissatisfaction under oppression on the other side (the side of the people) may yet produce in some other country, but of this I am certain, that it is the greatest possible blindness of great men (with the example of France before them) to run the risk of such a revolution when they could easily avoid it. I say easily, because very little, a very small share would satisfy the people. The Lord said to Adam in punishment of his unfortunate transgression, " Thou shalt earn thy bread by the sweat of thy brow." The people want no more. Let them till the barren and waste land for you that is on your estate and when they have tilled it and cultivated it, don't lay three rents and three tithes and three taxes on it to stall-feed those who have no industry. Leave their earnings with them and they will employ others. It is not such a very difficult thing to find employment for the people as some would fain make us imagine. Leave, I say again, but their honest hard earnings among them and they will employ each other, but should you refuse to do this, should you think you have a right to rob them and grind them down to the ground and sweep thousands of them off the face of the earth by starvation and want of employment, remember there is a God in Heaven, and remember also the example of France.

I may be told there is no other way to rule the people but by keeping them in poverty. That if they were allowed to become rich they would become ungovernable and would obey no law. I answer; look at the state of society and tell me where will you see people more amenable to the laws or that rears up their children with stricter notions of decency and propriety in every respect than those who have acquired a competence by their industry. And tell me, on the other hand, who are the promoters and ringleaders of riot and robbery and murder, and every breach almost of the laws, but those who have been reared in wretchedness, poverty, barbarism and slavery; aye, slavery and, if possible, ten times worse than slavery, for if the slave were forced to work he would be also fed and clad, but these miserable slaves have neither employment, food or raiment, and this in a country boasting of freedom. Leave them, then, the fruits of their industry, let them become affluent and comfortable and I, if my security will be of any weight, I will answer for the consequences. Should you still be in doubt of the bad effects of comfort and happiness among the human race, cast a glimpse across the Atlantic but take care it doesn't startle you too much, when you see the three and twenty United States and their millions of inhabitants in wealth and happiness, peace and plenty; where the labourer with his spade (spalpeens you call them) can earn from five shillings to seven and sixpence and sometimes nine shillings a day (while you screw your labourers down to sixpence or eightpence) and where he dines at the same table with his employer (or master if you please) and this in a country where they have none of those earthly deities called kings and nobles to make laws for them, and where they can change their rulers as easily as a man can change his shirt. Look at them, I say (if you can do so without being startled) and tell me does wealth and comfort and happiness make the people riotous and ungovernable. And if you are compelled (reluctantly) to answer in the affirmative, take a friend's advice in time, and be kind to your tenants and labourers, and make them comfortable as soon as ever you can. You have not a moment to lose. While you have them hoodwinked in ignorance is your time, for, if the shining light that has arisen in America and that has forced itself into France and is now spreading over Europe should once flash on them you might find to your cost that your pitiful, niggardly, reluctant favours would come too late.

As I said before, the people were going on gaily. There

was nothing among them but the greatest kindness and real " Brotherly Affection " and that to such a pitch, that they seemed to think they would never see a poor day, for there was no talk at all as yet of getting arms. This was too dangerous a string to touch in the beginning, for if it had been touched it would alarm the people too much and they wouldn't have joined it at all. For my own part, if such a thing had been as much as hinted, I wouldn't have joined it for all the men on earth. No, no, the people were first drawn in to swallow the bait and then to get a little intoxicated with the novelty and pleasure of the thing, and still there was not one word about war or warlike preparation.

One day my friend Bergan, who was out on business and who was always active and on the alert to bring me intelligence, came in and with a look of wonder asked me did I hear the news.

" What news ? " said I, catching alarm from his very look.

" Oh," said he " it's now we have the news in earnest; sure we're going to get arms."

"Arms ? " said I, " arms ! ah, what arms ? "

" Pikes," said he.

The very sound of the word struck me with horror. " Oh, man, don't believe it ! " said I ; " it can't be true."

" It's as true as you're there," said he.

" Why, who says it ? "

" Peter Ivers says it ; that's the very man says it."

" Oh, it can't be possible; sure he couldn't be such a madman ! "

" It is possible," said he ; " and get them he will, for he is fully bent on it."

" I'll take very good care he shall not," said I, " if it be in my power to prevent it." Inexperienced as I was and little as I knew of the world, I saw destruction in it at the very first sight. People in the beginning were so cautious of being in the power of too many, that one of them in swearing a new member would not allow a third person (even one already sworn in) to be present, but if the getting of pikes was persevered in, I plainly saw it would put hundreds in the power of each other, particularly the smiths that would make them and the persons that would buy and distribute them, to say nothing of the murder that was implied in having them at all.

Full of these melancholy forebodings, I made it my business to see Ivers without delay, not doubting (if the report was true) but I could without any difficulty make him sensible of the madness of such a course. As soon as we met, " Peter," said I, " I'm come to you to know if this report I hear is true ? "

" What report is it ? " said he.

"A report," said I, " that you are going to get arms made for the people."

" If it be true ? " said he, laughing and staring at me with as much wonder as I stared at him. " To be sure it is true. Why, what did we unite for ? What are the people organised for ? "

" Oh," said I, " sure it wasn't to murder any one we united; wasn't it to form a ' brotherhood of affection ' we united, and sure there is no ' brotherhood of affection ' in murdering any one ! "

" Oh, man," said he, " you don't understand it at all; now we are expecting the French here immediately, to emancipate us. There are delegates in Paris this moment about it. They have an exact account of our organisation and of our numbers and they of course expect as soon as they land, that we will be ready armed to assist them. Wouldn't it be a very pretty thing if they landed to-morrow, to find us unarmed, unable and unwilling to assist them ; but let them, after encountering the dangers of the sea, have to fight our battles for us and let us be tame cowardly spectators, till they were done, and then expect a share of the victory—why, it would be an eternal disgrace to us ! We would show ourselves fit for nothing but to be mean, abject slaves and it would be little matter if they did enslave us."

" But," said I, " do you observe the dangerous predicament you will place the people in by getting arms ? At present, there is no offence against the law by being United

Irishmen; but go one step further; let the getting of arms be tacked to it and you make it a capital offence. You put ropes round the people's necks from that moment; and all on the uncertainty of the French coming to assist us. And if we should get pikes (or arms as you call them) and that the French did not come, what could we expect but slaughter without mercy? Besides, I will show you for two reasons how they are no use at all."

" What reasons? " said he.

" First, if the French don't come, they can never be used; and if they do come they won't be wanting, for they will bring plenty of arms with them."

Here he burst into a loud *ha ha ha* and said, " they are irrefragable reasons, no doubt, but tell me, if they did land and did not bring the arms, how would we be? For, mind, we are to leave nothing if possible to chance; how would we be then? "

" Why, if it went to that," said I, " 'twouldn't give the people more than three days to get arms enough."

" How would they be got in three days? " said he.

" Take them," said I, " from every one has them, and that I am sure could be done."

" You could not be sure of it," said Ivers.

" Well, if I even could not," said I, " what is the reason a pitchfork wouldn't be as good as a pike; and there is no law against a man having a pitchfork. Get as many pitchforks made as you please, if you get anything. If it was left to me, I would get none at all, but for God's sake do not get pikes made, for I see some deadly danger in it that I am not able to explain."

Ivers, who listened to me with great attention, but who was not to be turned out of his course, replied, " If we never wanted them to assist the French, we would want them to defend ourselves against the Orangemen; don't you hear accounts every day of them murdering people in the North, and I'll engage we will soon have the same here among ourselves."

Though Ivers spoke in this manner, he knew right well

there was no danger at all of Orangemen turning out in this part of the country, because the Catholics here were too numerous for them, and because there was no part of Ireland where a better feeling of friendship existed between both Catholics and Protestants, nor no part where greater numbers of both were blood relations; so that there was no cause at all for having the least apprehension on that head. I told him so, but all in vain, for he was determined not to give up and I no sooner drove him from one position than he dexterously took up another and this being his last one, he put on a countenance of great gravity and said, " Why, man, you are speaking to me on this subject as if I was the inventor of it, or as if this was the first part of the country that was getting them; now, instead of that, I tell you we are nearly the last, and that there are few counties in Ireland but has them already ; and are we to set up our opinion in opposition to the wisest men in the kingdom and think every one fools but ourselves ? And if we even did refuse to join them, we wouldn't be a feather in the scale and would only get ourselves laughed at."

This settled the matter. I saw plainly there was no use in contending any farther, and I went home filled with the most alarming apprehensions for my unfortunate country and left Ivers exulting at the bad victory he had gained over me. I knew right well I had not made any impression that would have even a chance of turning him from so mad a project and a very little time proved it but too clearly, for pikes, that were afterwards to be our ruin, were making in every direction. I shuddered at the consequences but could not prevent them. The reader will here particularly observe the deep, the vital importance of this argument between Ivers and myself; how the destruction or welfare of Ireland depended on it, how exactly everything I warned him of came to pass, particularly the dreadful point of having things called "Arms" and no foreign aid to oppose disciplined armies of horse, foot and artillery, and what a vast difference there is between tinselled logic and a grain of common sense.

In some time after, another serious difference, and on a most important matter, happened between us. The quarry division, to which we both belonged, had its full complement of men and sergeants, but no captain, and it was considered full time to elect one. As the sergeants alone were the proper persons to elect the captain, I had nothing to do with it and, of course, did not mind much about it. However, my friend Bergan who, as I said before, brought me every intelligence, came in one day and, almost laughing, asked me did I hear any news lately.

"No, indeed, I don't recollect anything particular," was the reply.

"Indeed you did," said he, "but you are so close-minded you wouldn't tell a body anything."

At the commencement of these elections for captains, there was little or no precaution taken to examine whether the man chosen possessed the qualities requisite to fill the station or not; it was generally made a joke of, or treated as caprice or whim dictated. At one time a man remarkable for speaking with great warmth in praise of liberty and reprobation of tyranny was considered a very proper person for a captain. At another, a man that had the greatest number of United Men's songs and could sing them best was chosen. At another, a man that had plenty of money to spend and that was a good fellow and treating everybody gained the honour, with hundreds of other similar reasons; for at the time people in general were not aware that they would ever be brought into real action and thought that any one would do to be a captain, but a little time showed them the difference, for when they got arms in their hands (or things in the name of arms) they became so unruly that it became a very difficult task to keep them to order where every one should be captain and do as he pleased himself. On this account, it required more resolution in a captain of United Irishmen than in a captain of a regular regiment of the line, where men, so far from disputing the orders of their captain, should know nothing but to obey them.

PREPARATIONS AND PREMONITIONS

The want of this subordination was productive of the most melancholy consequences. Not satisfied with the unlawful arms they had of their own, they frequently attacked the houses of those who had firearms and did not leave one they could come at but they plundered, and these were considered such meritorious actions that a captain, if he happened to be a man of prudence and foresight that disapproved of them, he would in many cases have very little business to make an objection as, if he did, he would run the risk of losing his popularity and be branded perhaps with cowardice in the bargain. When the people once got possession of fire arms, they were not very long before they got an itch to try them; and woe betide the man that would say or do anything contrary to the rules and regulations of United Irishmen, or that would even express a doubt of their success or fear of their doing wrong. Any man that had the temerity to do so placed himself in one of the most unenviable situations imaginable; for the moment the "Brotherly affection" men heard it, they tried, judged and executed any sentence they pleased on him, in the most summary manner.

I shall just mention one out of a great number of various descriptions. There was a Mr. Bennett who lived at a place called Ballynocken, near Leighlin Bridge. He was in a most respectable station in life and though he did not rank so high as a first rate gentleman, still he was in the front rank of what was called gentlemen-farmers and as he was kind and familiar to those in the humble walks of life and very useful and skilful as a doctor, on many occasions there was a particular respect paid to him by everybody, rich as well as poor. This good man being in Leighlin Bridge one day, the company he was in began to discourse about the United business and to recommend it in glowing terms.

"I'll tell you what, my good friends," said he; "you are not aware of the kind of business it is at all and I tell you now that it will bring destruction on the country and on every one that has a hand in it."

They continued to praise it and he honestly but unguardedly continued to tell them the truth. The story got wind and was told of course with alterations and additions and in about three or four nights afterwards he was shot dead in his own house. Terror and dismay flew in every direction on the announcement of the bloody tragedy. Gentlemen were taught silence by his fate and even the thinking part of the United Irishmen could only whisper their sorrow to each other but to this day the name of Mr. Bennett of Ballynocken is mentioned with grief and regret by every one that knew him. In this dangerous and alarming state the county was, when the people of the Quarry Division of Carlow, to which I belonged proposed choosing a captain. As I belonged to the civil department, the thing did not concern me very closely any further than that I would wish to see a proper person in the station and of this I had no doubt; Peter Ivers belonged to the division and I was quite certain no improper person could be chosen, where he regulated all as he liked. My expectations on the subject, however, were very soon disappointed. As I said before, my friend Bergan, who brought me every intelligence, came in one day and with a look and tone expressive of disgust and regret, asked me if I heard any news lately. I told him I did not hear anything particular.

" Indeed you did," said he, " but you are so close-minded you wouldn't tell a body anything."

I assured him in the most earnest manner that I did not know of anything particular and requested if *he* did, that he would not keep me in suspense.

" Why," said he, " didn't you hear we are going to get a captain ? "

"A captain ? " said I, " a captain ! Ah, what captain ? Who is to be captain ? "

" Who do you think ? " said he, " you must guess now, or I won't tell you."

"I really do not know who to guess at," said I ; " maybe yourself ? "

"Oh, myself, indeed!" said he, "myself indeed! No such thing, but a greater man by far."

"Ah, who can it be?" said I, "let me know at once."

"Why, Henry," said he, "Master Henry!"

"Is it Henry Rogers?" said I.

"The very man," replied Bergan.

"Merciful God!" said I, "is it Henry Rogers? who says it?—who proposes him as a captain?"

"Peter Ivers says it," continued Bergan, "and will have him in the station and nobody else."

"I'll take very good care he shall not," said I; "I will not allow it! I'll do everything in my power to oppose him and he shall never get in."

"And how will you prevent it?" said Bergan dryly, and laughing at the same time.

"Speak to all the sergeants," said I, "and put them on their guard."

"That will never do," said Bergan, "for the sergeants will do nothing but what Peter likes."

"Then I'll speak to Peter himself," said I, "and sure it it can't be possible he will persist in putting in such a person."

CHAPTER FIVE

MEN AND SHADOWS

Before I proceed farther on this subject I think it necessary to give some account of this man who was afterwards so notorious a character in Ninety-eight.

Let no one imagine I take any pleasure in exposing any of my unfortunate countrymen who had the misfortune to disgrace themselves and their families in these times of persecution and terror and blood. No, I would willingly draw a veil over them if in my power, and will carefully abstain from mentioning any one of them, except such as are unavoidable and whose names are already before the public in as legible characters as any I could use. I know very well that few large families can be exempt from some bad members, but it would be cruelty indeed to wound the feelings of the innocent for the crimes of their degenerate relatives, which they mourn for and deplore more keenly than any other members of the community. For these reasons no person need be under the least apprehension, in looking over these pages, of finding their names recorded by me, as I fully adopt the sentiments of the great English Homer in that respect:

> Curst be the verse how well soe'r it flow
> That tends to make one worthy man my foe
> Give Virtue scandal, Innocence a fear
> Or from the soft-eyed virgin steal a tear.

It will be my endeavour to do all the justice in my power to the virtues of my heroic countrymen who nobly stood their ground in her cause, but to heave a sigh for those who failed in the dreadful trial, which was indeed almost beyond human endurance, and to let their ashes rest in peace and obscurity.

The man I now speak of was born in Carlow. His family

were, in days gone by, both wealthy and respectable, but as they were of that class and creed who were subject to the visitations of the Penal Laws, they could not make that permanent establishment for posterity which they otherwise might and which in all probability they would have done. The father of Henry Rogers, though having but small means, always supported the character of a decent tradesman and seemed to pique himself on the station his people once held.

As for Henry himself, from his boyhood he was too fond of that kind of education that is learned in the streets. He always wished to distinguish himself as a noisy little leader or partly a bully with those of his own age and as he had always an extraordinary share of loud talk for any subject and a considerable share of family pride, he generally had his way on every occasion with the company he kept, who were mostly of a class inferior in the world to himself. Though I knew him from his early years, I never liked his manner and would make no acquaintance with him; and if we did happen to meet, I always kept him at arm's-length, for of all persons there were few I disliked more than a braggadocio or bully.

When he grew up he enlisted in the militia, where he remained some years (I wish he remained there since), but was at length discharged for what reason I cannot tell (nor is it now material) but it was some time before the invention of the United system. Such was the man designed by Peter Ivers to fill the important station of captain at such a dangerous and critical period.

As soon as I could spare time, I went to Ivers and asked him if it could be possible that he intended to appoint Rogers to such a station.

" Possible ? " said he; " possible ? It is indeed very possible. Why do you wonder at it ? "

" I do indeed wonder at it; why now, don't you know him all his life and don't you know he does not profess one single quality to fit him for the station of a captain ? "

" Oh, you are quite mistaken," said Ivers; " there is

not a man in the town fitter for it. He was a wild foolish boy, to be sure, but the years he spent in the militia have quite changed him; he is not the same person at all that he was."

"I tell you he is," said I, "and he shall never be appointed with my consent, and if you suffer it, you will be sorry for it, depend on what I say."

"Why," said Ivers, "you speak to me as if I was doing it all myself, but I tell you it is no such thing, for the sergeants themselves are all for him and have proposed him to me and certainly, as he knows discipline and the use of arms so well, I do not know of any one so proper to fill it; and if he is rejected, can you tell me any man more fitting? If you can, I would be quite happy to hear it; perhaps you would like to take it yourself?"

"No," said I, "I will not take it myself; but if you want a proper man, a man to stand true on any emergency, appoint Mick Wall—that is the man to stand if a trial comes on."

As this man was very remarkable in the dreadful scenes that followed I consider it right in this place to give the reader some account of who he was.

His ancestors held large estates in the County Carlow nd in the Wars of Ireland held the rank of captains and colonels in the army. The cause they engaged in proved unfortunate and they lost all their property, but though they lost their estates and were obliged in the course of time to earn their bread, they did not lose the ancient nobles' spirit. They had naturally all those qualities that fit men for great and high stations. In athletic exercises, such as hurling, leaping, vaulting, etc., etc., they were first-rate, and as for valour in the field, no men could surpass them, although they were as careful in concealing this latter quality as others are in displaying it, and never showed it except when compelled by necessity; but when that happened there was no doubt of their being victorious. They were a protection to the people of their neighbourhood, for no one dared to inflict a wrong on the weakest neighbour in their presence;

they were my blood relations; the present man and my mother being second cousins, but not on this account at all would I recommend him but for the truth I knew was in him.

As soon as I mentioned his name to Ivers, "Oh," said he, "sure I know there is no better man than Mick Wall, but it will never come to that; we will never have such a trial as you mean."

"Don't be too sure," said I, "I think there is danger but, whether or not, there is nothing like having a man in a station that is fit to fill it."

"Oh," said he, "don't think that I am choosing Rogers. I have nothing at all to do with it; it's no interest of mine; only I see the people are all for him and the sergeants requested of me to have him appointed; that's all I know about it and you know the sergeants can appoint who they like in spite of me."

Notwithstanding all his cleverness in seeming so disinterested, I plainly saw he was (as usual) wedded to his own opinion and I instantly formed the resolution, if possible, to see the sergeants myself, unknown to Ivers, and prevent it; but he proved an overmatch for me, by calling the meeting so suddenly that I could not possibly have time to see them, as they lived so far asunder. The only resource now left me was to be at the house of meeting before they could assemble, and arrange matters with the sergeants as they went in, but in this also I was disappointed, for Ivers had them all in the room before I could get there, and Rogers along with them, so that I had no room to say a word; however, as I had spoke and sent word to some of the sergeants, I could not be certain how far my advice might be followed and I waited with great anxiety to see the result of the election and from the station I held as member of the baronial committee, I was allowed by Ivers to have the privilege to vote, which was done by writing the names on slips of paper and throwing them into a hat. But judge of my surprise when, on the papers being examined, there was not one came out with the name of Mick Wall on it but the one I put in myself. I was completely thunderstruck. Poor Wall looked over at me and gave a laugh and shake of his head, expressive of pity and contempt for the choice that was made; for my part, I was so full of sorrow and indignation that I left the room to themselves as soon as I possibly could, laughed at of course by Ivers and the rest but filled with the most gloomy forebodings of what had been done.

The reader will here also particularly observe how much depended on this election, how much the safety or ruin of the large and populous town of Carlow in particular depended on it, the dangerous trials that afterwards came on, and how widely different these two men acted.

In the course of some time afterwards, they wanted to appoint a lieutenant and Rogers's brother was proposed, but I protested against this with such vehemence that the claim was put aside and my friend Bergan appointed. We had now various baronial and some county meetings, at which nothing very particular occurred, until members were to be chosen from the county committee to go forward to Dublin, to form the provincial. This certainly was a grave business and when we met there were various opinions in private to know who would be the men. After much deliberation and consultation, the election went on. Larry Griffen from Tullow, a smart active middle-aged man, was the first chosen and I think a young man of the name of Matt Byrne from Rathvilly was the next. I now felt considerably for Ivers who (to me that knew him) seemed much disappointed at not being chosen second at least, though he assumed all the coolness possible and appeared to show he had no inclination at all for it and that he would rather some other person was appointed to a charge so weighty. However, the election went on. The names were nearly equal but the majority was for Ivers. A general burst of applause followed and Ivers himself (now that the thing was secured) could not conceal the satisfaction he felt. It was indeed what he wished for most ardently. Arrangements were now made by the new members to proceed to Dublin, the day to meet there was announced and money given by the treasurer to each member, to defray his expenses. I should have mentioned before that, on the admission of a new member, there was sixpence demanded of him as entrance and some trifle, about twopence monthly, to go to the fund ; but, as there was too much good nature among the brotherhood, they would not hurt the feelings of each other by pressing the demand too strictly, so that it was quite optional to give it or not and ninety-nine out of a hundred gave nothing at all but, if the rule was strictly enforced and every one made to pay, it would have made an immense sum, but people that did not know this gave out afterwards that certain individuals made large fortunes by it, but it was one of the grossest of falsehoods.

Everything being ready, the new members set off at the time appointed and met in Dublin. It was the grand theatre on which Ivers wished to display his talents, which he did ; first by a speech that drew forth the applause of the whole meeting, and afterwards by some resolution that was wanting to be drawn up in a very particular manner. There were several attempts made at it by different members but none of them would satisfy the meeting ; there was still some fault or other to be found. At length it was agreed on that a certain number of the most experienced and talented men should withdraw into a private apartment ; that each man should draw up a resolution to his own taste, and that of course would be the best chance of some one getting over the difficulty that opposed them. Ivers could not be idle on such an important point and while they were all waiting in the most anxious suspense for what the great mountain in labour would bring forth, he drew up one himself unknown to any one in the room.

After waiting a considerable time the wise men made their appearance. A dead silence followed. All were on the tip-toe of expectation to hear the wonders. Every man's paper was read in rotation. But to their great disappointment every man's paper had a fault and they were just now as badly off as ever. At this critical moment, Ivers stepped forward and said, " Gentlemen, here is a resolution I have drawn up on the subject and if you allow it to be read, perhaps it would come nearer to your wishes." The resolution was read and one general burst of acclamation followed from the whole meeting and from that moment Ivers from Carlow was known to them all and his name adopted as a password to their future meetings.

The business of the provincial meeting being over, Ivers came home with flying colours and gave a most flattering account of all he saw. He spoke with the greatest enthusiasm of the preparations that were making to obtain liberty and of perfect confidence in its success, and urged every one to increased exertions in the cause, and it certainly had come to a wonderful pitch, both with regard to numbers and the enthusiastic spirit that animated the people, and besides this it had found its way into the yeomanry, the militia and the regular regiments of the line, particularly in the two camps of Blaris and Loughlinstown, which, it was said, were all United Irishmen to a man, with very few exceptions and all burning with eagerness to be led on in the cause of liberty.

When the time approached for our members to go down again to Dublin, there were orders issued by the executive to all the provincial members of all the counties, to bring up all the money the county treasurers had and, besides this, to get as much voluntary subscriptions from every one as they possibly could, as there was some mighty measure on foot and money was absolutely necessary for putting it in execution.

This executive committee or council, or whatever else it may be called, was an invisible body, known to no one almost but themselves, and the more invisible it was, the more awe and respect did it command, for like Jack the Giant-Killer's invisible cloak, people imagined they could see and do everything they pleased and that no one could see or overcome them and accordingly, when they issued their orders, they were obeyed with the most scrupulous exactness, as people were very apprehensive they might bring their sword of sharpness to bear on any district or person found negligent.

When our county committee met, Ivers opened the business in the most persuasive manner he could. He spoke in glowing terms of the prosperous state of the business we were engaged in, of the great abilities of the great invisibles of the executive, of the complete organisation of every department, of the burning zeal of the army in Blaris and Loughlinstown and everywhere else, the great necessity there was for money to enable them to strike some important blow, and he was certain their power was so great they would be able to gain their liberty without foreign aid. Alas, alas, he never calculated that England was at that moment at the very height of her power by sea and land, that she had one of the most subtle scourgers of the human race (Pitt) her prime-minister, and that we had no more chance of conquering liberty, without foreign aid, than we had of pulling down the moon. Ivers was, as usual, quite sanguine in a contrary opinion and called on the county treasurer to produce his accounts and show what money he had on hands but it appearing that he had only the paltry trifle of about thirty-five pounds, he said it would be an indelible disgrace on our county to be so shamefully behind every other county in the province, and that, unless a weighty subscription was immediately entered into and brought forward, our county members would be ashamed to go forward to meet the great men, the patriotic men of the provincial committee, that probably the fate of Ireland depended on the measure now on hands, and that no man having a spark of patriotism and having means but should come forward and contribute to the utmost of his power. Some cheered his speech, while others were silent enough, but at any rate the subscription went on and every one present gave more or less. On the meeting breaking up, every one got directions to use all his influence with every man of wealth within his reach, to induce him to subscribe liberally, and to bring in all the money they could in the course of a week, as there was no time to be lost.

On the day appointed, we all met in the highest spirits and every man was questioned as to his exertions and success in raising the subscription but, upon the whole, the utmost that could be made out was only about seventy-five pounds, which was considered very small, but as more could not be had, our provincial members were obliged to stifle complaints and murmurs and take it with the best grace possible, but it left our treasury without a stiver. Ivers as usual was quite enthusiastic and expressed the greatest reliance on the profound wisdom and skill of the invisibles already mentioned and of his hopes, aye, and confidence of success, while others had their misgivings on the matter.

Everything ready, they all set off and met the other delegates in Dublin. The people at home, particularly those who paid their money, were in the greatest anxiety to know what the result of the mighty conference would be and when Ivers returned the curiosity and anxiety increased, as every one imagined he would instantly call a meeting to communicate the joyful intelligence but he did no such thing; he kept himself quite retired for some days, gave no information at all, and it was not till after he was urged to it that he reluctantly enough called a baronial meeting. The people, in the meantime, had very gloomy forebodings and when they met it was quite plain they had no less than reason for, instead of the enthusiasm always displayed by Ivers, he was completely chopfallen. He apologised for not calling the meeting sooner but alleged the fatigue he went through as the cause and, on being questioned on the outbreak that was so confidently expected, he said it had been debated by some of the ablest men in Ireland both for and against it and so evenly were both parties balanced that the weight of that (said he, showing a small bit of paper) would have turned the scale one side or the other; but, on the whole, it was considered best to make some additional preparations, in order to have everything secured beyond the possibility of doubt.

The instant he spoke the words, it occurred to me that they had lost an opportunity that they never again would have, for fortune is a very coy mistress and if not seized boldly when she presents herself, is very apt to take fret and leave us there. Besides this, the pass was sold at the very time to Government, as was afterwards well known, and they had their emissaries at the meeting to postpone matters, till it was their perfect convenience to draw the net on them. On being questioned as to how the money would be employed that all the counties sent in, he said that it had been lodged safely according to the orders of the executive, who were men of sterling worth and patriotism and would be employed by them without delay in forwarding the grand object that all had in view, and that they had sent down orders to the people to hold themselves in instant readiness for action; that every captain should provide himself with a strong car and horse for the use of his division; and that he should also have a pair of colours and every one of his men that could, should have the same that, in case they were attacked by cavalry, they should all unfurl their colours suddenly at them and by that means, aided by shouting, throw them all in confusion. I nearly sickened when I heard the story, as to me it had more the appearance of a humbug invented by some old ladies to amuse or astonish children than an official announcement from the invisible wise men of all Ireland.

Indeed, I must own it gave Ivers as much as he could do to give it any sort of a face and it was the first time I ever saw him distressed in delivering a discourse. He was evidently chagrined and disappointed at what he saw in Dublin and to any thing of a penetrating eye he could not at all conceal it. The committee listened to him in solemn silence and sorrow and astonishment, and it was the hold he had on their confidence and their respect for his abilities alone that saved him from hearing some very unpleasant remarks on the subject. As for the cars and colours and frightening cavalry, every one thought it the most prudent course to say nothing at all about them for fear of disheartening the people, while the stories of Blaris and Loughlinstown Camps were blazoned forth in the most glowing colours.

CHAPTER SIX

TREACHERY AND TERROR

EVERY day from this out became more and more gloomy. The magistrates and the army were more and more on the alert. The people were publicly insulted and trampled on. Different parts of the country were subject in some degree to martial law. Houses were broken open at night and the inmates beaten or sometimes put up and half-hanged to extort information, which the people in every instance refused to give, but the alarm caused by it had a serious effect, by damping the spirits of everyone. The members of committees and persons in other stations became more slow and cool in attending their duties and when the time came for having the next county meeting, it was under great apprehension they met. However, they did meet and though everyone was sensible of approaching danger, no one knew what remedy to apply, but depended implicitly on the wisdom of the " Executive " that they did not know and (for that very reason of their being invisible) placed the more confidence in them, for there was something in the name of the " Executive " that operated like magic and everyone considered them a superior race of beings who possessed individually the wisdom of Solomon but, when all joined together, formed a mass of wisdom capable of doing anything ; that there was no difficulty so great but the " Executive " would free the people from at once ; for the people were so credulous they never dreamed of treachery or perfidy, or what an Englishman could plan and execute too in this respect.

The Provincial Committee was to meet at the celebrated Oliver Bond's in Bridge Street and, as there was a man in Dublin of the name of McCann uncommonly active in the business, his name and Ivers's (as a compliment to both) were to be the passwords for getting admittance. Every member, as he came, had to mention them in the following manner : " Is McCann here ?—Is Ivers from Carlow come ? "—and immediately he was passed on to the meeting-room. They little imagined the pass was sold and that Pitt's agents had the words as well as themselves and that a guard was watching to take them. However, the plan did not succeed to the full extent that was contemplated ; for, whether it was too much tardiness on the one side to meet at the exact hour, or too much haste on the other to catch them, the party that was appointed to take them proceeded too soon to the place of meeting. However, they gave the passwords as well as the rest and, as soon as they were admitted, rushed at once well-armed into the room and made prisoners of every man in it.

Besides those that entered, there was a strong guard of soldiers in waiting, who immediately surrounded the house, so that no one could escape, and as it would have been quite useless to attempt it nobody did so. They were obliged to surrender at discretion with the loss of all their papers. The noise and terror and alarm caused by it saved the members who had not arrived and who were hastening to the place and whom a few minutes more would have been caught in the trap. Among those taken, were our two county members, Peter Ivers and Larry Griffin ; the others escaped.

The news of this adventure flew like lightning through town and country and we had it in Carlow early next morning, which filled us all with consternation. There was no county suffered a greater loss than ours, for Ivers was so very active and clever at arranging and managing, that he done everything himself and as none of us had any occasion or would attempt to meddle in such things while he was among us, we were quite a set of novices without him. One thing we were certain of : that he would never sell his country or his friends and though there were various offers made to him for that purpose, we did not feel the least alarm on it, as we were quite confident our man was too good game to bend to them.

There was one thing I forgot to mention sooner. A most ridiculous and nonsensical fashion was introduced of cropping off the people's hair quite close to their heads; and like every other fashion that the people blindly adopt, they put this in practice with the greatest eagerness. The graceful locks, so much prized before, were shorn in an instant and a young man did not think he would be considered polite or in any degree fashionable if he did not display a pair of large ass's ears and bared to the very skull, as if he had a fit of the scald. Verily, fashion, you have great power over some people. To me it appeared the extreme of folly and worse than folly, as there was danger attached to it. I always wished, even in ordinary cases, to have some sense or meaning in what would be done, but in this, which I looked on to be very important, I could see nothing but the height of absurdity and was quite disgusted with it. I, of course, thought it a duty incumbent on me to warn every one against the danger and, when I did so, I was laughed at heartily for my pains but I told them it was no laughing matter and that I thought a man might nearly as well wear a label on his breast with the words " I am a United man " on it, as do so; that there was no magistrate or no man of sense but would be of the same opinion, and that I did not think it right of any man to expose himself or make himself ridiculous without any necessity and when he might so easily let it alone. To this I was answered " to the d—— with the magistrates; who cares for them, and if it was only to vex them I'd do it the more. Is there any law to hinder a man of cutting his hair any way he pleases? Can a magistrate take a man up for it, without having a crime against him? And if he had a crime against him, long hair wouldn't save him. He'd take him up if his hair was a yard long, as soon as he'd take up a croppy." It is really astonishing with what pertness some logicians can take up a bad subject and with what obstinacy they can persevere in it in defiance of common sense or reason. However, the error of it was just as plain to me as it was before and it was with increased disgust and sorrow I saw the people persevere in it more and more until every one almost, except myself, was cropped to the very skull. Alas, alas, they little imagined they would rue the day they did not take my advice. I had no idea at the time in what it could have originated but I have now little doubt it was one of Pitt's plans to make them more ridiculous and the more easily known when the time arrived that he wanted to pitch-cap them and crop them in right down earnest.

Being left without Ivers, we were obliged to manage in the best way we could. The first blow was struck by Pitt and he was too skilful in the art of destroying the human race to lose any time, as he well knew, from England's great power at that time (but which she will never have again), that he had the battle in his hand when he pleased. It was indeed an extraordinary battle; a statesman to raise an artificial battle with his fellow-subjects, for the purpose of first murdering and then robbing them. Accordingly, consternation and dismay being struck into the people and the army, he attacked both at the one time as half-measures would not then be effectual. Blaris camp, which was considered the strongest garrison in the people's cause, was soon purged by the cat-o'-nine-tails. Every suspected man in it was flogged and transported, and that strong body of men, that combined were thought irresistible, were reduced with the greatest ease, when disheartened and taken one by one.

Loughlinstown Camp was reduced in the same manner and just so was every regiment in every part of the kingdom, and all this with as much ease and certainty as the juggler with loaded dice is sure of winning the game from the novice that engages him. The people, with all their organisation and all their *arms* (pretty arms, indeed), were treated with downright scorn and contempt, as well they might. The ransacking and burning of houses at night, the flogging and half-hanging of the inmates to extort information, that was commenced a short time before, was extended in every direction with increased violence; and if any of the unfortunate sufferers happened to get sulky or show any sign of ill-temper under the most brutal treatment, the pitch-cap was struck on and after being let to cement a little, was set fire to and the insolent wearer allowed to roar and tear it off as well as he could to the great amusement and delight of the spectators.

While these performances were going on, we, though bereft of our leader, did not entirely lose our spirits. The hope we had in the magical powers of the invisible committee in Dublin, called the " Executive," supported us. Our committees met, though not in such numbers as usual, for there were spies in every direction and we had need of using the greatest precaution. Besides, the town was full of army, a great number of whom displayed their Orange ribbons and their fifes and drums in every direction, playing " Croppies lie down " and every other tune that would insult or annoy the people most and though there were numbers of them that wished well to the cause, the people were engaged in, still they dare not budge, as they were as closely watched themselves and were certain of being brought to the triangles if they uttered a word in their favour.

At length the time arrived for calling a county meeting (which was always held in the town) and when the first of the members came to the place of meeting, they were so much in dread of being arrested, that they proposed having it held at a friend's house in the country, about three miles off, and which was actually agreed to, and they had just set off for the place a little before I came up. As soon as I heard of it, I cried out in the strongest manner against it to Mick Heydon, who was left behind to direct the members on, according as they arrived. I told him the country was as thick with spies as the town; that we would be suspected and watched by every one of them we met; and that such a number of strange men meeting at a house in the country could have no excuse; that there would be guilt in our very appearance; that it would be too plain we were about something wrong in such times; and that, instead of running from danger, we would be running into its very mouth; that we had a public house to meet at in town and if necessary we might meet in different rooms; and that if we even were attacked there would be less difficulty in having excuses, as a public house was free to everyone.

Heydon agreed with me immediately and dispatched a messenger after them, who brought them back, but as the majority of the other members failed in coming, we done no business that day, further than to appoint another day for meeting and send word to all members to attend.

In the meantime, the persecution of the people was extended in every direction and carried on with the greatest rigour. Every nerve was strained to force them to a premature revolt but the people bore it steadily in the hope that the " Wonderful Executive " would immediately commence operations and that they would be crowned with victory. Vain hope, which was never to be realised! Pitt had his direful plans too well arranged to leave any chance of it; town and country was one scene of terror and alarm and armies marching and counter-marching in every direction and leaving desolation in their track.

The day at length arrived for our county meeting and besides the forces stationed in the town, two regiments more were ordered on that very day to march in. As soon as the members arrived, they were informed of this and concluded at once that it was for the purpose of having them arrested so formidable a force was prepared, and they became so panic-struck that they agreed at once to leave the town and set off with all speed to hold it in the country. I came up a little after they went and was greatly mortified when Heydon told me what they had done and asked him why he agreed to it. He said he had done his best to prevent them, but it was of no use. They would listen to nothing but leaving the town and he had his choice either to have no meeting at all or follow them, and from the state things were in, there should be a meeting at any risk, to send members to the provincial, as if that was not done all would be confusion immediately and all lost.

I saw very plainly the truth of his remarks and though I was sadly vexed in the beginning and refused to go, still I yielded to his opinion and agreed to go, though I told him at the time the danger we were in of being seen and remarked on the road by any of the opposite party that might meet us. I set out first and took the high road. Heydon followed me but crossed the country. When I had got about a mile outside the town, I saw a man at a considerable distance riding towards me, which gave me some uneasiness and as he came nearer I found him to be a man from the town I was well acquainted with and an Orangeman, and though I greatly disliked meeting him, still there could be no flinching and I was reluctantly compelled to advance. As soon as we met, I gave the customary salute and thought to pass on, but he reined up the horse and put some very searching questions to me, accompanied with the most scrutinising looks, which showed plainly his suspicions of what I was about, but I endeavoured to appear as careless as possible and after evading his examination as well as I could, I bid him good-bye and went on a good deal vexed at being put (as I thought) to such an unnecessary trial. When I came near the house of meeting, one of the members I was acquainted with came out and met me, and after the usual ceremonies asked me in a friendly way what was the reason I hadn't my hair cropped. I was in bad humour at the time and thought it a most extraordinary question to put in the midst of such danger. I replied very coldly that I didn't choose to crop my hair and that I thought it was a very foolish custom from the beginning. He gave a hearty laugh at this and said, " Oh, then, my boy, you'll be cropped before you leave that house, as sure as you live, for they are after cropping two or three already and such diversion you never saw."

" Why," said I, " do they mean to insult me? If I thought they did, I wouldn't go in at all and I didn't think it was such treatment I was to get after following them here in such danger and I believe I will just turn back again and leave them there."

" Oh don't do that," said he ; " and since you are so averse to it, I am certain they will not press it on you, but take care one of them does not get behind you with the scissors and whip it off in a moment, for it is only all a joke."

"I won't go in one foot," said I, "except you go in first and tell them my determination that I will not submit to it on any account; they may make fools of themselves if they please but they shall not make one of me."

He accordingly went in and returned immediately and called me and said he had settled the matter to my liking. When I went in, I was received kindly by the gentlemen present who (as if they had no important business at all on hands) asked me very gravely what my objections were to having my hair cropped.

"Gentlemen," said I, "you all know that the line of business I am engaged in brings me in constant intercourse with gentlemen of rank and I do not wish to offend them or lose their friendship by telling them I am a United Irishman; and if I cropped my hair it would be telling it to them as plainly as if I told them so in words."

"But don't you see the first men in the kingdom doing it?" said one of the wise legislators; "and don't you see everyone here has done it? and do you think yourself wiser than us all?"

"I don't want to prevent any man of doing as he pleases and having his own opinion," said I, "and I think it only reasonable that I should be allowed to have mine."

The majority immediately cried out in my favour and they proceeded to the business of the day which was to elect members to go to Dublin, to meet the provincial committee. This was a serious business, indeed, and a dangerous one and so apprehensive were they all of it that several of them gave in their objections beforehand and said there was no use in electing them, as they could not possibly go; and in order to save trouble and prevent disappointment, it was proposed that the persons to go should be chosen first and then that the ballot might be gone on with, merely for form sake. This was agreed to for the best of reasons, because they couldn't help it and everyone was glad to settle the matter any way, so as he could keep out of the hobble himself, but who will the reader think was the first person chosen for so important and (at the time) so hazardous an enterprise? Some hoary veteran, to be sure, some champion distinguished for acts of daring in his country's cause? No such thing. You must guess again, my friend. You are miles astray; so I may as well tell you what you could never guess. It was no more nor no less a personage than myself, an inexperienced boy, that was chosen for the fearful purpose.

I was struck with astonishment and alarm at the announcement, for I knew very well I had gone far enough, perhaps too far in the business already, and was fully determined not to stir one inch farther. Entreaties or persuasions were all in vain. I stood firm to my point and would not be moved. They were then at a complete stand to know what to do and several others were asked the question, but all refused. At length Heydon told them that if somebody didn't go it was completely giving up the cause and sooner than that should be the case he would go himself, if they approved of it. They were all very glad of his offer and he was immediately elected but whether any one went with him or not, I cannot now recollect. When this was over (as was always the rule) they had to appoint a place for the next meeting but they were unanimous in declaring that there was too much danger in having it in Carlow and that they would not meet in it any more.

" Well, gentlemen," said I; " since it would not answer you to meet in Carlow, it is only right of me to mention that it would not answer me to meet anywhere else, so that there must be a person chosen in my place and I think the best person would be some one belonging to the country and as there is so much danger in attending meetings, you might appoint the different fair days in the country for that purpose, where there would be less suspicion and a better excuse if necessary for being there. And though I am resigning my situation, do not imagine I am giving up the cause entirely, as I will be always ready to do anything in my power to serve it."

They approved most cordially of my advice and we parted good friends.

Heydon set off immediately for Dublin and it was expected by everyone that as the Government was pressing the people so hard, the " Executive " (as it was called) would make some mighty effort and not suffer the people to be destroyed inch by inch, but in this they were sadly disappointed, for the executive knew too well the value of their own skins to do anything of the kind and besides it is not very improbable that some, aye, or many of the same Executive were in the pay of Government; but it is quite certain the pass was sold somehow or other.

When Heydon returned, every one was anxious to hear the news and the baronial committee were summoned to meet for that purpose though it was only thinly enough attended. He said there was great difficulty in getting the members of the Provincial to attend at all; that they were few in number and that every man in the room had a case of loaded pistols before him on the table and were fully determined to fight to the last if attacked, sooner than submit to be arrested; that the rulers in Dublin were not ready to commence operations for a little longer, but ordered every captain to have his men in a state of readiness. I almost sickened when I heard the tale and not one at the meeting but seemed to feel in the same manner, not excepting Heydon himself, who all the time he was relating it seemed fully sensible of its futility and childishness but what could he do? The pass was sold, but it wasn't his fault.

Pitt, the great English Iago, had the game now completely in his hand. He had no occasion to use hypocrisy any longer and therefore threw off the mask and was everywhere in city, country and town; that is, he was there in the persons of his bloodhounds who were running the people in full cry. They had already done considerable work by half-hangings, house-burnings, pitch-caps, etc., etc. but that was only children's play to what was to come on. The people stood out wonderfully under this species of torture and terror and could neither be forced out into open insurrection nor even to turn informers against each other under all their sufferings; but he (Pitt) had a nostrum in his pocket they little dreamed of. The panic was every day becoming more and more general. The baronial committee was summoned. Only very few would venture to attend. It was summoned again, but with less success and the apprehensions of the members increased so much that at last they would not meet at all. Fire and sword was in every direction through the country. Orange colours and Orange insults were everywhere shown to the people. Every party of army that came in marched to the tune of " Croppies lie down " and other insulting airs; and even at morning and evening parade, the same tunes were played through the streets to collect them.

The people were in the greatest consternation. They still expected great matters from the national or executive committees, but in this they found themselves miserably disappointed and left in a net they could not get out of. Their enthusiasm cooled by degrees, until they grew at length heartsick of the business and wished heartily they had never anything to do with it. But wishing was little use and the man (if he was a man) that made the net knew the use he designed it far too well to let them escape till he accomplished his object. The people, as I said before, could not, with all the tyranny used on them, be driven into open insurrection and as this was a point to which the great English Iago wanted to have them pushed without delay and as every other project for it failed, his last expedient his nostrum, the cat-o'-nine-tails, was introduced, and the town of Athy in the County Kildare and ten miles from Carlow had the honour of tasting them first. This was an operation the people never contemplated and had it been tried on them suddenly when they had an opinion of their strength and before their spirits were broken down might have produced serious consequences. But it was a master-hand in murder they had to deal with, who knew when and where and how far to go to the breadth of a hair and who, by the way he trampled and bullied and terrified them beforehand, showed them plainly what he could do. With this preparation he had no more difficulty in ordering a man, or any number he pleased, to be tortured, than a schoolmaster would in chastising his scholars.

Accordingly the triangle was put up in the public street of Athy and the work began instantly. There was no ceremony used in choosing victims; the first to hand done well enough. There was this difference, certainly, that though there were many Protestants engaged in it, they were all let to pass free, any trifling excuse was sufficient for them and the whole weight of the persecution fell on the unfortunate Catholics. They were stripped naked, tied to the triangle and their flesh cut without mercy and though some men stood the torture to the last gasp sooner than become informers, others did not, and to make bad worse, one single informer in a town was sufficient to destroy all the United Irishmen in it, for if they were superior to him in rank or that he never exchanged a word with them, all he had to do was to say, "take such a man up, he is a sergeant —he is a captain—he is a committee-man—he is the man can give you plenty of information," and it was done instantly and he was tried by the cat-o'-nine-tails who were his judge, jury and executioner at once. The terror and alarm produced by this operation cannot be described, but to any one of the least share of commonsense it must have shown plainly that the whole United system was completely broken up, and that, after all their boasting, the great and invincible Executive could do nothing. The men of Athy seemed to be fully sensible of it, for on the very first day's performance large discoveries of arms (or things called arms) were made and numbers of persons compelled to bring them in publicly and give them up.

CHAPTER SEVEN

EVE OF THE RISING

THE news flew like lightning in every direction but on its first announcement could scarcely gain credit. A very little time, however, showed plainly it was true enough, for notices were put up in every direction in Carlow, calling on the people to make an immediate surrender of their arms; that there would be ten days allowed for that purpose and if they were not all given up in that time, martial law would commence. This was a serious summons, but as we had no committee that would act, and as we had no information whatever from the great men behind the curtain in Dublin, every man was at liberty to give what opinion he pleased.

For my own part, I did not hesitate long, for if I was blind before, the affairs of Athy completely opened my eyes. And when we got the offer of peace by giving up things we were not able to keep, I was not at the least loss to know how to decide, but considered it a capital good bargain on our side; that we had decidedly the advantage in it, and that we were most fortunate in getting peace on such cheap terms. These were my opinions and as I imagined the case so clear that no man of commonsense could have different ones, I consulted my friend Bergan and my brother Tom, who without hesitation approved of every thing I said and we agreed that, as there was no time to be lost, I should go as soon as night came (for I dare not go sooner) to Mick Heydon, who held the highest command of any man in town and take measures with him for saving us all from the destruction we were threatened with. I thought the day rolled most heavily on and that every minute seemed as long as ten, I was under such anxiety about our dangerous situation.

Night came at last and I went off to Heydon on the important business, a business of nothing less than life or death. When we met, it was in his father's house. He was in company with a man I did not much like but on my entering the room, he hastily retired. Full of the great importance of the business I came on, I made no unnecessary preamble but began at once and said: " My dear Mick, I am come to speak to you on a subject that I think you would not at all suspect me for."

" What is it ? " said he.

" Why, it's nothing more or less," said I, " than to make an immediate surrender of the arms. The cause is lost and there is nothing else to save the peoples' lives."

He replied with the most apparent sincerity, " Oh yes, to be sure; that's what we're all about. The man that went out and I were speaking of it this long time and we have all agreed on it."

I was filled with joy at the announcement and said, " Oh, my dear Mick, I am most happy to hear it; the people, I hope, will be saved from destruction."

Here he gave a kind of contemptuous laugh and with the same kind of look and tone said, "Ah, then, are you serious ?"

" Serious ! " said I; " to be sure I am. Why, my dear friend, are not you serious ? "

" Why then indeed I am not," said he, with a most severe and determined look. Is it to give up arms ? Tut, man, we'll have orders down from Dublin immediately and we'll drive all before us."

" Don't believe it, my dear Mick," said I; " the cause is lost; look to Athy; look at the people's blood spilled. If the people in Dublin could do anything to save them they would not look on at such murder, and when they couldn't save *them* we have nothing to expect."

He seemed put to a considerable stand at this and replied, " Sure, if we give up the arms it is giving up the cause entirely and if the French landed the day after, we would not be able to give them any assistance."

" We have our choice," said I, " either to give them up

voluntary or give them up by compulsion and the people's lives along with them. If we give them up, we save the people. If we don't, we lose both. Only mark the consequence if we don't; martial law is to commence here in ten days. Let there be a triangle put up in any street and there will be as many informers in it as will destroy all the rest. You might stand true or I might stand true, or perhaps we would not if we were tried, but what end will it answer, tell me, to give up our lives and the lives of the people for nothing, when we can do no good by it? But mind what I say to you, if you don't join me and stop it, the streets will run with blood."

He had not one word of argument to advance against this but still adhered sulkily in his opinion and said, " Oh, man, I couldn't stop it; the people wouldn't stop for me."

" They would," said I; " you can do it if you please. I haven't as much authority over them as you have, yet I'll engage the people of my division will be guided by me. Don't let it be said you and I separated at such a time. Let us both go the one way and besides I will never part you till you agree to it."

I spoke with so much earnestness and was so deeply affected that he at length yielded a little but unfortunately for himself and others it was more to the friendship he had for me than to my arguments he yielded, when he said : " Well, I will speak to them to-morrow about it."

" Oh, no, my dear Mick," said I, " to-morrow won't do ; you must have them given up to-night, there is not a moment to lose. Give up as much as you can instantly. Make a beginning and I will go off straight and make the Quarry division do the same and the news will spread far and near to-morrow and when the country people hear we have surrendered, they will do the same and we will prevent bloodshed and have peace."

He promised me he would and I went back in all haste to my friend Bergan and my brother, who were anxiously waiting for me. I told them to go up instantly to the Quarry division and warn all the sergeants to give up their arms and to let them know Mick Heydon and I had agreed on it. They both refused, as it was so late at night and said it would not be right to be going to men's houses and disturbing them at such an unreasonable hour.

" Well," said I, " there must be something done at any rate and you must only give in the few you have yourselves, to make a beginning," and that Heydon should not find any failure on my part in the morning.

They then started an objection, and a very fair one, that they had no person to give them up to and did not know what way to manage or how to act.

" Oh, I'll tell you how you'll manage that," said I ; " throw them over such a gentleman's garden wall that can get no blame by having them found on his premises but on the contrary would receive great praise as being instrumental to it."

They still showed great reluctance at going on the business at all, but I pressed them so closely and pointed out the impending danger so strongly, that they consented at last and did as I directed them. Next morning the news flew like lightning in every direction. The gentleman who found them went with word to the barrack, where he was received with the greatest joy imaginable and was ordered a guard to bring them up.

It was the chief conversation of the whole town during the day and the magistrates and other gentlemen were in raptures about it and bestowed the greatest praise on the honest fellow that did it. Although I was highly pleased at the success of my trifling effort, still I was under great anxiety about Heydon and was in hourly expectation the whole day of hearing of his arms being found but I expected in vain, for he did not give up one. However, the men in power, thinking that this beginning would be followed up by the delivery of the remainder, actually gave the people ten days more for that purpose and I say it to the honour of the gentlemen of Carlow, that they showed plainly they did not want to spill the people's blood, when they made them such an offer and when they had such ample means in their hands for taking them by force; but there was no town in Ireland where there was a friendlier feeling between Catholics and Protestants and even a blood-relationship than there was in Carlow at the time.

I was highly gratified when I heard the additional ten days were given and was quite certain I would accomplish my object in the time and though I found Heydon would not act along with me itself, still I had no doubt of gaining over others of more experience. I accordingly exerted myself with every one I thought I could be safe in speaking to that had any influence over the people and among the rest to my friends Pat Kelly, who was captain in the town and his lieutenant John Berne, two unfortunate men who afterwards lost their lives. There could be no braver men than they were and as I considered them men of good sense, I imagined myself certain of their co-operation but, judge of my surprise, when I found them as immovable as blocks. In vain did I reiterate all the arguments I used to Heydon. In vain did I point out the horrors of martial law and the bloodshed of Athy and the certain loss of their own lives and those of every one else and the ready way of escaping if they only joined me. They seemed actually thrown into such a state of stupidity and torpor as to be incapable of either giving or taking advice. They did not, however, oppose me but stood stock still and would neither do one thing or the other although ruin was advancing with racehorse speed. No one attempted to oppose me openly but one and that was the celebrated Captain Rogers, who afterwards became so conspicuous in infamy. He protested loudly against it and called a meeting of his sergeants on the subject. My friend Bergan, who was his lieutenant, and my brother Tom attended. Rogers enquired who it was wanted to give up arms. Bergan, who was of my mind, replied that every man of commonsense ought to give them up. Were men to be waiting for a set of scoundrels in Dublin until they were whipped and murdered, without doing one thing or the other, and if people were not led on to fight they should give up at once and not be made fools of. Rogers said that in ten days the nation would be up as he well knew it, and that was not long to wait, and that no one would think of surrendering but a coward. My brother replied, " to the D—— we pitch the nation ! Will the nation themselves stand to be whipped and flogged for ten days ? And if a trial comes, perhaps the greatest boasters may prove the greatest cowards."

After a stormy discussion of this nature, the meeting separated ; some for keeping the arms, some for giving them up and others unable to give an opinion one way or the other. But in the main bulk of the people and even in those called leaders, it was quite manifest that every particle of enthusiasm and spirit was gone from them and that so far from being fit to take the field as fighting-men, they were completely heart-sick and fitter to lie down and die of fear ; and I really think it was the fear of some bugaboo behind the curtain in Dublin and the empty boasting of such fellows as Rogers that prevented them of surrendering arms and accepting the peace they could have had so easily and which they wished for so much.

The men in power, finding the first surrender of arms was not followed up, redoubled their energies to compel the people to do it through terror, but all in vain for, though they had lost all hope of being able to contend as fighting men against an army and dreaded even the very thought of it, still they seemed as if destined to be incapable of opening their eyes till ruin fell on them.

As I could get none of the men in power to assist me, I merely confined myself to grieving for the danger that was so fast approaching and making the closest observations I could on things as they went on.

I had no communication with Heydon from the time I made the proposal to him of surrendering the arms, for I saw it was quite useless, but I was informed he took Rogers into his confidence as a counsellor in my place and had sent him to Dublin as delegate for intelligence and I was also informed that Rogers had the pass sold on him very early. I do not give this as a fact but from the opinion I always entertained of the fellow and from the subsequent occurrences it would not surprise me very much if it was so.

The time at length expired for giving up the arms and there was great terror held up at one side and great dread and confusion on the other. Everything was expected from the great men in Dublin but when it came to the fighting point, it was like the mice putting the bell about the cat's neck; every one wished most earnestly to see it done but no one cared to do the job himself. Just so was it with the mighty Dublin "Executive." They took very good care of their mother's calf-skins but sent down word to a set of ignorant foolish countrymen to begin with sticks in their hands and while they were winning the battle and beating horse, foot and artillery, they would assist them with their orders.

With us particularly, as we were summoned to give up arms on a certain day and did not do so, there was no alternative but stand and strip to have our flesh cut off with whips or turn out and fight. The people did not like the former course and they were too much terrified to be of any use at all for the latter, and he must be a general of great abilities indeed that can infuse such a spirit into a poor ignorant terrified people as would make them fit for storming garrisons.

Heydon unfortunately undertook the task. The fatal orders came down from Dublin on the 24th of May. It was rumoured that Rogers was the bearer and that he either came with the night coach or a very early morning one. However, as soon as unfortunate Heydon received the orders, he did not lose a moment.

He merely delayed in town to give directions to as many as he thought requisite to prepare the people against night and then rode off full speed to different parts of the country to rise up the people there. I was told by a person who was present and, of course, knew it well, that the country people declined it and said, "Mr. Heydon, we are not fighting men. We are heart-sick of this business and would much rather give it up and have peace and don't bring us in to the town if you are not certain of help enough there to take it without us."

His answer was, "I have help enough in the town. I have nearly all the yeomen, nearly all the militia, ready armed, and a great number of the Ninth Dragoons, besides all the townsmen and you will have nothing to do but march in and give a shout and they will all flock to you in an instant and there will be no one to oppose you and the town will be taken without any trouble." This encouragement prevailed on some and as they increased in numbers, they compelled others who were wavering to join them also but before it was long in the day there was not a movement he was making but was as well known to the men in power in the town as he knew it himself.

Accordingly there was every precaution used and the men who offered peace very naturally prepared for war. There was no disguise. All was bold and open and manly. All the arms belonging to the loyalists were carefully inspected and they carried them in their hands publicly through the streets and encouraged each other resolutely in taking them to the gun-maker to be put in order and in bringing them back. This preparation had a most important effect and which probably they had in view of showing the townspeople their strength and the certain ruin of those from the country if they came in and putting it out of their minds to make any attempt to join them. Besides all this for the defence of the town, there was a strong force of the Ninth Dragoons in the barrack, a company of the Armagh Militia and a company, I believe, of the City Cork Militia in the town, besides a very strong Corps of Yeoman Infantry and there were two Corps of Yeoman Cavalry, Sir Charles Burton's and Sir Richard Butler's, quite convenient, that could be in the town in a few minutes' notice and every loyalist house in the town well armed and ready to meet any attack, and in the course of the day the militia were paraded and their arms piled publicly in the Main Street which showed them ready and determined for battle.

The people of the town saw all this very plainly and were

under the most terrific apprehensions for the consequences. Many were doubtful whether the people would come in or not. Many wished heartily they would not come in. But all wished there was an end to the business and that that peace would return which they once enjoyed and which they now looked back to in vain.

It was a considerable time in the day when by mere accident I happened to hear of it. My friend Bergan went out on business and brought me in the news. I could not believe it as first but he told me in the most positive manner it was a fact and asked my opinion of it.

"Oh," said I, "you know my opinion already and if you wanted anything to strengthen it, look at the preparations that are making. Why, man, if they do come in, they will be shot like rats in the streets. Look at every loyalist house in the town an armed garrison and tell me what chance a set of people with sticks in their hands can have of taking it. But it cannot be possible but there will be one man of commonsense among them that will point out the danger and prevent them and I hope they will not come in."

As the evening came on, the report became stronger and stronger of their determination to come in and there was a private whisper that there were boats ready on the Barrow above the town to bring the Queen's County men in, in that direction.

When it came near dusk, I consulted with my friend Bergan and told him I had a great wish to take a walk by the Barrow, to try if there were any boats waiting, as was said, to take the Queen's County people across, as that would give me some idea if they were really determined to come in. He agreed at once and I cautioned him to be very careful not to say anything for or against it if we got into conversation with any one, but to see and hear all we could and at the same time to be quite neutral. We walked down Castle Street and Coal Market over Castle Himm till we came to Graigue Bridge without seeing anything very particular except that there was some bustle with the people going backwards and forwards. We then walked up the track-line by the Barrow to the point we were told the boats were waiting, but there were no boats there. As soon as I saw this, " Come back," said I, " you see it is only a false report and they will not come in to-night, I warrant you."

We returned the same way, carefully watching if we could see any thing worth notice and just as we were going out of Coal Market into Castle Street, Bergan happened to turn about and spied John Berne near his own door.

" I will go back," said he, " and speak to John Berne ; perhaps he might give me some information."

" Don't," said I, " I have been speaking to him myself already and I know his mind. It is no use for you to go to him."

Bergan insisted he would and as all I could say would not stop him, I was obliged very reluctantly to give him his way and walked on slowly by myself. He very soon overtook me and was quite out of temper. I asked him what was the matter or had he heard any bad news.

" No," said he, " I heard no news at all. I never saw such a man ; as soon as he saw me, he cried out, ' Oh, Pat, Pat, don't come near me ! Ask me no questions ! I'm afraid we'll have terrible work to-night.' I told him I only wanted to know if the people had got any orders to be out and if he knew anything about it but he continued like a man distracted and said ' Oh, Pat, I know nothing at all about it ; leave me ! ; don't stay near me ! I know nothing at all about it.' I am sorry I went near him at all."

" Well, why didn't you take my advice ? " said I ; " but come home as fast as possible and if they are determined on destroying themselves, you and I have nothing to account for ; we have done our best to prevent it."

After we got home, Bergan, who was irritated before, got uneasy and said, " I will go out again and try if I can hear any news."

" Don't," said I ; " we want no news, we know enough already and don't go out upon any account."

It was in vain I strove to prevail on him. Out he would

and did go and I walked in greatly chagrined and sat down, musing in the parlour; in the course of about half an hour there was a rap at the door and my sister, happening to answer it, came in and said my brother and Pat Bergan wanted to take their leave of me. Nothing could exceed my astonishment. I walked out and asked, " what's the matter? What's the matter?"

They both replied, " We're come to take our leave of you; we are to be out to-night."

" Out where?" said I; are you losing your senses?"

" We are not," said they; " the whole town will be out and Rogers is warning all his men to be out and has warned us too and out we'll be; farewell."

"And do you intend," said I (stopping them) " to take the advice of such a vagabond as that before mine?"

" We do," said they; " we are sworn to obey him and we will and must be out."

" Yes," said I; " you are sworn to obey him as far as prudence will permit, but is there any prudence in rushing on certain destruction because he bids you?"

" Now you both know that I am higher in command than he is and I order you both not to obey him."

All I could say was unavailing and they were both going to rush out when I laid a fast hold of Bergan and said, " Now I tell you what, Pat Bergan; out of my hands you won't get to-night. There is no use in your attempting it for, mind you, I'm determined on it. No, not one foot you'll leave this house to-night."

After a very doubtful struggle, I providentially succeeded and by that means saved both their lives.

The unfortunate people had it laid out (by what means I know not) to march into the town in four parties through the four main streets; Heydon's party on the east to come in through Tullow street; the Queen's County people on the west to come in over Graigue Bridge and through Castle Street; the Garryhunden people on the South to come in through Burren Street and over Burren Bridge; and the people of the north district, under the command of

Rogers, to come through Dublin Street, and all to meet at the Potato Market in Tullow Street.

Colonel Mahon of the Ninth Dragoons had the command of all the military in the barrack and in the town and as every transaction of unfortunate Heydon was fully known to him, he made every preparation to meet the attack. There was a strong party of military stationed in the Court-house, within about sixty yards of Burren Bridge. There was another party with two small pieces of cannon stationed on the Bridge, with which they commanded the whole length of Burren Street and in case they were hard pressed and obliged to give way, they were convenient enough to the Court-house into which they might safely retreat. The post of greatest danger, as it was a long way from the Courthouse, was Graigue Bridge, which was the only pass from the Queen's County and from which, it was apprehended, a strong body would come in. There was an officers' guard of yeoman placed there and the command given to Doctor Fitzgerald, who was Lieutenant and the only Catholic Officer in the Corps, but the men under his command were both Catholics and Protestants. At the entrance to Dublin Street there was no military guard placed, as it was well known the party in that direction could not be very numerous but there were some large strong houses on the spot which were filled with loyalists, well armed, who if there was any attack there could do dreadful execution without being in any danger themselves. The entrance at the east, through which unfortunate Heydon and his party were expected to come in, was also left without any guard to prevent them but the barrack, with a powerful force of armed and disciplined soldiers was quite convenient.

CHAPTER EIGHT

WOE TO THE CONQUERED

In this way everything remained, till the fatal hour arrived which was to decide their fate and which was about two o'clock on the morning of the 25th of May. At this hour every party was at the place appointed. The Queen's County men and Garryhunden men, when they came up, received immediate information of the forces stationed on the two bridges to resist them. This was startling news to men who expected to take a town without any fighting. They immediately formed a communication with each other, by getting a man to swim the Barrow below the town and both parties very sensibly agreed that they would not run such a risk but that if Heydon chose to do so he might and they would wait the issue; and if he took the town and didn't want them they would then help him.

It was almost time for them to see the danger when they were just on the verge of destruction, but the wonder is how they could not see it a week or two sooner. If they could or would have taken advice, they might be sleeping peaceably in their beds instead of being there trembling for their lives. However, it was well for them they saw it then itself.

As Heydon's party were marching on, they had to pass by the house of the Revd. Mr. O'Neill, Parish Priest of Tynryland, a most exemplary man and famous even for his skill as a medical doctor and consequently a man of most extensive influence in the country. He came out of his house, stopped them on the road and begged of them, in the most moving terms, to desist. He even went on his knees and used every entreaty he could think of to prevail on them to go back, but all was useless.

The multitude of people was so great that those in the rear drove on those before them and the twentieth part of them did not hear what he said but rushed on like a drove of cattle, without being capable of knowing what they were about. When they came near the entrance of the town, they halted. All their fears returned and they called out to Heydon if he was not certain of sufficient help in the town, not to bring them in; that they were totally unfit for such a task; and some even went so far as to advise them to turn back, when a fellow of the name of Murray, a perfect stranger, who had been obliged to fly from some other part of the country a short time before, walked up and down with a blunderbuss in his hand, declaring he would blow the first man's brains out that would dishearten the men or prevent them of coming in, as he was certain of victory. Heydon also, in order to satisfy them, said he would not ask one man to advance a step, till he went in first to the town himself, to try if the people were ready to join them or not and if everything was not right, he would not allow them to go in at all.

This proposal was very well liked and he set off at once by himself on the perilous expedition. While he was away, the party he left behind were under the greatest terror and apprehension, so much so that many of them proposed to return home again and not wait for him but were prevented by Murray and others who, partly by threats and partly by holding out illusory hopes, caused them by much ado to remain but had they any idea of the preparation that was made for them, it would be impossible for any general on earth to make them remain, much less to bring them on. It is really wonderful that some person in town did not tell Heydon of it but he was so confident in the assistance of the United men that were in the Yeomen Militia and even the Ninth Dragoons who, he was certain, would run armed to join him, the moment he entered the town, and so blinded with the hopes of victory, that he would listen to nothing else.

Full of these vain hopes, he returned to the people and

marched them on. Never before, since the world began, did such an army march on to take a garrisoned town; a set of trembling, ignorant, country men, headed by an unfortunate, foolish, enthusiastic young man. There was no obstacle in their way to prevent their going into the town; the most trifling one would have done it. Had there been a single sergeant's guard before them, they never would have faced it. Unfortunately for them, there was no such thing and in they marched.

When they came to the potato-market, the place appointed, they halted and commenced shouting, as a signal for all their friends to come to their assistance, but they shouted in vain; the friends they expected were too much terrified with the preparations that were made to stir one inch. When they found this, that they were left alone, they were seized with a sudden panic and some of them proposed to march forward and bring in the Queen's County men but just as they made the movement to go on, there were two sentries at the collector's house, a little below them in Tullow Street, and one of them presented his piece and fired and killed one of the party and this single shot stopped the whole body. They then thought to go through Bridewell lane and get off that way but just at the moment Colonel Mahon, who had been closely watching them, ordered out a strong party of soldiers from the barrack who, taking them in the rere, had them covered the length of Tullow Street, from the fair green to the potato-market and opened on them a most tremendous fire of musquetry. The scene that followed could hardly be described; they flew like frightened birds; some down Tullow Street towards the Queen's County; some across the potato-market and down Bridewell Lane for the same place and fired at from the windows as they went along. Others were so overcome with fear that they were not able to run away but forced in the doors of about forty thatched cabins that were on the spot, to hide themselves. In vain did Heydon call out to them to stand and fight for their lives; he might as well be whispering to a tempest and was obliged at last to run himself when all was lost and saw his woeful mistake when it was too late. The army advanced, firing volley after volley, till they came up to the cabins that were completely filled with the unfortunate creatures that rushed in. By this time there was not one of those that came in to be seen in the street, except such as were killed, and they were lying in heaps.

The army, now having no enemy to oppose them, turned their attention at once to the cabins and made short work of them by setting every one of them on fire and all that were in them, men, women and children, innocent and guilty, even all burned together in one common mass. There has been great lamentation made, and very justly, about the unfortunate burning of Scullabogue, but here were forty Scullabogues in Carlow and very little said about it from that day to this. Besides those people who justly complain of Scullabogue ought to recollect that it was themselves or their party who first set the example and that there were hundreds of houses burned by them in every direction, and the inhabitants put to death before the deplorable case of Scullabogue happened at all.

In this affair of Carlow, some of the unfortunate people rushed out of the flames, thinking to save themselves, but they were instantly shot or bayoneted and even the people who ran out of their beds with whatever covering they could throw round them shared the same fate. I know one man myself, as peaceable and inoffensive a man as any in town, who ran out of bed in his shirt and an infant in his arms and was shot dead at his own door; for the orders given out were to spare no man that was not in regimentals.

When Heydon was compelled to run, he got by a back way into his father's house, which was quite convenient, took off the clothes he wore and putting on his yeomanry dress, came out with his gun in his hand, as if to assist the military and fired some shots. He got great blame for this conduct from some people, who reported that he actually fired on those he brought in, but the charge was false, as he was one of the last that run himself and by the time he got to his father's house, there was not one of them to be seen in the street, therefore he could not fire on them; and surely he afterwards suffered dearly enough for the part he unfortunately took, without calumniating his memory. I made the closest enquiry into the transaction and was informed by an authority that knew it well and that I could not doubt, that it was only stratagem he used to gain time to make his escape.

While the houses were burning, the rest of the enraged soldiers were in full cry through the town, dragging the terrified creatures out of every hiding-place they could find and either shooting them on the spot or hanging them out of gateways or signposts, whichever they chose. There was no opposition, as they were nearly dead with fear beforehand without touching them at all and to make bad worse a report was circulated that all the Catholics in town would be put to death at their own doors. The terror this news inspired was beyond any description. The shops remained all closed. No one would attempt to open till Colonel Mahon sent out orders to everyone to open their shops and go on with their business as usual and threatening the severest punishment on whoever gave out the report if he could find them out. The soldiers at the time had actually commenced racking the houses, the first of which belonged to John Berne; this they gutted in a hurry and everything it contained carried away in the shortest space of time. They were then at a stand to know whether the house should be thrown down or burned, when orders arrived for them to desist and that no house was to be racked or pillaged, but if any information appeared against the owner he should be made prisoner and brought to the barrack to be punished for it himself.

In the course of the day, all the cars and horses and carts that could be got were put in requisition for taking away the bodies of those that were killed in the streets and burned in the houses. As for the first part, taking off those that were in the streets, there was not much difference; but as for the burned bodies in the houses, they were lying in such heaps and reduced to such a frightful mass by the fire that it was actually terrifying and disgusting to look at them at all, but to move them or to touch them was so shocking that some of the men brought there flatly refused to do it, until they were compelled by the threat of instant death. As soon however as they began to move them and root them out of the burning ruins, the smell became so offensive that they were obliged to desist till pitch-barrels were procured and burnt in different directions and pitch put on the carts and clothes of the men to prevent infection. They then proceeded and continued drawing them away till night to a large sand-pit in Graigue called " croppy hole," where they threw them in and covered the bodies but did not finish their work, as it took them a great part of next day for that purpose. The computations of the number killed and burned were various, some calculating them at five, some at six hundred. The bodies found in the streets were easily counted, but from the state the burned bodies were in there was no possibility of counting them as they mostly all came asunder when they were stirred.

The barrack, by this time, was thronged with prisoners and I wondered greatly what they meant to do with them, for there was no battle, no resistance made to the soldiers, none of their friends killed to irritate them and so much bloodshed on the other side I imagined they would be turned home in contempt, after being shown so plainly their weakness; but in this I was sadly mistaken.

I should have said there was no occasion to wait for any information against the people, for any one they suspected was made prisoner and brought to the barrack, without the least trouble or ceremony. In the course of their search through the town, they at last hit on the noted Rogers, who had been so active the night before in warning the unfortunate people to battle. It was said he had sold the pass some time before and indeed, from the opinion I entertained of him, I should not much wonder at it; but, be that as it may, as soon as he was brought to the barrack, he did not hesitate a moment but began to give information at once against every person he knew. Fortunately for me, he knew nothing of me that could injure me, but on the contrary what he did know of me was strongly in my favour. In the first place, he knew that I endeavoured with all my might to cause arms to be given up and to make peace by making the people surrender, and secondly, he knew that my friend, Bergan, who was his lieutenant, or my brother Tom were not with him that fatal night, although he warned them to it which, coupled with the first part, should in all probability be placed to my credit.

This certainly was a dreadful day. Among the many prisoners brought in was a man of the name of O'Connor, from Tullow, and three brothers of the name of Maher, from very near the same place. I could never find out what crimes they were charged with or what occasion there was to send them from Tullow to this town (not to be tried, for there was no trial on them, but to be sacrificed) as I am pretty sure there were few towns at the time but had men enough able and willing to do such work themselves, without applying to others. But, however that might be, these four men were brought out to the triangles and were the first, I believe, punished in that way; for the blood that had been spilled, so far from satisfying the rage of the soldiers, seemed only to increase their thirst for more.

They began with the unfortunate Mahers and the youngest man of them was stripped and tied up first. They commenced cutting him with the cat-o'-nine-tails with all their fury for a considerable time but, this failing to extort any confession from him, they actually began to use the rough-riders' cutting whips on him till he was one wound from his shoulders to the calves of his legs. This torture was so excessive that he began to fail under it and cried out to them to stop, but as soon as the eldest brother heard him, he stamped his foot on the ground and exclaimed, "Oh, what are you going to do? Oh, let us die like men! Oh, let us die like brothers!" This had the desired effect; he uttered no complaint after to the last gasp. They then untied him and hung him up naked and bleeding as he was. The two other brothers were served the same way and stood it with a fortitude that astonished every one, as they never cried out during the whole dreadful operation. O'Connor acted a different part, for from the first cut he got to the last, he made battle with them as far as words could do it, by calling them murderers and every opprobrious name he could think of. This increased their fury to such a degree that they made his flesh fly in every direction, until the standers-by were fairly disgusted with the exhibition; even some soldiers accustomed to see men flogged turned away and could not bear to look on at the horrid tragedy. When their fury was fully satisfied, they untied him and hung him up with the Mahers.

What a pity it was and what a loss to any country, to lose four such men and to have them lost in such a manner. There could be no excuse, no palliation for the men that came into town as assailants. They came in with arms in their hands and though they did not use them, still they put people in terror of their lives; and no one, I believe, will deny that they deserved their fate. But these four men had no concern whatever with it but were sent in from Tullow, upon what charge I could never learn, but if they were even guilty of crime, surely taking their lives by hanging or shooting might be sufficient punishment, without, like savages, butchering them in such a horrid manner.

While all this was going on, my friend Bergan and I were studying every plan we could think of for making our escape but could not hit on one that would answer. It was almost impossible to do it, as any person seen going through the country could be shot on the spot, without any ceremony and no more thought of it than of shooting a sparrow, and no friend or relation dare conceal a person in his house without running the same risk and having his house burned, perhaps, besides; but, as soon as I heard the above horrible account, all my fears of being taken and hopes of making an escape vanished in an instant and I almost wished for death, as I did not think there was any use in being alive any longer.

For the honour of humanity, I am happy to say that all

men, even in these dreadful times, were not lost to feelings of tenderness and generosity and that it is no matter what a man's religious or political opinions may be, that a good man will be a good man in any case.

The first person I will mention as an instance of this and who so well deserves it, was Mr. Richard Budds, a man who had a good property of his own, besides being town-sergeant of Carlow and permanent sergeant of the Carlow Yeomen. This man was a Protestant, a Freemason and, I believe, an Orangeman—at least he used to wear the Orange ribbon. He and my brother-in-law, Mr. Andrew Fitzgerald, were in strict habits of intimacy from their early years which, if possible, grew stronger and stronger as years increased; and if one had a party at his house, he would not be happy if he had not the other with him; in fact, they were like two brothers. When Mr. Budds saw what was going on in the barrack, he came in haste to our house. As soon as he came into the shop, he took off his military cap, wiped his face and said, " Oh, I am almost ready to faint. Is there e'er a drop of spirits in the house ? "

" Plenty," said Mr. Fitzgerald; " come in."

" Oh," said he, " there is not a drop to be got in town for love or money. No one dare sell any of it."

They both walked in and as soon as he had taken some refreshment, " Oh, Andy, my dear," said he, " there is terrible work going on in the barrack. They are cutting these unfortunate people all in pieces. I was obliged to come away, I could not stand to look on, and they have Rogers informing and everyone that had a hand in it in town will be destroyed. Now do you examine all your boys and if any of them had a hand in it, I will get them protection."

" Oh, Dick, my dear," said he, " I have no doubt they had a hand in it, for they would never take my advice."

" Don't blame the foolish boys at all, Andy," said he; " they couldn't escape it. Why, man, some of the greatest men in town had a hand in it—old men that might be their fathers—and they will be all taken by and by. Oh, there will be dreadful work. Men you wouldn't suspect at all will be taken but I will get these boys protection."

"And how can you do that?" said the other.

"I'll tell you; Mr. Harman Fitzmaurice has just got the power from Colonel Mahon to give protection to a certain number and no one in town knows it yet but me and we can have them in first before his number is full. But they must have some kind of arms to give up, as no person can get a protection without doing so; and I will go with them myself to the barrack and it will be all over then. So now call them up and examine them. I would not wish to be by, as it might hurt their feelings, so I will go down street and be back by the time you are done."

I was the first called up, but I was so full of indignation at the accounts I heard I was consequently in very bad temper at the time to enter into a pacific discussion.

There was no one in the room but my sister and her husband and as soon as I walked in he began, "Oh, you unfortunate fellow, see what you have brought on yourself; but you wouldn't take my advice. They are cutting the unfortunate people in pieces in the barrack and will serve everyone in town that had a hand in it the same way."

"Let them do their worst," said I, in a loud and vehement tone.

He started and looked with astonishment at me and said, "Eh, what's that you say?"

"Let them do their worst, I say!"—and I repeated the words with (if possible) more vehemence than at first.

"See that!" said he, turning to my sister; "be positive now, as you were always. But Mr. Budds, who was here now, will get you all protections from Mr. Fitzmaurice and all you have to do is to take some arms up to the barrack to give him and your lives will be saved and if not you will be all destroyed."

"Is it me to take arms to the barrack, to get their protection?" said I, in the same tone and temper as before; "I'll do no such thing. I don't want their protection."

"You don't!" said he in amazement. "If you don't take it you'll be destroyed."

"I don't care a pin about them," said I.

"You don't?"

"No, nor if there was a cannon planted before me there this moment, I wouldn't turn aside from it."

The peculiar force and energy with which I pronounced this last sentence had such an effect that he and my sister burst into tears. It was a very unusual thing with him, indeed, for I never saw a tear from him before but, recovering immediately, he and my sister endeavoured to prevail on me but, finding it useless, he said, "You are an unfortunate young man, God help you, but since you won't take the offer go down and send me up Pat Bergan in all haste, for Mr. Budds will be soon here."

I went down and done so and as soon as he entered the room, Mr. Fitzgerald told him the offer made of getting us protection and added, "It is very probable your mother's house and all she had in the world is burned and your brother shot; and your mother, if she be alive, will have no one to take care of her or do anything for her but you, and if you take my advice you will take the protection and save your life, as I am sure there is nothing else for it." This discourse had such an effect on Bergan, that he burst into tears and consented. As soon as he came down stairs, he told me what passed and that he had agreed to take the protection.

When he told me this, it occurred to me immediately that if I persisted in refusing it and anything fatal was to happen to me, every one would say it was my own fault; that I was offered my life and wouldn't take it; and besides that, I would probably be accessory to my own death. The moment these reflections struck me, I told him to go back and say that I had agreed also and that my brother would do the same, but we all protested against carrying arms to the barrack.

By this time Mr. Budds had returned and was informed of our intentions. "Well," said he, "lose no time. There must be arms given up by every person that gets a protection. Mr. Fitzmaurice could not give one without it or if he did it would be no good, so try and get something at once."

Here we were at a complete stand and did not know what to do, as he had no arms of any kind. After some consideration, Mr. Fitzgerald recollected he had an old bayonet in the house and, in rummaging further, found an old rusty blade of a sword without a handle but this was quickly supplied by the first thing came in the way. We were now completely run out, for we could get nothing that would do for the third article and were greatly at a loss.

"Stop," said Mr. Budds, "I have an old gun at home that's not of much value and I will give that."

He also mentioned that he had been speaking to Mr. Fitzmaurice and that we would have no occasion to go to the barracks, as he would receive them at his lodgings in Burrin Street which was pretty convenient. When Mr. Fitzgerald heard this, he said as it would be dangerous for us to carry arms through the street, that he would pack them up like goods and take them himself and we could follow him. He did so and in a few minutes returned to let us know that, as Mr. Fitzmaurice considered it dangerous for us to appear in the streets at all, he would come and give us the protections where we were. This was certainly an extraordinary act of kindness and consideration for a man of his rank, but to anyone that knew Mr. Fitzmaurice, it would not appear much more than might be expected from his goodness of disposition. He was a Protestant gentleman of considerable fortune, but his family was far more considerable, as he was nearly related to the Earl of Shelburne and was Lieutenant in Colonel Rochfort's Corps of Yeomen Cavalry. He was about five feet nine inches high, fine shape, remarkably handsome countenance and something so grand, so kind and engaging in his whole mien and deportment, that even an ordinary observer should at once pronounce him as born a superior being.

This gentleman came in a few minutes and being ushered up to the drawing-room, we were called on to appear before him. It was indeed a painful and (notwithstanding the great compliment paid and the danger we were in) I felt it rather a humiliating task and was filled with trouble at it. As soon as we walked in, " Here they are now, sir," said Mr. Fitzgerald ; " three pretty fellows ! they ought to be ashamed of themselves."

" Not at all ! Not at all ! " said the kind-hearted young man ; " young lads that didn't know what they were doing. Why, Andy, my dear, they were all fools and when we see men that might be their fathers, aye, upon my honour, that might be their grandfathers, made fools of, what need we wonder at young lads like these ? Now, there are three as fine lads as you need ask to see in any regiment and if there was twenty thousand of them together, what would they signify before disciplined men ? Nothing ! They wouldn't know what to do but I hope they will have more sense in future and never be made fools of again. Eh, lads, I'm sure I may take your words you will never join anything of this sort again ? "

" Indeed you may, sir."

" Oh, I'm sure of it. Eh, Andy, we can't blame them too much. We did many foolish things ourselves when we were like them. But let us make haste and get the papers ready and, Dick Budds, do you draw the form of the protections as I am in a great hurry. It will expedite the matter and I will sign them."

This was done accordingly and, after administering the oath of allegiance to us, he departed ; but the kindness and delicacy and tenderness with which he treated us left a lasting impression. It was in fact more like that of a good kind father than an angry judge. He did not even ask us what part we took in it or what stations we filled though the amnesty was not to extend to captains or members of county committees, which, of course, excluded me, but I looked a good deal younger than I really was and he never suspected me of holding such a station. Besides, Rogers knew but very little of me except what was in my favour. In the first place, he knew I had done all in my power to have the arms given up and that my friend Bergan, who was his lieutenant, and my brother, who was his sergeant, both joined me in it. He also knew that neither of them were out with him that fatal night and that they acted under my influence, so that these circumstances would weigh more for me than against me if he mentioned my name at all.

CHAPTER NINE

JAIL JOURNAL

THE arrests were now going on with fearful rapidity in every quarter of the town and every hour brought news more terrific, if possible, than the preceding one, of some man being taken that no one suspected to have any hand in it and of his being brought to the barrack, while the accounts of the merciless floggings inflicted there were such that the most innocent man could hardly be sure of his life.

I have heard it said that the notorious Mr. Pitt, the English statesman, was the very man that planned the whole system, in order to rob the country of its parliament. It began by uniting men in a " brotherhood of affection " (that was the gilding that was on the poisonous pill) but it ended by cutting their flesh in such a barbarous manner as to compel them, by the excruciating torture, to tell something or other of some unfortunate person implicated in the same business, and also drove some of those that escaped to retaliate on their enemies in every way that came within their reach, until the whole country looked as if it was peopled with Furys after coming out of hell.

In the midst of all this terror and confusion, there was a Protestant clergyman, a Mr. Carey of Mount Finn, in the County of Wexford, obliged to fly with all his family, wife, children and servants, and take refuge in Carlow, to save their lives. Mrs. Carey was daughter to Sir Edward Loftus of Mount Loftus, in the County Kilkenny, and sister to Lieutenant Loftus of the Ninth Dragoons, who were quartered in town and as all the family dealt with us for their saddlery goods and had a particular friendship for us, they took up their lodging in our house.

I attended the shop as usual but it was only a mere show, for under the circumstances it may well be supposed I could not do much business, when on the Tuesday following the slaughter, which was the 29th of May and Whitsun Tuesday (I remember it well and I should have a bad memory if I did not) three magistrates Major Eustace, Mr. Henry Rudkin and Sam Carpenter, walked in. The two former, who were friends of ours, said nothing but Carpenter, who was the Major Sirr of the day, a man with sour countenance and sharp spiteful accent and who was known by the appellation of " Busy Sam," began and the following conversation took place :

Carpenter. " Mr. Fitzgerald, how many persons have you got in your house ? "

Fitzgerald. " No one, sir, but my own family and Mr. Carey's family that came here from the County Wexford."

Carpenter. " Oh, I don't mean them—your own family I mean—how many ? "

Fitzgerald. " Their names are here on the door, sir."

Carpenter. " Read them for me." He read them over, till he came to my name.

Carpenter. " That is the man I want."

Fitzgerald. " Well, there he is, sir."

Although Carpenter himself knew me very well, he should make the most solemn ceremony he could about it and said, " I have an order to take him, an order from Leighlin Bridge."

Fitzgerald. " Oh, sir, it can't be him; sure he knows no one in Leighlin Bridge, it must be some other person."

Carpenter. " My order is against William Farrell of Carlow, saddler. Is there any other William Farrell a saddler in the town ? "

Fitzgerald. " No, sir."

Carpenter. " Then he is the man. See here, I will read it for you; it is a letter from Colonel Rochford, to take William Farrell and Michael Heydon, but Heydon has made his escape, he is not to be found; but he will be taken; we will take him yet."

Fitzgerald. " Well, sir, but he has given himself up to Mr. Fitzmaurice and has got a protection."

Carpenter. "To Mr. Fitzmaurice! To Mr. Fitzmaurice! Ah, I don't know what authority Mr. Fitzmaurice had to give a protection to anyone. He could give no protection."

Fitzgerald. "Oh, he could, sir; he had an order from Colonel Mahon to give protection and he gave him one. Show your protection—why don't you show Mr. Carpenter your protection?"

I immediately pulled it out. "Here it is, sir," said I, handing it to him. He seemed as if he didn't like to see it and took it rather reluctantly, but as soon as he looked over it and saw Mr. Fitzmaurice's name to it, he was completely disconcerted and did not know what to do but, recovering a little, he said, "Well, I see Mr. Fitzmaurice's name is to this paper, but I can't tell who wrote it. Any one else might write it for what I know."

Fitzgerald. "Oh, no sir, I was present when he wrote it and I wouldn't tell an untruth."

"Show it to me," said Mr. Rudkin; "I know his handwriting"; and just looking at it, said, "Oh it is—that is his handwriting—no doubt of it."

Major Eustace said the same.

Carpenter. "Well, but I don't understand protections, nor I don't know how far this may or can protect him, d'ye see, Mr. Fitzgerald?"

"I do, sir, but at the time Mr. Fitzmaurice gave it to him he said he need not be in the least uneasy, that no one had any power to meddle with him."

Carpenter. "Mr. Fitzmaurice had a duty to perform and I am sure he performed it very properly; and I have a duty to perform also. My duty is to take him and lodge him in the jail and if Mr. Fitzmaurice, when he hears of it, has any power to take him out, I am sure I won't have any objection. But he must come along with me."

As soon as I heard this I put on my hat and walked out with him. To attempt an escape would be worse than useless, as I would be fair game for the first armed man I met (and they were in every direction) to shoot or stab me to death on the spot and if I even did escape that, no friend dare give me shelter except at the risk of his own life, and perhaps having his house burned and family destroyed. Besides this, I was not in a temper for trying to escape; I actually scorned it; and besides that, I had my protection in my pocket and the amnesty excluded me from any pardon, on account of the station I filled still, from the part I acted all along, particularly in my endeavours to prevent bloodshed and to cause the surrender of arms. From these circumstances, joined to Mr. Fitzmaurice's interest, I considered I had good reason to think myself entitled to a speedy liberation. Under these impressions, I went on with him, till we came to the Market-cross where, meeting some armed men, he said to them, " Here, take this man and leave him in the body of the jail."

When I arrived there, all was terror and alarm, as the executions were going on in the barrack-yard with the utmost violence and there was no need of information against any person, for whoever the soldiers pitched on was stripped naked and put to the torture without any ceremony, to force him to tell something of himself or of somebody else; and in many cases the cries and agony of the victim were turned into complete mockery by those engaged in this dreadful work.

As they had a great number of prisoners in the barrack at the time, there was no call on the jail for any victims on this day and, indeed, the jailer had plenty to do without it, in regulating all that came in and in endeavouring to find places for them. When night came, there was not beds sufficient for all the prisoners but the jailer, Robert Kirevan, who was a kind humane man (qualities rarely found with men in his station), did everything in his power to accommodate them. There was some straw shook on the boards of the room where I was and five of us lay down on it in our clothes which, with some pieces of old blankets to cover us, did well enough. In fact, we did not much care about a bed and felt no more inconvenience than if we were sleeping on down for no one could tell but that night would be his last.

Next morning came and passed on gloomily enough. Even the appearance of breakfast made no great alteration. Whatever came first was handed round to every one as far as it went and so on to the last, and the spirits of any kind were strictly prohibited, yet there was hardly a jug of tea came in but had some in it, while our jailer Kirevan, an honest Protestant, never prevented it, though he would tell us he run great risk in permitting it, but, as I said before, a good man will be a good man any where, no matter what his creed or conviction or station may be. However, it had but little effect as the conflict we might be engaged in during the day was so strong in our minds that it quite prevented it.

In the course of the day, which was uncommonly warm, there was a bottle of Curran whiskey sent me by a friend, and a soldier of the Armagh Militia was employed to carry it. He was a great United man and, being sturdy and active and sharp north, he gained admittance, which was a difficult task enough, and while speaking to me, slipped me the bottle very dexterously, unperceived. When I returned to my room, I took it out and was just going to divide it among the prisoners, when one of them said, "Ah, there is a poor fellow in the next room, I wish he had a glass of this. Oh, he is after being cut to pieces!"

"Who is he?" said I hastily.

"He is a man from Painstown or Oak Park, as they call it."

I was almost afraid to enquire further, as I had a most painful apprehension of who it might be, but I could not stop; though with dread and difficulty, I asked his name. Oh, my conjectures were too true; it was the very name I dreaded to hear.

"His name," said he, "is Wall."

This was the very man I proposed to Ivers to be captain, and my near relation. He was a man of powerful strength in his youth but for the present dreadful occasion was rather in the decline of life. He might be about fifty and appeared too much worn to be fit to stand the trial he went through, but the spirit of his family was never worn, it was the same at any age. As soon as I heard his name, "Ah, then, he must have some of this," said I.

" Why, is it going to him you are ? " said one ; " don't attempt it. There is strict orders against it. No one is to go near him or see him or speak to him on any account."

"Ah, then I'll see him and speak to him too."

Here several spoke together in great alarm of the hazard, the certain ruin, if I was seen speaking to him, and endeavoured in the most pressing manner to dissuade me from it. But, without giving any reply, out I stepped with the bottle and glass in my hands. I had to step very lightly along the corridors and watch sharply till I came to his room door, which was the middle room in the upper storey and was called the Straw Room as it was in it the straw for the whole jail was kept. Prisoners were never kept in it except on extraordinary occasions and he was put there in order that no prisoner should have any communication with him. There was a half-circle cut out of the top of the door to give passage to the air and when I came up, after looking closely down the corridors and stairs, I looked in over the door and saw him standing at the window and leaning the weight of his body on his arms which were folded under him, for there was no chair or seat of any kind in the room. I called him softly but he didn't hear. I called again, but no answer. I was then obliged to raise my voice and call louder and I then perceived him endeavouring to raise himself up and turn round. He then strove to advance but he was weak and staggering, his eyes sunk and hollow and his face so pale and ghastly that death itself was firmly printed in it. When he made his way up to me I asked him how he was. He strove to look up at me and said in a tremulous voice, " Bad enough ; who is this ? "

I replied, " It is I ; don't you know me ? "

He strove to look up again but his sight was too much gone to discern me and he said, " Why then, I don't. Is this Pat ? "

" No, it is I, William Farrell."

When he heard my name, he seemed to forget his own

situation and to feel more concerned for me than for himself and exclaimed in a lamentable tone, " Pooh, pooh, what brought *you* there ?—but what need I ask you—that villain Rogers, to be sure, that murdered us all."

By this time I had a glass filled out and handed it to him over the door and bid him take it but as soon as he saw it he turned against it and said, " Oh, I couldn't take it."

" But you must, man, don't you see it is nice Curran whiskey ? "

" Oh, I see but I couldn't take it, don't ask me."

" But you must, man, it will do you good and I will take no excuse."

At length he took it out of my hand and by much ado drank about half the glass but would not on any account take a drop more. I saw his determination and did not press him further, as I knew it would be useless.

After recovering a little, "Ah," said he, " this was a bad business. I was well off, I wanted for nothing, I was worth a hundred pounds, a few acres of land and five cows, besides my trade. I was as happy as I need wish. I wanted no man's share. Whatever brought me into this unfortunate business ? But do you think they'll take my life ? Though I believe I could hardly live now if they let me off itself."

"Ah, Mick," said I, " don't be thinking of that at all. Keep God Almighty before your eyes and don't regard their worst. But tell me, were you out that night ? "

" I was, to be sure," said he.

" Well and what did you all do ? "

" Why, we were all warned by our captain to meet above at Rahenapish and we obeyed, of course, as we were sworn to do."

"And what did you do when you met there ? "

" He desired us all to wait till we got the signal to go in— that was when we'd hear the shouting, but as soon as ever we heard the first three or four shots he cried out, ' Oh, boys, its all over ! Let every one go home and save himself as well as he can ! ' But if I knew as much as I do now," said he, raising his arm and clenching his fist and giving a slight groan. He had no occasion to finish the sentence, for I knew right well his meaning; that the captain would not then be telling tales of him. During the whole time, I was under the greatest apprehensions of being seen and here the generous-hearted man, in the midst of his own sufferings and affliction, became apprehensive for my safety and said, " Take care you are not staying too long with me. If you were seen, it might ruin you, so don't stay any longer." We then parted, never, never more to meet in this world.

This day was dreadful. The murder and butchery raged in full fury. The guards were actively engaged bringing victims from the barrack to the jail and taking others back for execution and, among the rest, Wall was sent for again. As soon as his name was called out, there was a general expression of sorrow among the prisoners for him, such as " Oh, sure they're not going to murder him."—" Oh, sure they couldn't cut him again." While others gave expression to a hope that he might be let off entirely. Alas! Alas! It was no such thing. He had to walk out and I had the deep regret to see him go on with the guard, with his shoulders quite contracted and his head down, and oh, how deeply did I feel that I could give him no assistance! When they arrived at the barrack-yard, he was brought to the triangle and after tearing off his clothes and tieing him up, they commenced like demons in cutting open his old wounds and making his flesh and blood fly in every direction, till the torture was so excessive that he called out to them: " Oh, shoot me! Shoot me! Kill me! Kill me!" But they as repeatedly cried out to him to give information, particularly against Sir Edward Crosbie and they would take him down, but this he refused to the last gasp. Finding all their tortures could not bend him in compliance, the savage scoundrels stopped and untied him, when one of them, a fellow called Sergeant Martin of the Ninth Dragoons and afterwards called " the walking gallows," slipped a rope round his neck and gave him so violent a drag that he fell (naked and bleeding as he was) on the coarse gravel. And then this wretch, this scandal to mankind, getting the rope over his shoulder, dragged him along the gravel, bleeding through a thousand wounds, till he came to the lamp-iron, on which though he was dead at the time, he hung him up. Thus ended the sufferings of one of the bravest and honestest men that Ireland ever reared, a man that gave up wife, children, property, aye and life itself in the midst of tortures, sooner than bend to a dishonourable action. Requiescat in pace, Amen. He was thrown naked as he was into Croppy hole and covered up there, but the time might yet come when his bones would be sought for and a trophy raised to his memory.

It might seem wonderful to some people and almost impossible to conjecture what reason there could be for taking the lives of men in such a savage manner who were incapable of making any resistance. It is universally allowed that good soldiers are never cruel and that, even after a hard-fought battle where hundreds of their comrades have been killed and wounded they scorn to take the lives of the very men that done it, when they submit and are no longer able to make resistance. How then did it happen here, where the soldiers lost none of their friends and the unfortunate people lost so much, that they should use such savage barbarity on the defenceless beings that fell into their hands. Ah, there was a reason for it that takes the dishonour in some measure off the character of the soldier and fixes it on the cold, unfeeling, calculating statesman.

The wise man that directed the affairs of England at the time wanted to rob this country of its parliament; and he knew very well that the Protestant gentlemen who exclusively composed it at the time would never consent to let him do so if he did not throw the country into the most dreadful state of terror and convulsion and confusion. And he knew very well the lives of Protestants should be sacrificed in the attempt as well as the lives of Catholics; still (though he was of course a very pious Protestant himself) that did not stop him one bit. He hallooed them at one another like bulldogs to tear each other in pieces; and if it was not for his horrible orders, soldiers would never turn hangmen nor

gentlemen holding the rank of officers stand by to see it
done. Let us not then lay all the blame on the wretched
Martin, "the walking gallows," that cut and mangled
Michael Wall and dragged him on the gravel to the lamp-
iron. No, no, Mr. Pitt, my good Englishman, you are the
man I arraign for it. I trace it to you as plainly as I trace
the assassin's murder to the employer that paid and directed
him how to do it. You were long skilled in the trade; you
murdered and robbed India of her immense wealth to fill
the voracious maw of your vicious craving country, a
country where virtue and honour are laughed to scorn
and successful villains applauded. They swallowed it all
and got millions in debt besides, making good the old adage
that "what's got over the back of a certain personage goes
under his belly." They wanted more and you, who were
reared up in that deadly English school where the villainous
craft of Ulysses the Grecian, as drawn by Homer, and the
more deadly villainy of Iago, the Englishman, as drawn by
Shakespeare, is taught to such perfection and copied so
closely through life by Englishmen of every class. You laid
your trap to catch Ireland and you succeeded. You robbed
her of her parliament, her natural guardian and protector,
and you continued robbing her till the day of your death;
and your country continued it after you till this day, being
a period of forty long, long years. She has been sucking
the heart's blood of Ireland and murdering thousands by
actual starvation. But what is your country the better of
it now? She is eight hundred millions of pounds in debt,
such a debt as was never before heard of since the world
began. Her once mighty power is reduced nearly to half
what it was. Her manufactures are a drug which she hawks
through the world, begging for customers. She is hated and
despised by all countries and placed in such a perilous
situation at this moment, that a single blow might knock
her down, never to rise again. And what has become of
yourself, Master Pitt? Why, after robbing every country
in the world that came within your reach, and dipping your
hands in the blood of millions of human beings, you ended

it (as was reported) by dipping them in your own and in that state rushed into the presence of your great Creator, there to undergo the important trial whether you were fit or not to be admitted into that holy place where nothing defiled, where nothing with spot or stain can enter. Oh, wretched being, how was your doom fixed for an endless eternity! Oh, that you had not been born for a statesman! Had you been born to " till the ground from whence you were taken " or to ask an alms from door to door, your fifty or sixty years of life might have passed over without crime or a dreadful account before you in a strange country, without a single friend to plead for you and where your own vain eloquence and sophistry was no use; and besides all this, you are to be called on to attend another judgment where Wall and thousands of others that have been slaughtered like him, in every quarter of the country your orders reached, will be there along with you. You cannot help appearing. It will be all in vain to refuse. The hills and the mountains will not, they cannot cover you. You might have some excuse to plead had these men been foreign enemies that invaded your country, to lay it waste by fire and sword; but they were not. They were your own fellow-subjects, who were living quietly and peaceably and who deserved your protection and whom you should have protected. But instead of doing so, you laid the plan, oh, the dreadful, the horrid plan that ruined them and perhaps has ruined yourself for ever.

CHAPTER TEN

THE EXECUTIONS

THE executions now went on with such frightful rapidity that I could not at a distance of forty-three years pretend to give anything like a regular account of them. Certainly, for some years afterwards, I could have gone pretty near it, as the impressions were strong and my memory, thank God, pretty good; but I could not at present and must confine myself to some particular persons.

Among the foremost I think I may fairly begin with Michael Heydon, as he was highest in office here and, besides that, had the misfortune (wholly against my advice) of conducting the party into town. After the slaughter was over (for there was no fight) and all hopes lost, he changed his clothes and succeeded in making his escape across the Barrow about half a mile above the town, and fled to Killeshin in the Queen's County, about three miles from Carlow, where he got shelter at a farmer's house who was his namesake. But the search for him was so keen that his pursuers were soon in sight and surrounded the house. He then endeavoured to escape through a back window but in this he failed and was instantly made prisoner. He was brought straight into town and his capture was considered by his enemies as a great triumph. He was lodged in the Blackhole of the barrack and was brought to trial by courtmartial next day. It was reported that he was offered his life by giving information but, let the faults arising from his inexperience be what they may, no one could ever prove the charge against him with endeavouring to save himself by such means and he was sentenced to be hanged and beheaded the same evening. He was full six feet high, about twenty-two years of age, light sandy hair, fresh complexion, apparently of great strength and of courage the most undaunted. I saw him going out to execution, as the upper windows of the jail commanded a view of that part of the barrack-yard. He walked from the Black-hole to the place of execution with an active quick step and an air seemingly as unconcerned as if he was going to some place of amusement. When he came to the lamp iron, there was but a few minutes delay in fixing the rope round his neck and he walked up the ladder, seemingly with as much resolution as he walked to it. He merely got time to turn round and face the people present, when he was pitched off with great violence and in a very short space of time the rope broke and he fell flat at full length on the ground. He lay for a short time, apparently insensible, but got up again and stood till the rope was adjusted, when he walked up the ladder again and went through the same scene as at first but the rope broke no more. He was hanged till quite dead, when his head was cut off and kicked about the barrack-yard and then put on a spike.

This tragedy ended the proceedings of this day but to mention the number that fell besides would not be in my power and the terror struck by them would also go beyond any power of mine to describe. Next morning as usual, about eight o'clock, the whole of the prisoners were let out in the yard to refresh themselves, but there was gloom and horror on every countenance. As I walked about the yard, I observed one man that did not come down. It was Pat Kelly, whom I mentioned before. He was a resident of the town and a particular acquaintance of mine. He was deeply connected in the United business, as he was a member of the baronial committee and held the rank of captain.

I saw with some degree of surprise, not unmixed with pain, that every way I went he still followed me with a most scrutinising eye. At length I got a little vexed and, looking up full at him said, " good morrow, Pat."

" Morrow," said he, in a dark distant tone.

This increased my surprise and I said again, " Why don't you come down ? "

" Oh, I won't mind it," said he in the very same tone as before.

I turned away immediately and seemed to take no farther notice of him, but I could not at all surmise what could be his meaning. However, I soon found it out. It was customary, in order to spread terror the wider, to give out false reports that different persons were giving information and among the rest it was thought proper to mention my name as one of that description. This came to Kelly's ears and occasioned, on bare hearsay, the coldness I have mentioned.

When the time came for us all to go upstairs to our places (for there was a flight of winding stone steps down to the yard) I took care to be nearly the last for I still wished to meet him and as I came up the steps he was leaning in a most pensive gloomy manner against the iron door where I should pass and viewed me up and down from head to foot, as I came near him, and as I was quite certain he had something to say to me I walked up and spoke to him, but to my astonishment he seemed quite cool and not the least inclined for conversation. When I saw this, I got angry and made a hasty reflection that if he would not speak I wouldn't care about him nor try to force him to it and I stepped on with the rest, but he immediately called me back and said, " I have something to say to you ; wait till these are gone by." I was rather uneasy, for fear the keepers should observe me staying there too long and as soon as all passed, I said hastily, " Well, Pat, what is it you have to say to me ? "

He then looked earnestly at me and said, " I have something to say to you, and sure you won't be angry with me ? "

" Not at all, man, why should I be angry with you ? "

" I am afraid you will," said he.

This raised my curiosity to the highest pitch and I replied hastily, " Not at all, man. Let it out whatever it is. Tell it to me, I don't care what it is."

He then paused and after a visible struggle said, " Why, they are saying things of you and sure you'll say nothing of me ? "

Struck with contempt and surprise I stared and said, " Did you ever know me to be guilty of a scandalous action ? "

"No," said he, "but now I see you are angry."

"Not a bit, not a bit, but why should you suspect me?"

"Well," said he, "do you say nothing against me and I'll say nothing against you."

As these words showed he still doubted me, I replied, "Oh, if that be all, Pat, begin as soon as you please, for where there is but one to swear against me, I'd be glad there was fifty, that I might be put out of the way at once." For the torture at the time was so horrible that we considered the man that only lost his life got off very safe if he escaped it. Just at the moment, his wife came up to the front door, through which there was a round hole so as to allow prisoners to see and speak to their friends, and here followed one of the most touching trying scenes I ever witnessed. She was a comely, interesting young woman with fair hair and they had been married only a few weeks before. After some conversation his utterance got choked. His voice failed, the big tears chased each other down his manly face, his very soul was in agony; he struggled to recover himself and then, assuming a bold manly tone, he gave her some particular directions and finished by saying "And don't you come near me any more." The guard at this time was hurrying her from the door but he called her back and said, "As you are going down the street, tell every one it's all lies they're telling about William Farrell, that he never said a word about anyone."

Though some might take this as a flattering compliment, yet, for very particular reasons, I'd rather at the time it had been spared, for the danger I and every one else stood in was so great I cared but little about empty praise or unjust censure. I had one point to mind, one duty to perform, on that my whole attention was fixed, and so as I could perform that faithfully and honestly, I wanted no more.

Kelly and I parted and on coming to my room I began to reflect with the deepest attention on what passed between us and though some might think from a few weak points in his conversation that he had a notion of failing, yet I had no such opinion of him.

THE EXECUTIONS

The window of the court-martial room opened as usual at nine o'clock and it was then *Have a care!* Shortly after, the guard appeared in sight coming to the jail but, as no one knew who was to be the victim, every one was on the rack till the name was called out and then whoever it was should be off in quick time. No hesitation, no delay was allowed and at times there would be two or three different guards in motion, coming to the jail and going from it, but then there would be seldom more than two men to a guard and they were quite sufficient. On this day they were kept busily employed, until at length Kelly was called for.

There was something very particular in his case and which also concerned me most intimately and was as follows. Sometime before the unfortunate eruption, there were some prisoners in the jail who were in much want of subsistence, and one of the number happened to be high in office. They all, and particularly this man, sent to Michael Heydon for money to support them, as he was treasurer for the county. Very shortly before this, there was a call—the call I mentioned before—from Dublin on the different counties, and all the money Heydon had in hands, besides a subscription, was sent them by Ivers. When Heydon was called on by the prisoners every shilling he could get he sent them until at last he was fairly run aground and as they were clamorous for assistance he was obliged to call a baronial meeting to try what could be done. But such was the terror and apprehension under which people in general laboured from the number of spies that were in every direction, that not a man of them attended but two and myself and Heydon. When I went into the house I met Heydon and asked if they were come. "Only a few," said he, "go upstairs and I expect the rest immediately." When I went up, I saw but two members in the room, Kelly and John Berne, but to my great astonishment who was with them but the noted Rogers. As soon as I saw him I turned with disgust out of the room and went down to Heydon and asked him how Rogers came to get admission, as he was no member. He told me he did not think it any harm as he was a most zealous and active man. I replied that neither his zeal or his activity entitled him to a place there and that it was quite wrong to admit him on such an important occasion where men's lives were at stake.

" Well," said he, " I had no hand in it. He was brought by another person but, if you choose, I will call him out of the room ; but if I do so, it may offend the man that brought him in."

" Oh, if that be so," said I, " don't mind it. It concerns me no more than any one else."

So Heydon and I walked up, but I was fully resolved in my own mind not to say or do anything in his presence that could in the least criminate me.

When we went into the room, the business was opened at once and it was agreed there was no way of getting money but by borrowing from some person and Mr. McDonnell, the brewer, was the man pitched on. Mr. McDonnell was one of the wealthiest men in town and besides that possessed a kind and generous heart and was remarkable for his liberality and charity. The next point was to know who would go to him to ask the money and Kelly at once volunteered. In case anyone would go with him, he was desired immediately to make a choice of any one he pleased, and I was the person he pitched on. I did not hesitate a moment, but refused at once. Entreaties and arguments were used to prevail on me, but all in vain. I was determined on my point and would not surrender it ; when, after some hesitation, John Berne said he would go and actually did go along with Kelly and got the money from Mr. McDonnell.

On the present awful day we were all prisoners ; but Mr. McDonnell, on account of his great wealth and liberal principles, was particularly aimed at and the greatest diligence was used in every quarter to get any kind of information against him, but kind providence protected the worthy, honest, good man, for though Rogers knew right well he gave the money, still he was not present at the time and could not prove it so as to affect his life. John Berne was after being shot to death in the barrack-yard and there was no one could prove anything home against him, but Kelly. His life was in Kelly's hands but he had a real good man to depend on for Kelly was the right sort. When his trial came on, though there were several charges that could be brought against him, still I knew right well they would dwell particularly on the one concerning Mr. McDonnell, to try if possible to get Kelly to save his own life by joining Rogers to prosecute him; and I was also quite certain that Kelly would not do it but would deny the transaction altogether. I was in no doubt of him. Well, what then would the enemies of Mr. McDonnell do? Why, to try if possible to find out some other person that could strengthen the evidence of Rogers and contradict Kelly and to force that person to do it either by fear or dint of torture; and there was no other person but myself.

It is really astonishing, when they had Kelly in their power and wished so much to take Mr. McDonnells' life and property, that they did not put Kelly himself to the torture (as they did the other men) in order to force him to prove against the good man but they were completely blinded (as if by the power of the Almighty) in their fury, and missed their prey. Had they done so, the affair would not have concerned me so much and would have saved me from a deal of anxiety and danger their bungling occasioned.

The above-mentioned circumstances were so strong in my mind that I was almost certain of being called on and I knew right well, if I was once brought to the triangles, I would never be let go while there was a gasp of life in me. I reflected on the horrible butchery committed on the Mahers and O'Connor and Wall and, "Oh, God Almighty," I would think, " am I to suffer more than any of them? Or is the whole vengeance that was discharged on them separately to come collected and with all its force on me?"

While the noble Kelly was on his trial, the guards were coming and going quickly, sometimes bringing back a prisoner, sometimes taking one, and every guard I saw coming, I was almost certain was coming for me, as I had no doubt my name would be mentioned. This had such an effect on me and put me to such torture of mind, that I moved from the upper window that commanded the view of the guards and barrack to a dark corridor in the centre, where my sight at least should not be tortured till the moment I was actually called for, but the agony I suffered here I could not describe, for, though I could not see the guard coming up, though I was somewhat eased of that part of the torture, still I could hear the rapping at the door and had an ear quick and ready to know who was called for and if it was myself, out I should be in an instant. Over and over again, I envied the very dead. "Oh, how happy are they," I would think, "lying in their peaceful graves. Happy the man marching up to a cannon, with the match lighted, ready to blow him to pieces. Oh, that I were in his place, sooner than be sacrificed in such a manner!" Over and over again, these reflections crowded on my mind and it all happened exactly as I conjectured; and out I would have been brought and sacrificed, too, if it was not for the interference of a Protestant gentleman and that gentleman was Lieutenant Loftus of the Ninth Dragoons, as I afterwards knew to a certainty.

In this state I continued during the trial and it was a long one. At length there was a rapping at the door. I listened attentively but heard no one called for. I then could not be certain but they met the one they wanted convenient and were going off with their victim. I still listened and after a long, long interval of suspense, I heard it said Kelly was brought in. I endeavoured, as well as I could, to give God thanks for my great deliverance as I knew I had nothing more to fear for that day.

After some time, I went very slowly downstairs, when I was informed that Kelly was put down in the dungeon. I had a particular wish to see him, as the sting he gave me in the morning was not entirely healed. I walked down to the yard and as I passed by the dungeon door, I saw him on his knees, in most profound prayer, and three more along with him. These were Richy Heydon, Laurence Byrne, and James Hollogan, all under sentence of death and preparing for it. I passed on, for, though I wished to speak to Kelly, still I could not think of disturbing him in so awful a situation, but on reflection I resolved to stand in a part of the yard where he could see me and then, if he wished to speak, to give him the opportunity. I accordingly done so and it was not very long till he observed me. As soon as he did, he got up off his knees and called me. I advanced a few steps towards him and stopped.

"Come on, come on!" said he.

I did so and as soon as I came within reach of him, he thrust his arms through the bars and drew me to him saying, "Come here till I kiss you."

"Well, Pat," said I, "who swore against you now?"

"Oh, don't ask me!" said he.

"Oh," said I, "sure it can be no harm to tell it now. Tell me, can't you, who it was."

This, I observed, raised a conflict in him, but after a short struggle: "Rogers," said he. "It was Rogers swore against me and your name was mentioned, too. You won't be long after me, but while you are in it pray for me. Adieu, God be with you."

Just as I was parting him, the others got up off their knees and came over and kissed me and bid me farewell. I returned immediately to my room and from that till evening, I never saw such silence or sorrow observed by every one in the prison. Kelly's prayer could be heard distinctly from the dungeon to the very uppermost room and indeed it was a most extraordinary one. It was the following one: "That Almighty God may give me the hardest death ever any man got for my sins." This prayer he pronounced in a devout, firm, manly tone. He was always a man of a religious disposition, wore a scapular and in this last trial seemed raised above all fear and as undaunted as a lion.

The guard came over for them in the evening, and to guard these four men to death there was not a single man on the guard (as well as I can recollect) but four; and they were quite sufficient in those dreadful times, for the prisoners had no idea of making an escape and no friends dare be near to attempt a rescue though one of the prisoners, James Hollogan, was one of the ablest and finest looking men that could be seen. It would be hard to get a finer looking man in a parish and from his character for courage and action I suppose he would singly beat the four men that were guarding him, though he went like a child with them, knowing right well it would be quite vain to do anything else. The whole four were hanged together and the undaunted Kelly's head cut off and put on a spike.

Let no one imagine these were the only executions of the day; oh, no, the triangles were kept in constant employment, where human flesh was cut off and human blood spilled like water. Poor John Berne was shot too, as I said before, and when I mention him I mention one of the best men could be named. He was about five feet eight inches high, of the most perfect symmetry for elegance, strength and action, courteous, kind and gentle in his manners, and though bold as a lion if required, still he always took the greatest pains to conceal this latter quality. He was by trade a chandler. About thirty years of age, two or three years married and was just beginning, by dint of close industry and application, to rise in the world when he met his fate, leaving a wife and one child to mourn for him. When he received the first shots, he jumped upright on his limbs (and he had fine ones). He was ordered to kneel down again and the second discharge he did the same, but the third discharge finished him. His friends got leave to take him away to his burying-ground at a place called "The Graves," just adjoining the town and I was told by a person who saw him lying naked on the grass, after the blood was washed off, that he had a bullet hole through one of his hands, several more through his body and one through his head and that he had a skin as white as snow. Kelly's remains were brought to the same place and they were both buried side by side. Each could have saved himself at the expense of Mr. McDonnell, but both preferred honourable graves. May they rest in peace, amen, and may their memory live with honour in the country they died for.

Amidst all these scenes of horror and confusion, we were all astonished (if anything in such times could astonish us) at hearing of a prisoner that was after coming in. It was no less a personage than Sir Edward Crosbie, a gentleman of rank and fortune, that lived at Viewmount, convenient to the town, and a Protestant gentleman besides. Had Sir Edward been one of those fawning sycophants that could stoop to any meanness or any oppression of the poor or any plunder of the public, he would have been quite safe. The name of his religion alone, in case he never went inside a church or never prayed to God at all, would have been a sure protection for him. But he was not one of these. He did not approve of making the poor man and his little offspring wretched, and he sympathised with them in their sufferings and privations. He lived rather a retired life, was kind and affable to those in the middle and humbler ranks of life, who always were joyful and felt no alarm when they met with Sir Edward Crosbie. He seldom associated with those in power and when he did, he assumed a dignity and consequence suited to his rank. At one public meeting (I forget now for what purpose it was convened) Sir Edward delivered his opinions freely. They happened, however, not to be well relished and were warmly opposed and words ran so high between him and Counsellor Burton, son to Mr. Burton of Burton Hall, that a challenge was the consequence. They met next day. Sir Edward received his fire but did not return it and the matter was made up, though not entirely to the satisfaction of some persons. Old Mr. Burton was the most popular gentleman (and deservedly so) of any in the County Carlow. He always represented the county in parliament. He was a gentleman of such strict honour that his word was considered equal to a bond and though his fortune was not one of the largest, still he managed with such economies to keep up a splendid retinue and see the very first company and entertain them in the style of a nobleman. In short the " Truth and Honour " which was the family motto and the kindness and hospitality of Burton Hall were proverbial, and Sir Edward having a dispute with one of the family, no matter whether right or wrong, raised him a host of enemies and though it might not be prudent for them to avow it openly, they could not abide him afterwards and he was now fully in their power.

One of the first arrangements he made, after coming in to prison, was to send orders to all the tradesmen and shopkeepers in town that he was indebted to to furnish him instantly with their accounts and among the rest he owed about twelve pounds to Mr. Fitzgerald, my brother-in-law. In the course of the day, my sister, Mrs. Fitzgerald, came to see me and after some conversation she handed me his bill and desired me to go to Sir Edward Crosbie's room and give it to him. I looked at her with astonishment (as I had not heard of his orders) and told her I thought it would be a most indelicate and improper thing to bring a bill to a gentleman in his situation, and that I would not do it on any account.

" It is his own direction," said she, " or I would not do it, no more than you."

" How could that be ? How could he give directions and he confined here ? "

" He sent a person to the house," said she, " and to every creditor of his in town and several of them have sent here already."

" I wonder how they could come here unknown to me," said I " but, as you say so, I will go to him."

I immediately went up stairs and rapped at his room door. He desired me to come in which I did with some diffidence, and after bowing respectfully said, " Here is a bill, Sir Edward, that Mr. Fitzgerald sent you and he would not have done so at present but a person called on him and said you ordered it."

" Oh, he is very right, very right; I did send to him. Just leave it with me and as you are going down street, call to Sykes[1] and tell him to send me his bill."

---

[1] Sykes was a watchmaker and ironmonger.

"Oh, they would not let me go down street, Sir Edward."

"Why," said he, looking at me with astonishment; "are you a prisoner?"

"I am, Sir Edward."

"Well, well, you had better not remain here. If you were seen with me, it might not serve you." I bowed again and retired.

Sir Edward lost no time. He was unceasingly employed in making preparations for what was to come on. Lady Crosbie, too, attended him with the utmost diligence. Her carriage was repeatedly at the jail door and no woman could show greater anxiety or activity than she did. Oh, she was an honour to her sex! She had powerful interest and made every exertion and every application to save him and if she only had time would infallibly have succeeded. His enemies knew this right well and were fully resolved he should not have the time requisite and (as well as I can recollect) he was brought to trial on the third day after his apprehension. The principal charge brought against him was that a party of the rebels assembled at his house on the night of the attack and that he knew of it and encouraged them. The principal witness brought against him was his servant man that he reared from his boyhood and was always kind to. This unfortunate creature certainly did not give voluntary evidence against him. He was driven to it reluctantly, and through dint of the terror of tortures and death, but with all this I never could learn that he was able to prove anything that could (or ought at least to) affect Sir Edward's life. There were some of his workmen put to the torture to force them to swear against him and all that could be obtained in this way was as follows: one of them proved to a party assembling at the house and on being questioned as to whether Sir Edward was among them or not, he said he could not be positive as to that point, that he was some distance from the party at the time and that he saw a man about Sir Edward's size walking actively among them and giving them directions and that he then went up the steps of the hall-door and stood there and that the dress he wore was exactly the same as

Sir Edward's. This brought the charge home against him although he was not in it at all.

Sir Edward at the time had a man of the name of Tom Myler, who was his steward and gardener. Myler was of the United Irishmen and in size and shape resembled Sir Edward very much and might readily and at night and at a distance be mistaken for him, and Myler was the very man that went among the people and up the steps of the hall door and stood there, as related by the witness. I have the account of it several years afterwards from Myler's own mouth. After relating to me the almost miraculous escape he made himself, he proceeded as follows : " Sir Edward Crosbie was never a United Irishman. No person dare propose such a thing to him and if the United Irishmen happened to be mentioned in ordinary conversation, he would remark, "Ah, they are foolish people ; I pity them ; they do not know what they are doing " ; (and that was as much as any gentleman of them could say at the time with safety to himself) but as respects the night of the insurrection, it was a rule with Sir Edward, when the business of the day was over, to go into his study and when he once went in we saw no more of him till next morning, and he knew no more of what was doing in the house or about it during that time than a man twenty miles off. On the unfortunate night in question, he was as usual in his study and the people of the neighbourhood assembled and came to me, as I had some arms concealed in the garden which they wanted. I begged and entreated of them and used every argument in my power to cause them to desist ; but all in vain and at last they threatened to break open the garden door and take them by force if I did not give them. When I found this, I was obliged to open the door and give them and I then went from them and went up the steps of the hall-door and stood there as was sworn. And to make the matter more unfortunate for Sir Edward, I happened to wear a coat that night that he had bestowed me some time before, and in which dress I might be easily mistaken for him, so that the kindness of my good master to me was partly the cause of his ruin, and he lost his life for what he had no hand, act or part in."

Whatever was wanting in proof against Sir Edward was made up by probability and he was found guilty and sentenced to be hanged and beheaded.

He was not sent immediately from the court-martial to execution; he got till late in the evening to prepare and was attended by two Protestant clergymen, the Revd. Doctor Hobart, a venerable-looking old gentleman and his son, the Revd. Benjamin Hobart, a gentleman much esteemed as a man of high honour and spirit, and both paid him every attention in their power and seemed to feel very much for his situation. Sir Edward walked out with them with a firm step and the prisoners could see them from the upper windows nearby the whole way through the street and up through the barrack-yard, till they came just to the court-martial room door. We all wondered greatly at this, as we imagined he was going straight to execution but when we saw him stop there we thought it looked as if there was some hope of saving his life. A considerable crowd soon assembled on the spot and they seemed as if engaged in an important debate which continued a long time and in which I am certain the clergymen used their utmost endeavours for him. At length they all came back again towards the gate and when we perceived they did not bring him to a lamp-iron for immediate execution, our hopes of his acquittal grew stronger and stronger; but when we saw the gate opened and the crowd coming out, we jumped for joy and cried out, "he is saved! he is saved! his life is saved!" The new jail was building exactly opposite the barrack-gate at the time and we watched anxiously to see them turn the corner of the wall which hid them from our view. We thought they were a very long time coming and wondered greatly what could be the reason, when to our utter astonishment and dismay we saw them walking up the steps that led to the fatal apparatus of death. A few minutes more ended the tragedy. We heard the dreadful noise and fall of the board. He was hanged till dead and his head was then cut off and placed on a spike with the others.

It was a sad and gloomy evening's work for all the prisoners, for we all very naturally concluded that, where such a gentleman as Sir Edward Crosbie got such usage, that the chance of those in the humbler walks of life must have been precarious indeed.

There was another transaction I omitted, but which I think deserves to be mentioned in this tragical narrative. It was the case of Mr. Pat Kehoe of Leighlin Bridge. He carried on extensive business in the linen and woollen drapery line and the spirit and grocery line and as he had a large connection of the most wealthy farmers in the country his near relatives, he done great business and was accounted one of the wealthiest men in Leighlin Bridge. He was taken and sent prisoner to Carlow and as soon as he was, his whole establishment was ransacked and plundered and everything worth taking carried away; a proceeding that would not be allowed at all in Carlow, as bad as it was. When he arrived at the jail, he was placed in one of the middle rooms where I was and which was a flagged room and generally had but two beds, and as the prison was crowded, there was a pallet laid down for him. From the very commencement, he seemed to have a presentiment of his fate, for he was up at an uncommon early hour in the morning and with prayer-book in hand, walked the room, seemingly in deep devotion, as if he was certain of death, although he never took any active part in the business that I could learn except, unfortunately, being a United Irishman.

In the course of a few days, some alterations took place in the prison and he and I were removed to the upper rooms, which had better air, a fine view of the country and were boarded. Mr. McDonnell, the brewer, a wealthy man, had the best of these rooms which was at the upper end of the building over the river Burren and Mr. Kehoe, being another wealthy man, was put there along with him and I was put into the next room to the landing place, which was not so good but was good enough, as I was careless enough where I was. Here we remained a few days, when Mr. Kehoe was brought to a sort of a trial but, as we all knew he never took any active part in the unfortunate business, we were under no apprehensions for his safety and thought it would be a mere matter of form, and he came back without any sentence being passed but all was uncertainty as to his fate, and things remained in this state for a few days. Trials and executions were going on as usual. During this time I began to get uneasy for my fate, for I expected all along that Mr. Fitzmaurice's interest would have liberated me but as it did not, I concluded he could not accomplish it with all his endeavours (for I had no doubt of his goodness) and that without his help I could not possibly escape.

One day, while I was under this impression, the Guards were coming and going with such fearful rapidity that I became fully convinced it would be the last day of my life and from the anxiety I was under and from the heat of the day, my mouth got quite dried up, not a particle of moisture in it; and just at the moment Mr. McDonnell and Mr. Kehoe walked into my room and after a few moments gloomy conversation I saw a guard coming on hastily. The moment I saw them, I concluded to a certainty they were surely coming for myself and I had not a drop of water in my room to wet my mouth and as there was not a moment to be lost, I stepped out of the room without any ceremony and down the long corridor to Mr. McDonnell's room, where I was certain I would find it and commenced a rapid search among jugs, mugs, glasses and decanters, but could not succeed. Just at the moment, Mr. Kehoe came in after me and asked me what I was looking for. "Just a drop of water to wet my mouth," was the reply.

"Oh," said he, "you shan't take water, you must take a glass of spirits."

"No, no," said I, "I would rather take water" (which I really would at the time).

"But there is not a drop in the room, so you must take this," and he handed me the glass, which I took with great reluctance and just tasted it and handed it back, but he refused it and said, "Drink it, man, you must take it."

I still refused but he pressed until I was obliged to take

about half the glass and then desired him to finish it, which he did, and just as soon as he drank it, the thundering came to the front door and he was called for. As soon as he heard the call he clapped his hands and said " Oh, I am off," and without hesitation he was obliged to walk out and face instant death. I endeavoured to give God thanks as well as I was able for protecting me in such dreadful danger and walked slowly and heavily into my room.

As soon as I went in, Mr. McDonnell asked me (but not in an angry tone) what I was doing in his room. I told him the plain story, how I was certain the guard was coming for myself, and that I wanted a little water so much and the case so urgent, I couldn't stop to ask his permission. " Oh," said he, " it's not on that account I speak, only there was something so strange in it I was curious to know."

I then told him what passed between Mr. Kehoe and me in his room, to which he listened with wonder and then in a tone of devotion said, " Your time wasn't come. Almighty God has been merciful to you."

The rest of the evening passed over in gloomy conversations on the sad affairs that were taking place and it was not more than about one hour when the unfortunate Mr. Kehoe was brought by dead on a car, which made such an impression on us that we did not much mind any other occurrence of that day.

CHAPTER ELEVEN

INTERROGATION AND INTERCESSION

From the time I was sent to prison, I entertained hopes that Mr. Fitzmaurice's interest would have me liberated and I pressed my friends at different times to apply to him for that purpose, which they did, but Mr. Fitzmaurice had been apprised of the mistake he made in giving me a protection at all and that it could be no use to me, on account of the station I filled, and he told them so, but that he would use all his interest to serve me and that he did not despair of success when the storm would get a little calm. I now began to be very doubtful of it and did not well know what to conjecture, when one day an officer's guard of horse came up to the jail and I was called for. As I was just convenient at the time, I went to the door without my hat. The jailer desired me to go back for it, as I was wanting. I did so and when I returned, "Come here," said he, "till I put you up behind this man."

"Where," said I " are they going to take me?"

"I don't know," said he, "but never fear they won't let you go astray."

He immediately lifted me up behind a dragoon and the party moved on.

This was so unusual a proceeding, as no such guard was sent for anyone else, that I was filled with wonder and astonishment and could not by any means conjecture what could be the meaning of it. Cornet Lowther of the Ninth Dragoons commanded the party and they brought me up through the potatoe-market, down Tullow Street, till they came to the Market-cross, where they halted. I was ruminating the whole way on what they were likely to do with me and it occurred strongly to me that as I was so deeply concerned in the United business they were going to put me to death without giving me any trial and that they would make some public example of me. When they halted at the cross, I looked about to see if there was any stage erected or any other apparatus for an execution, but there was none. I then thought it probable they intended to cut me down with their swords and were only waiting for orders, as several of them, during the long time they kept me there, were going and coming in the direction of the inn, which was quite convenient; so fertile is fancy in drawing the most dangerous images on these frightful occasions. In the meantime a car was drawn close by me, with the naked corpse of a man on it who was after being flogged and hanged in the barrack-yard. I did not observe the horrid spectacle till it passed me a little and then I saw there was nothing under it in the car but the bare slats, which caused it to be shook and jolted at every step. There was no crowd with it nor any person but the one that led the horse. The people might look out from their houses, but no one dare go near it. I heard some one say his name was Curran and that he was from Timard and they were sending him to be buried in the place called " croppy hole."

Cornet Lowther, who had been away for some time, now returned and coming up close to me, said, " Farrell, you are to go on to Leighlin Bridge.[1] Your sister is getting a chaise. It will be ready in a few minutes."

" Oh, sir," said I, " I am well enough, I don't want it."

" Oh, but your sister means to go with you and she can't go without a chaise."

When I heard this, I assented, of course, though I greatly disliked the proceeding, as I could not see what use there could be in such ceremony, as it only tended to put my sister and myself to greater sorrow, and as regarded myself, I was quite careless of my own convenience or inconvenience, but I had got a new subject to meditate on, as I could not, for the life of me, conjecture what the meaning could be of sending me to Leighlin Bridge.

As soon as the chaise was ready, my sister and I went in

[1] A small town about six miles off.

and they set off with us, though I was greatly chagrined at having her with me, as I thought my own trouble quite sufficient for me, without having her to share in it, but she would not on any account stay behind and only for dint of interest, she would not be allowed to go at all.

As we went along the road, there was not a human being to be seen. The most death-like silence prevailed and all nature seemed petrified with terror. The trees, the bushes, the very stones seemed to shrink and tremble. The only exception was the cock, who crew and strutted about as bold and undaunted as if nothing was amiss. Oh, how I admired and almost envied his resolution!

Our family burial place was at Dunleckny, about a mile and a half from Leighlin Bridge and as it looked as if fate was drawing me to the spot, my poor sister broke out into the following loud lamentations; "Oh, must I leave you in Dunleckny! Oh, are they taking you—are they taking you to Dunleckny? Oh, that I could die in your place! Oh, that I could give my life and go into the grave for you!"

I remained silent the whole time. I made no reply; but, glory be to God Almighty, foolish and inexperienced as I was, He did not let me sink under the danger, in His great mercy He was pleased to fill me with the most profound contempt of the world and with the most brilliant prospects of a glorious eternity. I almost panted to be freed from a world that appeared to me as changed into a den of demons in human shape and to join the happy inhabitants of that glorious Country whose blessed citizens know not persecution.

In the midst of these reflections, a thought occurred to me which may seem rather a singular one in such circumstances; I recollected I owed a few shillings and I immediately became uneasy about it. I knew very well my sister would think nothing of paying it and still I feared it would increase her grief if I mentioned it, as it would look something like making a will. However, it should be done and after a little reflection, I said with as much apparent unconcern as I could command, "If I should not come back, pay a few shillings for me to such and such persons."

As we were travelling at a smart rate, we shortly after arrived at Leighlin Bridge, and as we drove up the street there was not a living creature to be seen and as dead a silence prevailed (excepting the rattling of the chaise and horses on the pavement, which was like thunder) as if every inhabitant of the town had been dead and buried twenty years before. We were driven up straight to the inn (where the courts-martial were held) and as we came near it, I observed in the square before the door the whole apparatus of death or torture, as the case might be, viz. : a triangle, rope and cat-o'-nine-tails appended to it, for it was in the public street before the men and women, old and young, that prisoners were stripped naked and executed.

When we came up, the carriage door was opened and I was ordered to go in. I did so and was brought into a very large parlour, where there were about fourteen or fifteen gentlemen, all officers of either the Yeomanry or standing army, who all knew me, as every one of them dealt at my brother-in-law's shop and as I had the name of being a good workman in them times and made it my study to give general satisfaction, every gentleman that knew me was my friend and I had no enemy. As soon as I walked in, they all seemed astonished.

" Oh," said some of them ; isn't this Andy Fitzgerald's man ? Isn't this Farrell, that worked at Andy Fitzgerald's ? By the law, it is."

" Yes, gentlemen," said I, " I worked for you all."

Just at this moment, Lieutenant Higgins of the Ninth Dragoons walked in and said, " Gentlemen, I came in to inform you that I have received a good character of Farrell and besides that I can say from myself that I have been frequently in the shop where he was and that I always saw him civil and obliging." Two or three others cried out, " We can all say the same ; and one of the best workmen in Ireland," and then said to each other they were very sorry for me.

After these observations, one of them said, " You have been brought here to make a full acknowledgement of your guilt concerning this dreadful business, that has brought such destruction on the country."

This appeared to me to be a very weak announcement from a great man in power and I replied : " There was no occasion, gentlemen, to bring me here for that purpose, as I made an acknowledgement of it already, when I gave myself up to Mr. Fitzmaurice and got his protection."

I was particular to mention the circumstance of having got a protection, to try if it would stop any proceedings against me, or in case they should go to extremities with me, that they should have no room to plead ignorance of my having such a thing. They, however, made no observation whatever on it, but went on and the officer who spoke first said again, " Yes, but we mean besides that you will give such information as will tend to put a stop to it and which, of course, it is in your power to do, from the extensive knowledge you must have had of it."

I replied, " It is not in my power to give any information that could be of any use and there is not one of you all gentlemen but knows as much about it now as I do."

"That is impossible," said the officer, "and it's a duty you owe your country to give any information that will stop bloodshed and there is no way of stopping it but by such information as you can give."

Here all the officers in the room, from the friendly way they spoke at first became violent, and repeated, " It is a duty you owe your country to give the information, though you may think it would be a disgrace to you, but in that you would be quite mistaken ; on the contrary, it would be to your credit to be instrumental in putting a stop to the dreadful scenes that are now desolating it. We wish to show you all the kindness in our power, but the information you must give."

I replied again, " There is not one of all you gentlemen would be more willing to stop it than I would. I would stop it this moment all over the world if I could, but I know of no plot, no conspiracy against any one ; nothing that could be of any use ; nothing but what you are all in possession of."

As soon as I said this, they all became exasperated and attacked me together and with such heat and earnestness that three or four of them would put their questions to me at once. This, however, so far from confusing or embarrassing me, was rather a service, as it enabled me to evade any dangerous question and give my reply to the person whose question was not dangerous, but the questions and answers were so rapid that I could not at all recollect them at present, but the whole tenor of them was an attack upon one side to urge me to give information and my defence on the other to resist it.

At length Captain Stewart of the Leighlin Yeomanry, a large, coarse, strong-looking man, who was writing at a table at the far end of the room, called out to me to come to him. I did so and as soon as I came up to him, he looked at me with an air of determined severity, and with a voice as sharp as a sword, said, " Now I'll tell you what, my good young man ; we have met with persons here as obstinate as you and we made them tell and we'll make you too. So tell at once, now ; there is no use in any further hesitation."

I felt my life touched the instant he spoke, for his plain meaning was : "Tell this moment or out you must go to the torture of the triangle, to have your flesh cut off and your blood spilled." I felt, I say, my life touched and I instantly exclaimed in a loud voice and with most earnest feeling, " Oh, gentlemen, I have no information to give ; I know of nothing could be of any use except I told of some other unfortunate person and *I know of no one worse than myself.*"

These words, with the tone and manner in which they were delivered, had such an effect that there was not a man present but was just as if he was struck dumb and as dead a silence followed as if there was not a man in the room.

The gentlemen lower down now formed a group and were consulting privately, when the door suddenly opened and in walked the celebrated Jack Kelly, alias the Switcher. He was a member of the county committee and we knew each other well, having often sat together on business. He was a man full six feet high, fresh complexion, black hair, sandy whiskers, wore a blue jacket, nankin pantaloons, and was on the whole a remarkably fine-looking man. I was completely astonished on seeing him, as I could not at all conjecture what the meaning of bringing him and I together could be, except to make one of us inform against the other for it never occurred to me, the thing was so sudden, that it was on his information I was taken. As soon as he advanced, the gentlemen drew up in lines at both sides of us and every eye piercing us with the most intense scrutiny for the result. I viewed him up and down alternately, to try if I could discover or make any guess at his intention, but I looked in vain; he appeared bold and unconcerned and did not betray the least sign of guilt. At last one of the gentlemen broke silence and asked me " Did you ever see that man before ? "

" No, sir," said I, but then, turning on the word, I said, " I've seen him before, but I have no further knowledge of him."

" Did you ever sit on a committee with him ? " was the next question. As an answer to this question in the affirmative would be a direct information against Kelly and would break down my own character for ever, I replied firmly, " No, sir."

" Kelly," said he, " did you ever sit on committee with him ? "

" I sat on committee," said Kelly, " with a man of the name, but I can't say it's him."

The instant he spoke, I knew what he was and I pitied him from my heart; the unfortunate man was tortured into an informer and his now evading to prove against me, though he knew me right well, showed plainly he did it reluctantly. After some further observations which I do not now recollect, he was ordered to withdraw and the attack on me commenced again with great fury. Major Cornwall was most conspicuous in this part. He got into a violent passion, thrust his hand inside his coat as if to draw out a pistol, exclaiming, " I'll shoot you dead this moment, you hardened villain ! "

"Do, sir," said I, opening my breast to him, I'd be glad you would."

"No, you villain, I won't now," said he; "I know you'd be glad of it, but you shan't get off so easy. Here," said he, "take him off to the guard-house and at nine o'clock to-morrow morning—mind that, now—at nine o'clock to-morrow morning, I'll give you the most exemplary punishment that any villain ever got."

I was immediately taken off to the guardhouse. It was quite convenient to the inn and, I believe, had been one of the stables. It contained twenty-one prisoners before me, the most of whom had sore backs, after coming from the triangle, and were lying on some dirty straw, and four out of the number were to be shot next morning. These were Paul Cullen, Jack Hughes, Jack Brenan, brother-in-law to Cullen, and Michael Carroll, who was clerk to Mr. Hanlon of Bagenalstown. The three first were respectable farmers. Carroll was one of the county committee and was heavily punished to make him give information but though he was a mild, delicate-looking, young man, still he stood it to the last and would not do it. He was lying behind the door as I went in and was apparently in a dying state. The marks of the cats were on his face and as soon as I saw him I exclaimed, "Oh, my God, is this you?" and stretched out my hand to him. He just turned his head to me but was not able to raise it and endeavoured to speak, but I could not well understand him. Jack Hughes was also greatly flogged, but he was a stout robust man and bore it manfully to the last. Paul Cullen and Brenan escaped the torture, they were not flogged at all. Cullen was an uncommonly fine young man, about twenty-two years of age, sandy complexion, and about five feet nine inches high. He was remarkable in the country for being one of the foremost in those feats of activity such as leaping, vaulting etc. so much practised and prized by young men in those times. He was one of Sir Richard Butler's yeoman cavalry and a soldier every inch of him, if wanting, and what may appear very extraordinary, he never was a United Irishman. How then did he come to be under sentence of death ? Simply as follows : he was so well liked by the people that at one of their meetings they appointed him a lieutenant. He was not present, but was told of it afterwards. He refused to act. He would not join them. But because he did not give information against them, he was sentenced in the very prime of life to suffer death. Such were people's ideas of law and justice and honour in those dreadful times. But surely, surely they had foolish young people enough to make victims of that really were concerned in it, without going out of their way to make a victim of one that was not. Had he given information against them, which the laws of honour and honesty forbid, he would surely have lost his life for it on one side ; and because he did not do so, he was to lose it on the other. Alas, alas, how hard is the fate of some !

During the day we were all making the best preparations we could to meet the next awful morning and when night came we were allowed candle-light. We were all on our knees, engaged in the most earnest devotions and supplications to the Almighty for mercy, and Garrett Kinsella, who was first cousin to Cullen, giving out the Rosary and litanies, when we were suddenly attacked by a party of the Wicklow Militia, who rushed up to the door vociferating in the most furious manner and the most dreadful oaths and imprecations : "Ah, you croppy vagabonds, its a fine time for you to be praying ! You are praying now but you didn't pray in time ! What is the reason of allowing light to such rebels ? Let it be put out immediately."

Here Garrett Kinsella on his knees begged of them to leave the light a little longer, in which request the sentry at the door joined, but they continued, " Yes, a fine thing indeed to see light with such vagabonds, common rebellious villains ; sure flesh or blood can't bear it ! They're snug and warm there within and loyal men standing out in the cold but I'll have a life, by the ——, I will ! I'll charge my piece this moment and fire it in among them. I don't care who it hits, but a life I'll have, by the —— ! "

Here some one interfered to stop this fellow from putting

his threat in execution when another fellow ran up with chains which he jingled, crying out, "Eh d'ye hear that? That's the way the chains of Hell will be jingling round your souls to-morrow night, for in Hell you'll be surely!" This discourse was interlarded with such volleys of horrid oaths and yells that a pack of demons from Hell could hardly outdo them, for these wretches seemed to think that cursing and swearing dreadfully was a great sign of valour and I believe it was very much on that account they practised it so much; but if the matter was to be decided sword-in-hand next day between them and the same number of the men that were praying, I fancy there would not be more devout men anywhere than it would make them. After some time longer, the light was put out and every one lay down without caring anything about the want of a bed or bedclothes.

We were all awake early next morning and a beautiful soft summer's morning it was; but it had no charms for us. We were all sunk in the deepest gloom and melancholy apprehension of what was to come on. Four were surely to die and, as for my part, I would by far sooner have made a fifth, than be tied to a triangle to be mangled in the manner the others were.

It was now about four o'clock and in the midst of our sorrow and despondency, one of the yeomen, and a Protestant too, came in and spoke very friendly to some that he knew and told them in a whisper, if they wished for a glass of spirits, by giving him a shilling he would bring a good bottle from the distillery. Though there were some wealthy men present, yet none of them happened to have any change, which caused some dull countenances. After some doubts and pauses, one of them stepped over to me and told me the story. "Have a care," said I, "its not a trap to see who would give the money and punish him for it afterwards."

"Oh, no," said he, "its no such thing; for though he is a Yeoman and Protestant, and perhaps an Orangeman, still he can be depended on, for he is well known to be as honest a fellow as any in Ireland."

"Oh, if that be so," said I, "I can give a shilling."
"Well, come over and give it to him."
"No, I will not," said I, "but here is a shilling for you and give it to him and don't let him know who gave it."

As soon as the yeoman got the shilling, he set off and stayed a very, very long time away; so long that there were some very doubtful surmises concerning it and I began to think my conjectures were not wrong. At length, when we had nearly given up all hopes, he appeared coming in haste with it and as soon as he entered gave a fair reason for the delay. He handed the bottle to the man that gave him the money who immediately walked over with it to me. I looked very sour at him and asked, "Why do you bring it to me? I don't want it. Take it yourselves and make the man that brought it drink first." There was now no glass and it was agreed to take it by guess out of the bottle and when they had done so, it was again handed to me and after I took a reasonable share, I gave it back. The man looked at me and asked, "What will I do with it now?"

"Hand it round to them all," said I, "as far as it goes."

While this was going on, I was meditating on the punishment I was threatened with at nine o'clock and wished very much to have a little spirits to take before I went out but would not mention it, for fear it should prevent anyone getting his share, but exactly as if they knew my thoughts, the bottle, after going round to every one, came back to me with something better than a glass in it, which was quite sufficient and was like as if I had received a treasure, and I hid it immediately behind a smith's bellows that had been taken from some one and brought in. The moments now rolled over with prodigious swiftness and breakfast to the different prisoners began to come in very early, until they were all supplied, as every one had some friends to bring it to him but me and though I had money, I did not know who to ask in such times to get anything for me, as every one was in such dread. There were different persons near me that pressed me to take share of theirs, but I would not, as I considered what was brought to any one person was little enough for himself and that it would not be right to intrude on it. The men that were to die and their friends all breakfasted together and for their use there was a large pewter dish full of bread and butter and a tin gallon full of tea and as soon as they perceived I had none, they called out to me to come over and breakfast with them. I hesitated a little but they called out again, " Oh, you must come over ; there is plenty here ; don't spare it." I accordingly stood up and went to them but it was indeed a sorrowful breakfast and I actually grow weak when I think of it.

As soon as it was over, some of their relatives came to see and take their last leave of them. The first were Hughes's two sisters, Mrs. Donahoe of Clocristick and Mrs. Hawe, two respectable women and married to rich farmers. As soon as they came in, they burst into tears and lamentations but he, poor fellow, endeavoured to pacify them ; but all in vain, they would not be pacified and proceeded to take off his clothes and shirt to put a clean shirt on him, but as soon as he was stripped and they saw the way his flesh was cut, their cries and lamentations were redoubled and even himself, when he looked at his breast and saw the condition it was in (for he was cut on the breast as well as on the back) could hold out no longer but burst also into tears. Cullen's brother Garrett came next. They were both in the prime of youth ; one about twenty-two years of age, the other twenty, and the breed of real good soldiers and men of action. As soon as they saw each other, they ran together and clasped their arms round each other with all their strength, while the wild cries and agonising shrieks and exclamations they used were almost sufficient to rend a rack.

Let us turn for a moment from the sickening scene and open another concerning myself. My sister, who had returned to Carlow, could take but little rest that night. She was up early in the morning and filled the house with lamentation. Through the excess of her anguish, she took a violent bleeding at the nose and as she considered this a bad omen, it increased her cries and moans. Fortunately, there was a lady lodging in the house who overheard her.

This lady was daughter to Sir Edward Loftus of Mount Loftus, in the County Kilkenny, and sister to Lieutenant Loftus of the Ninth Dragoons, and was married to the Revd. Mr. Carey, a clergyman of the Established Church, who resided at Mount Finn in the County Wexford. As soon as the rebellion broke out there, they were obliged to fly with their lives and as my brother-in-law was well known to both families, from many years of dealing, as soon as they arrived in Carlow, they came straight to his house with all their children and servants, to take lodgings, and were of course most kindly received. Mrs. Carey, on hearing my sister's cries, ran downstairs and seeing the condition she was in, exclaimed, " Oh, my dear Mrs. Fitzgerald, what's the matter with you ? "

" Oh, ma'am, enough is the matter with me ! This unfortunate boy is to be destroyed to-day in Leighlin Bridge and if they'd shoot him itself, I wouldn't think so bad of it. But to make a public spectacle of him, to mangle his flesh and sacrifice him, oh, I can't bear it ! "

" Be patient, my dear Mrs. Fitzgerald, be patient ; God Almighty is good," said the kind-hearted lady ; " and who knows what may be done ? Who knows but I can do something myself ? I will go off this moment to Colonel Mahon and see what can be done."

She immediately ran to the door and seeing one of the Ninth Dragoons going by, she called out, " Soldier, soldier, come here ! " The man came immediately. " Do you know Lieutenant Loftus ? " said she.

" I do, ma'am."

" Well, he is my brother and you must come up with me to the barrack ; I want to see Colonel Mahon."

" Oh, by all means, ma'am, I'll go with pleasure."

She got ready in a twinkling and set off. When she arrived at the barrack, she sent at once to enquire if the colonel could be seen and received for answer that he was not up. " Go back," said she, " and let him know there is a lady here waiting for him and that I will stay here till he comes."

Colonel Mahon had to get up instantly and when he came down, she explained the business to him at once and begged and entreated of him to interfere for me. "My dear Mrs. Carey," said he, "I am extremely sorry you have not made some request that would be in my power to grant, but I could not by any means interfere in this case. Is it to interfere for a man that has been so deeply implicated in bringing such horrors on the country? If I even wished to do it, it is not in my power. The law allows no pardon to a man that filled the station he did."

"Ah, Colonel Mahon, but a boy, a foolish young boy like him, you know you must make some allowance for that. And it is not for him alone I plead, but for his sister, Mrs. Fitzgerald, whom I am deeply concerned for, and beg it as a most particular favour that you will do something for her."

In this manner the debate continued for a considerable time, she entreating and he refusing, until at length she seized him by the arm and said, "I insist on it, Colonel Mahon, and I'll never part you till you come down with me and see the state poor Mrs. Fitzgerald is in, and you can't get over doing something"; and as she said it, she kept her word and brought him the whole way through the town to the house where she made him sit down and write a letter in my favour to Colonel Rochfort, who commanded at Leighlin Bridge. My sister, as soon as she received it, took a chaise and set off in full speed; and just in the midst of the scene I was describing in the guard-house, the chaise rolled up to the inn door and she alighted and walked in. The noise of the chaise drew some persons to the door to see what it was about and one of them called out to me, "That is your sister is after coming in the chaise," and while he was speaking some one came running from the inn and said, "Your sister is after coming and I'm sure she has good news. I think I know it by her."

I was knocked in amaze at the news and did not know what to conjecture but stood suspended between hopes and fears, when a messenger came from Colonel Rochfort, telling me to come along, that he wanted to see me. I left the dreadful scene in the guard-house and walked on, almost tired of being alive and uncertain what fate awaited me. When I came to the inn, I was brought upstairs, where the Colonel was at breakfast in a very large oblong room. My sister was sitting nearly opposite the entrance and the colonel a considerable distance farther on and at breakfast by himself. He was a very fine-looking man and one of the most accomplished gentlemen in the country. As soon as I walked in a few paces and his eye caught me, I bowed most profoundly and stood still. " Come on," said he, " come on."

I walked on a few paces more and bowed and stopped as at first, being under great apprehension, not knowing what sentence he was going to pronounce.

" Come on, come on," said he again, " come up to me. Oh, my God, if one of Thy creatures can inspire another with so much awe, what apprehensions must we be under, when Thy thunders roll and Thy trumpet calls us to come to trial before Thyself in all Thy awful majesty."

I then walked up close to him. " Sit down there," said he, pointing to a chair that was at one side. I did so and he began in a calm dignified manner, asking a variety of questions, but through the whole he never used either a harsh expression or threat or menace and in particular he never used the slightest insinuation to me to give information. I answered all his questions in the most clear intelligible manner I was able and in the fewest words, in order to avoid drawing on a scrutiny or repetition of the questions, some of which were extremely close and searching. I do not now clearly recollect them, a lapse of forty-three years having nearly obliterated them from my memory, but they chiefly related to certain resolutions drawn up by United Irishmen and would not be very interesting to people in general, if even I did remember them.

When we had finished this subject, " Now," said he, " I clearly foresaw from the beginning how all this would end and I did all in my power to prevent the people under me from having anything to do with so foolish a business. My plan for serving them was by giving them employment and for this purpose I began a new road in such a place, and other kinds of work in other places, on which I expended large sums of money and I frequently cautioned the most intelligent of them against the business that was going on. I cannot say, indeed, I was completely successful in my efforts and some of them might have been drawn into it; but at all events I acquitted myself in using my best endeavours to prevent them joining what I knew would be their ruin, and if they have not done so, they must only blame themselves."

Every word he said I knew to be true; and I knew more: I knew what the colonel, with all his learning and eloquence was completely ignorant of; he did not know that for the very exertions he made to serve the people and stop that fatal business he would have lost his life but for the very person he was speaking to, for so great was the infatuation of the people, that any one that advised them against it, though even with the best intentions, was looked on as a deadly enemy and if he was not very fortunate, treated as such. Had Colonel Rochfort known to a certainty he was so deeply indebted to me, no doubt I would have been liberated at once, but I could not mention it, because I knew if I did he would either have considered it a make-up story to serve my own purpose or else he would have insisted on me telling the particular circumstances and mentioning the names of those concerned in the plot to take his life, which I could not or would not do; and on that account I was obliged to remain silent.

During our conversation the drums began to beat, to collect the soldiers for execution of the unfortunate men in the guard-house, when he started up and said, " I must go to this execution. It is a melancholy business but I must attend it. Do you stay here till I come back."

When he went away, my sister in a hurried manner, told me of Mrs. Carey's interference for me and her obtaining the letter from Colonel Mahon in my favour, which directed that no decisive punishment should take place on me. This left me still in a state of great uncertainty of what would be done with me but it stopped the punishment I was threatened with, which was doing a great deal, and I made no remark on it, for fear of giving my sister uneasiness. Hearing great bustle abroad, she went to the window and said in great alarm, " Oh, the soldiers are all collected. Oh, they are going to the guard-house. Oh, they are bringing them out. Oh, they are coming. Oh, see poor Paul Cullen. Oh, see his poor father and his brother Garrett. Oh, they are gone."

I was on my knees the whole time and as soon as they were out of sight, my sister dropped down on hers and we both remained in earnest prayer. It was not more than about fifteen minutes till we heard the shots fired that ended their sufferings in this life and sent them into the eternal world. Oh, my God, with what salutary dread does the generality of Thy creatures think of that awful journey and how little do others of them think of thrusting their fellow mortals into it ; perhaps at the moment they least expect it or are least prepared for it ; torn from every tender tie and never, never more to come back.

As soon as my sister heard the noise of the people coming back, she got up off her knees and went to the window again. " Oh, there they are," said she, " with poor Paul Cullen. They are carrying him and he is bleeding at the nose. And there, oh, see his poor father and he is following him. And there, oh, there is another, I believe it is Jack Hughes, and they are carrying him, too, but I don't see Carroll or Brenan. I suppose they are taken some other way."

Very shortly after, Colonel Rochfort returned and seemed very much agitated and distressed at what he was after witnessing and made some severe observations on the punishment the men were after suffering who were far less implicated than I was. I made no reply but was as dumb as a statue, well knowing the dangerous precipice I stood on. The chaise and a guard of two horsemen belonging to his own corps of cavalry were now ready at the door, with orders to take me back to Carlow and without further delay we were sent off.

CHAPTER TWELVE

THE LOTTERY OF DEATH

WHEN we got about a mile of the road, I grew uneasy to know where they were taking me or whether I was entirely free or not. I was almost afraid to ask my sister the question, lest it might give her any trouble. However, as the notion pressed stronger and stronger on my mind, I was compelled to it and after a considerable struggle I asked her where they were taking me.

" They are taking you to my house," said she, in a confidential tone.

"Are you sure of that ? " said I, in a tone that could least alarm her.

" I am," said she, with as much confidence as before. This did not satisfy me and I told her she had best call one of the horsemen and ask him where he was taking us. She did so and received for answer in a loud voice, " To the barrack-yard."

" Oh, no," said she, " Colonel Rochfort told me he would send him home to my house."

"And he told me," said the horseman, " to take him to the barrack and there I must go. I know my orders."

All my hopes were now blasted in an instant. My expectations of liberty vanished like a dream and destruction, certain destruction stared me in the face. I took especial care, however, to conceal my tortured feelings from my sister, lest it should put her on the rack also and I seemed just as unconcerned as before, but the agony of my mind, the sufferings I underwent at the thought of facing the barrack-yard of Carlow were hard indeed to describe. Hell itself seemed hardly capable of more horrors, for if there was a hell on earth, it was Carlow barrack-yard. In the midst of my anguish, I would frequently ejaculate in my heart, " Oh, happy, happy Cullen, you are safely landed on the shores of eternal happiness. You are beyond the reach of the torturers. You are in the land of peace. Oh, that I had the good fortune to be shot with you, this day in Leighlin!"

The day was excessively warm and such heaps of dust on the road as I never saw before from the long continued heat and drought. The horses and chaise raised it in such clouds that we were obliged to keep the glasses up and when we went on a little farther we heard the noise of horsemen approaching us. They very soon came up and when both parties met the dust rose in so thick a cloud that we could not distinguish who they were but we distinctly heard the word " Halt ! " given in a loud and commanding voice. The chaise and guard instantly stopped and the same person in the same commanding voice called out, " Where are you going ? "

" To Carlow," was the answer.

" Have you a pass ? "

" No, I have not."

" Then I can't let you go on. Turn about the chaise instantly."

" Colonel Rochfort's orders to go on with a prisoner is my pass," said the guard, " and I won't turn back."

" But you must turn back, for I won't let you go on, so turn round instantly, I say ! "

Words now ran so high and swords drawn on both sides, that I thought every instant they would have come to blows, which, if it did happen, would probably have caused my destruction, as being (though against my will) partly the occasion of it. At this critical moment, the dust having cleared away a little, my sister let down one of the windows and looked out, when who did the person prove to be that stopped us but a Sergeant MacKay of the Ninth Dragoons and a private of the same regiment. MacKay happened to be billeted at our house some time before and was treated with particular civility, as he well deserved. He was a good soldier and he was so remarkably genteel in his manners and person that he seemed more fitting to fill the rank of officer than a sergeant.

As soon as my sister recognised him, she cried out, "Oh, Sergeant MacKay, sure you won't stop us!"

A cannon-shot fired unexpectedly near him would not have knocked him in greater amazement. "Oh, my dear Mrs. Fitzgerald," said he, "is it you that's in it? I beg your pardon a thousand times. Had I known it was you I wouldn't have stopped you. And my dear William, oh, my heart bleeds for him (and the tears actually gushed from his eyes) and if I could be of any service to him, I would turn back again and go with him every foot to the town, but I could not. And you, gentlemen (addressing the guard), I hope you will excuse what has happened; I'm extremely sorry for it. Adieu, Mrs. Fitzgerald; and my dear William, may God be with you and protect you."

Though I was much gratified with the grateful and generous conduct of MacKay, still it could not make a deep or lasting impression; for the situation I was placed in, after escaping prison and torture and perhaps death in the morning; and the hopes I received of my pardon and liberty being suddenly blasted and a worse scene, if possible, than I escaped in the morning staring at me, immersed me in such a sea of suffering that I would have considered it a happiness indescribable if some hand of friend or foe would have shot me on the road. The incautious Indian whose frail bark unfortunately has passed the marks that should have warned him of danger, as he sailed the Great St. Lawrence river, could scarcely feel more horror when he heard Niagara roaring his destruction, than I did as I approached the barrack-yard of Carlow.

I remained silent as we went along and endeavoured to conceal what I felt from my sister. I made no remark whatever on the disappointment I met, as I knew it was quite useless and I considered, as Colonel Mahon interfered in the business at all if he intended to liberate me he would have done it at once and as he did not do so, I had nothing for it but prepare for the worst. We very shortly arrived in Carlow and though our guard travelled smartly along the road, they went at an easy drawling pace through the town, giving every one that pleased an opportunity of gazing at us, till at length we arrived at the fatal barrack-gate. It was fast closed as we approached but soon yawned open like the grave to admit us. As we went in, I observed some dead bodies lying outside the gate, some more lying inside and others hanging up, but whether dead or dying I could not tell. The triangles were at full work and the very stones seemed petrified with the horrors of the place.

As soon as we got in, the gate closed on us like the tomb and we were brought on towards the court-martial room, but stopped a short distance from it, where our guard left us. Immediately after we stopped, one of the Ninth Dragoons came up to the carriage door. This man's name was King. He was an old and a good soldier, who had served abroad for many years. He was a man of great action in his youth, but years of service in a foreign climate had visibly impaired his constitution and replaced the natural colour of his skin with a yellow hue, but still he was fit enough for any home duty. As he had been frequently at our shop getting work done, he of course knew us well and when he came up to the carriage door, he seemed considerably affected and said " I'm sorry, indeed, Mrs. Fitzgerald, to see you in this place; and indeed I'm sorry for William, too, but if it was my brother had a hand in such business, I could not excuse him."

While he was speaking, two more of the soldiers ran up in a hurry and asked, " Who have you got here, King? Why don't you bring him out? "

" He is not to be brought out," said my sister; " he is brought here by order of Colonel Mahon."

" We don't care for that," said they; " out he must come."

" Mr. King," said my sister in great alarm, " I want to go up to the gentlemen and will you stay here till I come back?"

" I will, indeed," said King.

"And I will depend on you to let nothing happen him until I come back."

"You may indeed, Mrs. Fitzgerald" said he in a sorrowful tone; "I'll engage not a man shall lay a finger on him."

Away she went, as fast as ever she could, and a little after, three or four soldiers came running up like furies from the butchery they were engaged in at the triangles and one of them called out, "What are ye about? Why are ye not bringing him?"

"Oh," said the other, "sure King here won't let us; King is hindering us, but I'll have him, by the ——, in spite of King or any one else!"

"And I'll be d—— if you do!" said King, "or if I let any man lay a finger on him."

Here the whole set joined against him in one uproar and with volleys of oaths and imprecations called out to him, "Are you going to take part with a rebel, King? You are not a loyal man, by the ——, you are not! And we'll drag him out, by the ——, and no thanks to you!"

When King saw their fury and determination and in particular their number, he was obliged to take them another way, and said, "You all know I am a loyal man, that never took part with a rebel, but I pledged my word to Mrs. Fitzgerald I would let nothing happen him till she came back, and would you want me to break my word and honour? Don't you know it wouldn't be the part of a soldier to do it? She is only gone up to the court-martial room and you'll only have to wait a few minutes, and sure that isn't much, and when she comes back, do what you please; my honour will be safe."

This discourse of King's had the desired effect, though it was with great reluctance they agreed to it, for bloodhounds never showed themselves more savage for prey than they did.

In some time my sister was seen hastening back and as soon as she came up, she said, "I'm much obliged to you, Mr. King, you have behaved honourably and like a soldier."

"But is he saved, Mrs. Fitzgerald?" said King, in a friendly and feeling tone.

"He is!" said she; "he is to be sent on to the jail."

"I'm very glad of it, indeed, Mrs. Fitzgerald," said the worthy, honest fellow.

"But how are we to know that?" said the executioners, evidently grieved for missing their prey; "are we to take your word for it?"

"You'll know it in a moment," said she.

The honest and generous King, although a Protestant (and in those dreadful times, I suppose, could not escape being an Orangeman) politely handed her into the carriage and shut the door and if ever any of his descendants (as he is now probably in the grave himself) should ever meet this account, they may boast with honest pride of having a good soldier and a man of honour for their ancestor.

When my sister got into the carriage, she was nearly exhausted and as soon as she recovered a little, she said, "Well, it was with the greatest difficulty your life was saved. Mr. Phil Newton was the man that saved you. If it wasn't for him, you'd have been torn in pieces." I made no reply and never uttered a word during the whole scene.

Some one now came up, who ordered the carriage to drive on to the jail and as it turned round, I heard the bloodhounds, who were disappointed of their prey, attacking King with the most bitter epithets. Tigers themselves could not show more savage ferocity but King was a man not to be frightened by the threats of such miscreants but treated them with the most profound contempt, and they knew him too well to provoke him too far.

The carriage moved on slowly to the horrid gate, which, though it opened freely to let us in, now seemed reluctant to let us out. There was a considerable pause and some consultation on the point, till it did open slowly at last, but the driver became so stupefied with fear that he was unable to rise the reins or urge the horses in the least, so that they only went on at the slow drawling pace of the slowest snail. We at length passed out, but had only gone on about forty yards when some one came running after us and shouting out "Come back, come back! Turn the carriage round, I say! You must come back!" I now gave up all hopes and expected nothing but instant destruction when, just as we were up again at the gate, I heard some one in the crowd cry out in a loud and commanding voice, " Who brought the carriage back ? What scoundrel had the impudence to do it ? By the ——, if I knew who done it, I'd cut his head off ! Turn round the carriage and go on to the jail ! Turn it round, I say, and go on ! D——n you, are you stupid, go on when I bid you ! " I did not know at the time who was speaking, but was told afterwards it was my good friend, Mr. Fitzmaurice.

The driver, after a good deal of bungling, got the carriage round again but was wholly unable to drive the horses one bit faster than he did before ; and the distance from the barrack to the jail was only about three or four hundred yards, yet a man might reasonably drive two miles in the time he took to perform it.

When I went into the jail, I saw an unusual gloom and horror on every countenance and was soon informed (almost in whispers) that there was dreadful work going on while I was away and that several of my acquaintance (young lads of the town) had been heavily flogged and others put to death. Among the number was Pat Dowling, whose father, some years before, was one of the wealthiest and most respectable merchants we had in town. He kept a most extensive linen and woollen warehouse, besides a very extensive brewery. He reared up a large family of sons and daughters in a suitable style and Pat, his eldest son, was brought up to the profession of an apothecary. He was at the time about twenty-five years of age and of the most polished manners and though he never, that I could learn, took any active part in the United business, farther than taking the unfortunate oath of forming a " Brotherhood of affection " with everyone, and which no one thought could have any harm in it, yet he was flogged unmercifully and as he was a young man of delicate constitution and quite unfit to stand such punishment, it had a terrible effect on him. He was as pale as death itself in the face. There was even no necessity for punishing him in such a manner, as the rebellion was completely put down at the time and the people unable to make the least opposition but those in power were so accustomed to the spilling of blood that they done it as if for mere pastime.

Pat Farrell was the next. His father was at the time a very wealthy man. He held the customs of the town; kept a very strong cloth shop besides a considerable share of land; he, too, reared a large family of sons and daughters, the eldest of which he had settled respectably, as he was well able to do. He was gay, friendly and affable among all his neighbours, rich and poor, over whom he never assumed any superiority on account of his wealth, but lived within his means and wisely minded the main point of keeping carefully what he had acquired by honest industry; not that he ever had the least tincture of the miser for if any of his neighbours wanted any assistance in his power, they were as free to go to honest Myles Farrell for it as they would be to go to the parish pump, and as sure not to be disappointed. His two eldest sons were bred to different trades, but his youngest son, Pat, he kept at home, having plenty of employment for him in attending to his own extensive business. He was a young, soft boy, about eighteen or nineteen years of age and not very firm in his health, having something like a touch of asthma but this did not save him from being brought out and tied to the triangle, where he was heavily punished. As soon as his back was healed, he obtained his liberty by enlisting as a private soldier but though his father speedily purchased his discharge, he never recovered the punishment he got, for after lingering for about two years, it brought him to his grave.

John Neill was also heavily flogged. He was born in the army. His father held the station of master-tailor and a sergeant in it for many years and reared a large family decently and respectably. He was frequently employed on the recruiting service and no man was more fitting for it, as he was possessed of an exhaustless fund of wit and pleasantry and though he enlisted hundreds of men, no one could ever say that honest Sergeant Neill ever crimped or took an unfair advantage of any man. His son, John, was about twenty-two years of age, a fine smart-looking young man, formed for strength and action, with a quick intelligent countenance and the glow of health on his cheek. He was by trade a shoemaker and was remarkable for the gentility of his manners and dress, which certainly were of a superior order. All this, however, did not prevent him of being stripped naked and tied to a triangle, to receive that punishment too barbarous to be inflicted on the lowest slave and which is now in progress of being abolished in every country professing Christianity and which no man with a particle of humanity would inflict on a dog, to tie it to a post and cut it with whips while there was a gasp of the life in it. Neill, however, though he was heavily flogged, did not pine as much after it as the others, his natural strength and goodness of constitution supporting him, and though some of the healthy hue was taken out of his cheek, still he maintained the same bold, careless manner as before. He obtained his liberty like Pat Farrell, by enlisting, and is alive and well to this day.

Of those who suffered death, I shall first select the case of Jack Murphy, which was a most pitiable one, indeed; his father was a rich farmer and in early life bound him apprentice in the most respectable house in Tullow to the linen and woollen drapery business. He had not been very long there, when, some dispute happening between him and his master, he ran away from him and enlisted in a regiment of light horse, where he served as a good soldier for many years. How he obtained his discharge, I do not recollect, but at the time the general raising of the yeomanry commenced, he was married and living in Carlow. As he was well skilled in military discipline, he applied to Sir Richard Butler of Garryhunden for a situation, which he readily obtained, as permanent sergeant in his corps of cavalry. In this corps he conducted himself to the entire satisfaction of both officers and men. He was cheerful, hearty and jocose, and everyone liked the company of honest Jack Murphy.

At length the curse of Ireland, the United business, made

its appearance and as numbers of his friends were unwarily drawn into it, he was importuned by them over and over to become one. At first he refused it bluntly and said he would insult the first man would ever mention it to him again, but his friends were not to be put off that way. They watched every opportunity, studied every plan for coming round him, selected the men most likely to prevail on him, till at length he was so harrassed and importuned by men who really wished him well that the only excuse he had to offer was that it was contrary to the oath of allegiance he had taken. When he stopped to reason with them at all, he was undone. They produced the form of the United oath and defied any man to say that " Forming a Brotherhood of affection with Irishmen of every religious persuasion " was contrary to the oath of allegiance or to any other oath ; and being silenced on that point, he was drawn unfortunately, like thousands of others, into the great state dragnet.

This was the only crime ever committed by Jack Murphy either against Church or State, for he never attended a meeting or had hand or part in it farther. And yet, for that alone all his former services as a soldier and a yeoman were forgot. There was nothing more required than merely to prove that against him. And for that alone honest Jack Murphy, that served his king and country faithfully and honourably and that never hurted as much as a chicken belonging to a neighbour and that would scorn to stand by and see it done, was sentenced to lose his life and did lose it by being hanged in the barrack yard of Carlow.

His brother, Dick Murphy, shared the same sad fate. He was left in possession of a good farm by his father. In fact, he was left a rich man. He was cheerful and hospitable ; fond of company and being an active able young man, was foremost in every kind of amusement. In short, there was no such thing as a frown to be seen on the countenance of any one while in company with Dick Murphy. He was, of course, a United Irishman. There was no trouble at all in getting *him* to join it, for the warmest wish of his heart was to form a " brotherhood of affection " with all the world. He was also a yeoman in Sir Richard Butler's Cavalry, along with his brother, but all his good qualities did not avail. He was taken prisoner (so little was thought of men's lives at the time) and tried for being an United Irishman and in the prime of life received sentence of death and was shot to death in the barrack-yard. Alas, alas, humanity, honour, where were you at the time?

There was something very extraordinary happened, respecting the death of this young man. He had a brother at home at the time in a bad state of health and long confined to his bed. This lad, not receiving his visits as usual, became very uneasy and made strict enquiries for him. The persons who had him in care were afraid to tell him the sad story, lest it might prove fatal to him. They therefore invented various excuses, but all would not do. He insisted on seeing him and that very night the brother did appear to him and in a mournful voice said, "Ah, Hugh, they shot me in the barrack-yard. Look at the hole in my side. See my blood. And I was buried in Killinstown. My grave is fresh and you will easily know it."

Next morning the young man got up and dressed himself. Those attending him were astonished and asked the reason he did so. "Ah," said he, " you were deceiving me about my brother but I know it all now. Yes, he was shot in Carlow and is buried in Killinstown."

"Don't believe it," said they; " who told you that story? "

" He told me himself," said he. " He came to me last night and told me all. Come along with me and bring help to open his grave, till I see my brother and take my last farewell of him."

They could hold out no longer. It was all in vain to refuse compliance. He brought them to the spot, had the grave opened and found him just as he described. Some people may call this superstition or any other name they please, but I had the story from the man's own mouth, and he not only gave it as a fact but said that, if necessary, he'd give his oath for it on the Bible. But the feeling and affecting manner in which he related it left as little doubt on my mind of its truth as if I had seen him give his oath on twenty Bibles.

The murder continued to rage with unabated fury and Phil Kennedy was led to execution while I was in the barrack-yard. Fortunately for me, I did not see it, but was told it afterwards by my sister. He was steward and gardener to Sir Richard Butler of Garryhunden, and a most respectable man for his station in life, and until this time had the esteem of everyone in the country, rich and poor, and such was the punctuality and honesty of his dealings joined to a particular kindness and affability of manner, that Phil Kennedy's " word would pass for more than he was worth." He was rather elderly and might be drawing towards fifty at the time. His sentence was pronounced aloud by Major Dennis in the barrack-yard, in the following words : " You are to be hanged by the neck till you are dead and your head to be cut off and put on a spike." Kennedy did not seem to notice him in the least, but kept his eyes fixed steadily on his prayer-book as he walked along to his place where he underwent the dreadful sentence.

Among the other various scenes of blood that took place (the half of which I cannot recollect) was one of a very singular description. It happened to a young man of the name of John Dowling of Graigue, Carlow. His father was a respectable man in the tanning and currying trade, but he was not regularly bred to it himself, except he might do a little for his amusement. He was brought to the triangle and severely flogged in order to extort information from him, but neither " hopes, fears, rewards or punishments " could compel him to give it. He was at length taken down and naked and bloody as he was, a gentleman (or one who held the rank of a gentleman) Arundel Caulfield Best, Esq., who was present, as an additional punishment for his obstinacy, struck him a violent blow with a stick. Dowling instantly made a sudden rush and endeavoured to wrest a sword from the next person to him, to drive it through his body but was prevented. It is very extraordinary he was not put to death for it on the spot, but wonderful are the ways of Providence; instead of being served so, he was sent off to the jail and put down in the dungeon.

The executions in different shapes continued without intermission. The guards were coming and going with victims the whole day and in the evening Dowling was sent for again. He was not ready in a moment, when he was called, as he was endeavouring to get some of his clothes on, and they again shouted and called violently for him as follows: " Why don't you come? What's delaying you?"

" I'm going, I'm putting on my clothes. I'll be with you in a moment," was replied in a weak tone. This, so far from appeasing them, made them if possible worse and they vociferated more violently, " Why don't you make haste? Go down and drag the scoundrel up!"

" I will!" said one, " by the —— " (uttering a tremendous oath and making a violent rush down).

" I'm coming," said Dowling, meeting him. " Oh, don't drag me, don't drag me! I'm not able to go faster," said he, in such dying tones, joined to his emaciated appearance, that the savage hearts of his enemies were softened and they let him take time to get up the narrow winding flight of stone steps, which he accomplished with great difficulty, as he was quite exhausted. Every window in the jail was crowded looking at him, as we all expected he was going to immediate execution, and he seemed to have the same notion himself, for as he was coming up the steps, he looked up at the windows and called out to us all, " Oh, boys, pray for me."

He went on very slowly with the guard (he was not able to go fast) and to tell the truth they neither pushed him nor hurried him; for we could see him nearly the whole way from the upper windows. But what was our astonishment, in a very short time after, to hear that as soon as he got to the barrack-yard he was liberated and sent home. The reason, I suppose, of this was that they had no information against him and that they flogged him just on chance, to try if they could obtain any from him, for they were quite at liberty to do it and if they even took his life, they could do it with perfect impunity; there never would be any more about it than if it was the life of a sparrow was taken.

But blessed be Providence, that in the midst of the bloodiest field saves some and though in the variety of ways, thousands will be killed and wounded, others will come off without a single scratch. And though an unerring Providence does all this, to many it looks like chance or the motions of a lottery-wheel, that turns prizes up to-day and down to-morrow. Just so had it happened with all the great actors in those bloody scenes; not a man of them that I know of, Mr. Best and all included, but have gone down to rot in their silent graves, while John Dowling is alive and well to-day, and all this in the course of forty-three poor years.

This evening seemed like an evening of wonders and of exceptions to the horrible scenes that were going on, for in some time after John Dowling's affair, another came on, nearly as extraordinary, and happened at a time, too, when we thought all the worst of the day had been finished.

The court-martial room had been long closed and it was getting near dusk, when we observed some persons collecting about the lamp-iron at the corner of the barrack-yard just convenient to the court-martial room, which was at the right wing as you entered. From the smallness of the crowd and their very little bustle or ceremony, we did not at first think it of much consequence, but in some time there was a ladder brought and the crowd increased. We now began to wonder and make various conjectures on what it could mean, but we had not the least idea in the world that a man's life could be in question where we saw such apparent carelessness. At length we observed a man stripping off his coat and standing for them, while they fixed a rope round his neck. He then went up the ladder and the rope was thrown over the lamp-iron and secured. We were now filled with horror and astonishment, as we became certain that it could not be a mockery and that they were really going to put him to death, but just as the rope was secured, there was a pause and we saw him coming down again. We immediately gave God thanks, as we imagined he had got a pardon, but he did not come entirely off the ladder and after stopping a little, as if speaking to some person, he went up again. This was strange, indeed, and we were now, we thought, certain of his fate. When he got to the height required, he turned round, settled himself on the ladder and opened wide his arms. Our eyes were now strained, watching to see him pitched off. But there was an unexpected pause and we still watched with the closest attention, expecting every second would be his last and praying fervently for his soul, but he still remained in the same manner. Nothing now could exceed our anxiety and astonishment and at last we began to entertain some hopes of him. At length, to our inexpressible joy and wonder, we saw him come down the ladder and put on his coat. We instantly gave glory to God, with all the fervour and affection of our souls, though we did not know at the time who the man was, but it was not long after till he was brought into the jail and told us the whole story himself.

He was Laurence Nowlan, a respectable farmer, who lived at Ballinacarrig, within about two miles of Carlow. He was also one of Sir Richard Butler's Cavalry Yeomen and it was most wonderful, from this circumstance alone, how he ever escaped. But he happened, luckily for himself, to be a good land surveyor and in that capacity was a highly useful man in the country; for, when any dispute happened to arise respecting surveys, he was generally appealed to and so clear and so honest and so impartial were his decisions, that he had the rare happiness of generally pleasing both parties and on this account was in the highest esteem with the gentlemen of the country, so that they would have considered it almost an irreparable loss to lose him. In fact, it was the chief cause of saving his life.

He told us it was proved against him on his trial that he was a United Irishman and had attended a baronial committee. I am not certain now whether he admitted the first part of the charge or not, or whether he said it was as an inducement to him to become a United Irishman he was brought to the committee by a friend, who relied on his honour. The charge of attending the committee he did not deny, but defended himself ably on it. He said he was intoxicated at the time and did not know where the person was bringing him and that, when he was brought into the room, he took no part in the proceedings but merely sung a song.

" What song did you sing ? " said an officer (ironically) ; " was it ' God Save the King ' you sung ? "

" No, sir, it was not."

" Well, what song was it ; will you sing it for us now ? "

" No, sir, I could not sing it now, but I'll tell it to you. It was this song, sir :

> When I was a youngster and lived with my dad
> The neighbours all called me a smart little lad
> My mother she called me her white-headed boy
> Because with the girls I used to toy."

It was certainly the song, for I was present in the room at the time he sung it and happy it was for him there was nothing disaffected in it. Had it been " Erin go brah " or some of the other productions of the time, it is very probable the bare circumstance (trifling as it may appear now) would have decided his fate, for he stood " on the sharpest edge of death or life."

He then described accurately the state of every part of his farm, whether for tillage, pasture or meadow and showed them clearly there was not a spot of it but owned the hand of industry and improvement and called on some gentlemen who were present to testify the truth of it, which they did. He then concluded, " There, gentlemen, there is the work I was employed at and not in fomenting disaffection or rebellion."

When the trial was over, he was sent to the guard-house or black-hole uncertain of what was to follow and in the evening late was ordered out to execution as described. Fortunately for him Sergeant Martin, commonly called the " walking gallows," was the principal acting man on the occasion. Martin had been under some compliments to him and had a liking for him and when he brought him out, he saw a considerable number of gentlemen in a distant part of the yard who seemed engaged in some very earnest debate. Martin conjectured at once that it was something favourable to the prisoner was going on and delayed the execution purposely, till the order came to save his life. Thus, wonderfully at times does Providence interpose for some individuals.

Though the destruction and bloodshed and terror continued every day with unremitting fury and nearly the same, still every day had some variety or other. The next unfortunate victim I mention was Dick Heydon, who was one of the Carlow Yeoman Infantry. He was reared up to a country life about three miles from the town. He always had a taste for supporting a respectable consequence and certain respect was always cheerfully granted him (though his means were not more extensive than the generality of his neighbours) chiefly because he was of a decent, honest stock of people and trod in their footsteps. He received as good an education as could be procured in his time and was even taught music by the celebrated Tom Callanan, the finest violin-player our country could than boast of.

Before the breaking out of the rebellion he held the situation of overseer for Colonel Rochfort of Clogrenan, as he had various works going on and a great number of men employed and besides that he kept the public business going on in town. Various were the attempts made on poor Dick Heydon to induce him to become a United Irishman but, like Jack Murphy, he would not listen to it at all in the beginning. However, as a man's dearest friends were always selected in these cases, he was attacked and importuned in every direction until at last he was unfortunately sworn in. He never went one step farther than that; he took no active part, never attended a meeting, for I really believe he was sorry all along for joining it.

When the arrests were going on, he was made prisoner as well as the rest and sent off to jail. After he was brought in, his friends (and he had many of them) exerted themselves most strenuously for him and as the charge against him was so very light, people in general imagined he would be liberated without any trial. Things went on this way for about a week but to trial he was brought at last, where nothing that I knew of could be proved against him except what I have related. When the trial was over, he was sent back to the jail without knowing the sentence of the court and remained there a day or two, during which time his friends redoubled their exertions and it even went so far that they obtained a promise (from what quarter I do not now recollect) that by giving large bail he would be liberated and that his sureties should come up to the barrack for that purpose. Every preparation for this purpose was now made. A guard came from the barrack for poor Heydon, who went with the expectation of meeting his friends and being restored to his family. Two wealthy respectable men from the town went up to be his bail but to their utter astonishment, when they went into the barrack-yard, they saw him hanging dead.

CHAPTER THIRTEEN

SUSPENSE

In the midst of all this horror, a new and unexpected scene opened suddenly on us all. It was nothing less than the visit of Major Dennis of the Ninth Dragoons to the jail. The very name of Major Dennis at the time was the terror of both town and country, as the rank he held of being next in command to Colonel Mahon imposed the duty on him of attending all the courts-martial and executions that took place. If his name in every other place was so terrific, what must it have been in a place where every unfortunate inmate was supposed to have committed some crime against himself by the bare circumstance of being a United Irishman, and whose life he could dispose of in any way he pleased. As might be expected the announcement of his name was like a shock of electricity through the whole jail. Every one stood aghast and scarcely ventured to whisper, " What can it be about ? "

He was accompanied by one magistrate (Mr. Samuel Carpenter, the very man that took me prisoner) and a dragoon. As soon as he walked into the jailer's room, he did not delay a moment but ordered the jailer to bring every prisoner he had in rotation before him, as he wanted to examine them and make such enquiries of them as he thought proper. It was no sooner said than done and the first that were called before him soon sent the news flying among the rest. Every one was knocked in amaze at the news, for no one could tell what questions would be put to himself and all he had for it was to make the best guess he could and prepare accordingly. For my own part, I felt myself in a most awkward and embarrassing situation, as I was quite well known to Major Dennis, as he was frequently at our shop, where he dealt pretty largely and at times would speak to me with kindness and affability. On this account, it was almost like facing death itself to me to face him, but there was no flinching from it; go I should. After a good many had been examined, it came to my turn at last and I was called. Before I proceed it may not be amiss to give some description of the person, etc. of Major Dennis.

He was a man about five feet eight inches high, broad and strong made, very much in flesh all over, but particularly prominent in the belly, remarkably full in the face, which was as red as scarlet and he might be about forty years of age. He was particularly attentive to every article of his dress. He always had the very finest and highest coloured scarlet cloth in his coat, white Marseilles waistcoat, blue pantaloons and cocked hat and feather and though he might be near sixteen stone weight, still he showed a great deal of action and strength, and so extremely haughty in his gait and mien as if he thought the ground was not fit to carry him.

As soon as my name was called, I had to step on smartly; no one dare delay; and when I entered the room, he was seated in a chair but instead of presenting a full front to me, he sat in such a position that he should view me with a side look. He was leaning back in awful majesty in his chair, with his arms folded, his hat on and the side cock foremost, his large swollen face and coat so exactly of a colour that there was scarcely a shade of difference between them. In short, he appeared to me one of the most awful-looking beings I ever beheld. The most potent monarch of the East could not assume more terrific dignity in presence of his most trembling slaves. The dragoon was seated at a table quite near but rather behind him, with pen, ink and paper to take down the examinations; but Mr. Carpenter was nearer to the door and standing.

As soon as the major's scowling terrific eye caught me, I bowed to him most profoundly and he without delay said in a most awful sonorous voice, " I am more surprised at seeing you there than any one that has come before me yet;

one I have known so well; I have been so frequently in your shop and "—here he paused while his eyes seemed to flash lightning, before he added the words—" to think you had it in your mind to assassinate me!"

A cannon suddenly fired close by me could not have astonished me more than such a charge, the charge of assassination or intended assassination, the foul crime I always so much detested and which I always endeavoured so strenuously to prevent, to be charged with it at such a moment roused all the fire of my nature (and there was some in it) and I replied both with vehemence and the very strongest emphasis, " I never entertained a notion of the kind, sir."

"What, sir?" said he; "didn't you know of them coming in that night?"

As I thought the meaning of this question, from the station I held, was didn't I plan it or encourage it, I replied, "No, sir," and as soon as I said so he looked over at the magistrate and said, "Oh, Mr. Carpenter, there is no use in asking this man any more questions;" and, turning to me, said, "you may go out." I knew full well the meaning of his last words and the dangerous consequence of being sent out of his presence as a liar and I quickly replied, " I knew nothing more of it than the common report of the town, what every one knew, but I had no hand in bringing them in, but did all in my power to prevent it."

"Now I tell *you*, my friend," said Major Dennis, "tell me the truth and nothing but the truth for if I find you out in a lie I'll give you the most exemplary punishment ever a man got."

"I'll tell you the truth, sir," said I, "and nothing else. And I did do all in my power to prevent them of coming in and the arms that were given up and brought to the barrack it was I caused them to be given up and if every one had done as I did there would be no bloodshed since, but when they wouldn't take my advice, what could I do by myself?"

This declaration made a visible impression on Major Dennis. He listened to it with the greatest attention and it was quite evident his whole demeanour was softened by it. When Carpenter, who was a compound of spite and bitterness, saw this, he interfered and said in a sour, waspish tone, " You should have applied, sir, to a magistrate."

" I did not know, sir," said I, " what to do."

He then went on and asked, " Hadn't you a brother? "

This question astonished me greatly, as I could not see any meaning in it and I replied, " I had, sir."

" Where is he? " was the next sapient question.

" He was at home, sir, when I came away, but I don't know where he is now."

" Well," said Major Dennis, " you may go out now and send in such a person " (telling me the name).

I bowed instantly and retired to obey his orders and upon the whole had reason to think I got off tolerably well. One thing I was certain of, let what would happen, that there was not one word I said could be contradicted by any one if they went to ever so rigid a scrutiny on it.

The examination continued and though there might be about seventy or eighty prisoners in all, still Major Dennis never left the jail till he examined the last man of them, which of course took up a considerable part of the day, and when he was gone we all had our own private and gloomy consultations on it and no one able to make any conjecture what the consequences would be and every one uncertain of his own fate.

It was in the midst of all this confusion and terror that the Revd. Mr. Travers, Parish Priest of Baltinglass, was brought in prisoner and lodged in the black-hole of the barrack. He had neither chair, table, or bed in it, nor as much as a lock of straw under his feet, and he might either stand or lie down on the damp flags, whichever he pleased, and in this state he was kept for two days and a night. This would agree but badly enough with the youngest and most robust constitution, but he at the time might be advancing towards fifty years of age and of course quite unaccustomed to such usage, and on that account it had a most terrible effect on him. He was a kind-hearted, worthy gentleman to any one that wanted his assistance. He kept a most hospitable house and no poor traveller was ever let to go away hungry or dry that called to the house of Father Travers. He was particularly attentive to any soldiers and their families that passed the way and when all this came to be known, it weighed so much in his favour that he was ordered to be taken out of the black-hole and sent to the jail, but he was so affected by the treatment he received in it, that when he arrived at the jail he was like a man completely deranged.

He uttered the most bitter invectives against king and government and particularly was most unsparing in his abuse of Orangemen. In short, he stopped at no treasonable expression and seemed like a man actually courting death. The jailer, Robert Kirevan, though a kind-hearted, humane man, could not listen to it without resenting it, nor dare not in those times. He told him if he did not desist he would commit him to the dungeon and load him with irons, that it was good enough for any man would use such language and at any rate that he had no other place for him, as every part of the prison and every bed in it was occupied, and that he would give him some straw there to lie upon, and that he should do with it as well as he could. Words now ran so high and violent on both sides that Larry Nowlan, who happened to be below at the time, came running upstairs to me in the greatest terror and alarm and told me the whole story and dwelt particularly on the point of putting him in the dungeon and giving him no bed and concluded by saying, " I'm afraid he will be killed among them and bring destruction on us all."

Larry and I at the time used to sleep together in a good bed belonging to the jailer, for which I paid him five shillings a week, for my part, and I suppose he paid the same for his. There was a room next to ours called the straw room, as it was put to no other use but holding straw for the whole prison and this room was so infested with the multitudes of fleas from the heat of the weather that, when the turnkey wanted to get out straw, he would not on any account venture in himself, but picked out the most daring wicked fellow he could find in the jail for that purpose, to whom he should promise some premium or other for bringing out the straw, and all the while this fellow would be in it he would be cursing, swearing and roaring from the number and venom of his assailants. When I heard Nowlan's alarming story, I said, " What do you think if you and I would give him our bed ? "

"And where," said he, " would we sleep ourselves ? "

" In the straw room."

" In the straw room ? " said he, staring at me, " why, man, we'd be destroyed with the fleas."

" But," said I, " what harm could a few fleas do us ? For my part, I don't think a pin about it" (and I really did not at the time, for as I could not be certain of being alive till night I was quite careless about it).

" Well," said Nowlan, " if you are satisfied, so am I, so go down and tell him to come up."

" I will not," said I ; " I don't know him at all, but do you go down, as you were there before and saw him and it will come better from you than from me, as I don't know him at all."

Nowlan did not hesitate a moment but went down at once, where he found them all in full battle (as far as words went) and stepping into the middle of the fray, invited Father Travers to come up and have our bed and room. He no sooner uttered the words than the jailer and turnkey fell at him with such a torrent of abuse and used such threatening language and terrified him to such a degree that, in order to save himself, he threw the whole blame on me and said it was I sent him. The turnkey, who was a powerful athletic man, instantly ran upstairs to find me and from the unusual force he ran with, I knew at once his business and prepared myself at once (as well as I could) for the attack. He dashed into the room with fire and fury in his countenance and bawled out, or rather roared out, to know how I dared have the impudence to meddle with their affairs. I affected as much surprise as possible and asked " What's the matter ? What's the matter ? "

" Oh, aye, what's the matter ? What's the matter ? Oh, how d——d innocent you are ! " said he. " Didn't you send Larry Nowlan downstairs to tell Father Travers he could have this room and bed ? Wasn't it the d——'s impudence of you ? What right had you to give this room to any one, or how dare you do it ? But I tell you it's the worst job ever happened you ! Stay till the gentlemen hear it to-morrow and then you'll see how it will be ! "

I saw the danger and extent of the last sentence in an instant, for the court-martial, triangles, blood, and perhaps death, were all comprised in it, and I endeavoured to soften him by replying in the most submissive tone possible that I did not think it was any harm, but I soon found I did not make the least impression on him, for he went on in the same raging passion as before and said, " Oh, no, you didn't think it any harm, because it was a priest was in it, and you wanted to show yourself so mighty loyal, but I tell you again, it's the worst job ever happened you, and stay till the gentlemen hear it, and then you'll see how it will be ! "

My alarm was now raised to the highest pitch and I felt there was not a moment to lose in making it up with him and it occurring to me that the danger of losing two weekly payments for the bed might be the chief cause of his passion, I was resolved instantly to touch that string, to try if I could pacify him by showing that instead of losing he would gain by it. I accordingly went on in the same submissive manner as before and said, " Sure I only told Larry Nowlan that he and I could sleep in the straw room ; and sure there could be no harm in that, when he and I will pay the same in the straw room as if we had the bed, and the priest will pay you besides."

The instant I mentioned this, I perceived that a shock of electricity would not have performed its operation more effectually. He was a changed man in a moment and though he did not seem to give up his passion at once, I saw plainly it was only affectation when he said in a subdued tone, " Who pay ? Is it the priest pay ? He hasn't a farthing to pay any one."

" That may be," said I, " but wait till his friends come to know where he is and then I'll engage he'll have plenty."

" Well," said he, " how will you and Larry manage to sleep in the straw room ? "

" What management is in it ? " said I; " isn't there room enough ? "

" Yes, indeed," said he, " there is room enough and about fifty million of fleas in it. How well you'd like to be among them ! "

" I don't care a farthing about them; do you put us in and never mind that. A great matter, indeed, about a few fleas; what great harm they can do us ? "

" Well, but how will I manage for bed-clothes ? I have neither a blanket nor sheet nor anything."

" No matter, the weather is warm and we can do without them."

" Well, I must go down and tell Robert and if he is satisfied you know I don't care; but I must tell you now," said he, in a friendly tone, " he was very angry with you and you know you were wrong in what you did."

" I know I was," said I, " but do you tell him I didn't know what I was doing and make us friends, if you can."

" I will," said he, going off, " but hadn't I better bring up Father Travers ? "

" Oh, certainly," was the reply and thus the battle that began with so much violence ended in peace.

Father Travers was immediately ushered upstairs and with all due ceremony introduced to his room and bed. The turnkey got the straw room put in order for us, by removing as much of the straw and fleas as he could; he also contrived some way or other to procure us a pair of sheets, a blanket and a quilt, and left us to manage the rest ourselves. We accordingly set to work and made our shake-down on the boards on which we slept as soundly as if it was a bed of down, and though to some it may appear superstitious, yet

I declare most sincerely that all the time I was in it, a flea never bit me.

It was about this time the alarming report arrived in town that eight thousand County Wexford rebels were coming in from Killcomney with four pieces of cannon, to storm the town. There was about eight or ten of us in one of the upper rooms at the time and standing just convenient to the window, which commanded an extensive view of the barrack-yard, and as we looked over we observed an unusual bustle with the soldiers and their wives, who were running backward and forward, apparently in great alarm. We were a considerable time looking and expressing our wonder to each other at what it could mean, when the turnkey came upstairs, walked in hastily, and said, " Bad news, bad news I have for you to-day. Eight thousand rebels are coming in from Killcomney with four pieces of cannon, to storm the town." Instead of this being considered by us as bad news, we looked on it in quite a different light, as it let in a ray of hope that we might gain our liberty by it, although we did not or dare not say so, but he quickly damped our expectations when he added, "And I have worse news than that for you." Here he made a pause and we stared and listened, when he exclaimed, " Oh, there's no use in concealing it. I may as well tell it at once. There is positive orders given that every man in the jail is to be turned out in the yard and if the rebels come in, the first thing the soldiers are to do is to put all the prisoners to death." Some of the prisoners imagined he was only joking and striving to alarm us and told him so, but he replied quickly, " Oh, it's no joke at all. I wish it was ; and you'll see me now turning every man of them out in the yard. But what will I do with you here ? I don't know what to do. At any rate I won't put you down in the yard. Here, take the key and lock yourselves in, but don't make a noise or go to the window. Robert is gone down street and will be back immediately and if he doesn't miss you, well and good, that's all I can do."

Off he went and we locked the door and stood like so many statues, not knowing what to do. In a few minutes all the middle rooms were cleared and the prisoners moved down to the yard, amid cries and lamentations and followed by the turnkey. He then proceeded to the lower dungeons, turned out every man and locked the doors after them, for fear they would go in again.

By this time the jailer had come back and immediately set to work hammering all the bars and bolts of the front door, to make it secure, and every blow they gave sounded like a death-knell in our ears. As soon as this task was finished, he looked over a railing into the yard to try if the prisoners were all turned out and having missed us he asked the turnkey where we were. There was no evading the question and he was obliged at once to own the truth and tell him. As soon as the jailer heard it, he ran upstairs with a large oak stick in his hand, with which he rapped loudly at the door and called out to have it opened. We in the meantime had a short consultation in which some of the prisoners came to the determination of not giving up or surrendering our position and accordingly there was no answer made to the jailer's first summons. He thundered again at the door and shouted to have it opened but received no answer. He then called out, " If you don't open the door instantly, I'll call in the guard, so open it this moment !" This threat had the desired effect. We all saw at once how vain it was to hold out any longer and we accordingly made signs to the man that held the key to open the door, which he did without delay. As soon as the jailer came in, he turned to give blame to the man that had the key for keeping him out, but we all excused him and said he could not open the door without our leave and that we wouldn't let him and that we were all as much to blame as him. " Now, you unfortunate set of men," said he ; " see what you have brought on yourselves. My heart bleeds for every one of you, but what can I do ? I have orders to put you all down to the yard and there is no saying against it and if the rebels come, in that moment you lose your lives, and they are in full march on the town. Go down before me, go down, go down, you unfortunate men, God help you."

We made no reply but walked downstairs with slow steps and heavy hearts until we came to the front door, where we met the turnkey. Just at the spot where he stood, there were two passages, one going down to the yard, another to a place called the Women's Walk, exactly opposite the front door. Here he stopped us and told us what passed between him and the jailer and that he could not help telling where we were.

"But at any rate," said he, "I won't let you go down to the yard, let the consequence be what it will. Here, turn down the Women's Walk and go into the Terret[1] and close the door, but don't fasten it."

Into this place we all went as a great favour, although it could not afford us much protection if soldiers came in and attacked us, for the window was so large that they could point their guns at us and kill us in any direction; but there was this chance, that if they came in and went down to the yard, in the slaughter and confusion that would ensue, they might probably think they killed all the prisoners and so go away without knowing anything about us. However, as soon as we got into this room, there was an immediate consultation to know whether we should fasten the door or not, but the majority were of opinion it would be quite useless and that it would be better for us, whatever time we had to live, to employ it in striving to make our peace with God and preparing for death.

As soon as this resolution was formed, we all went on our knees and with all the earnestness of dying men crying for mercy to God and expecting every moment would be our last, particularly every time we heard a rap at the front door or the least noise about it. But where would be the use of such a waste of human life and blood? To prevent us forsooth from joining the rebels? If the rebels approached the town and were beaten off, what a reflection would it be for the victors that they had murdered so many men that they need not have murdered and that they would be branded

---

[1] A large room for holding female prisoners but which was unoccupied by women at the time and the men that were in it were after being put down to the yard.

as murderers for it during their lives. But in case the rebels were victorious and came and viewed our slaughtered bodies and the place running over with our blood, it is very easy to suppose what fearful vengeance would probably follow. But who would be to blame? Them that set the bloody example, or them that copied after it? Besides this, there was blood enough shed already, the blood of five or six hundred men, women and children, between those who were killed and burned in the town and sacrificed in the barrack-yard, without adding the heartless cold-blooded sacrifice of us, unarmed and defenceless as we were, to the horrible catalogue and adding another Scullabogue to the many we had in Carlow. But glory be to God Almighty that ordered it otherwise, for after we were kept in this dreadful situation for the space of three or four hours, trembling on the sharpest edge of death or life, word came in that the rebels changed their design and had marched to Castlecomer, upon which we were all ordered back to our different apartments.

We immediately returned thanks with all the fervour of our souls to the Almighty for our deliverance from the bloody tragedy that awaited us, and making the most gloomy reflections on the situation we were placed in; for, if we escaped death one way, we could not tell the moment we would meet it in another.

Our time passed on in this manner until the time arrived at night when the jailer came his rounds to lock us up. As I said before, there could be no more tender or humane man found in his station, than honest Robert Kirevan, although he was a Protestant, an Orangeman and a free-mason. His harsh word was never heard to the unfortunate prisoners under his care, even at a time when he would have been applauded by some in power for ill-treating them and when several mean creatures went far out of their way seeking opportunities to display their loyalty by using every violence and doing all the mischief in their power to those who were even suspected, and sometimes to those who were not suspected at all, of being what was called rebels.

When he came in he was accompanied by William Supple,

the turnkey, and his dog " Danger," a large, ferocious, black bull-dog, who was the terror of the whole prison, as he would make free with no one but his master and answered most appropriately to his name. As soon as the jailer had counted us over, " I have bad news for you to-night, you unfortunate men, God help you," said he.

" Oh, what is it, Mr. Kirevan ? " said someone.

" Bad enough, bad enough," was the reply. " How it grieves me to be looking at you there, my old friends and neighbours and to think that not one of you may be alive in the morning. Yes, the news has some in that the rebels are to come to-night from Castlecomer, joined by all the colliers, to take the town. The instant they appear, the drums will beat ' to arms ' and every house must have lighted candles in the windows to assist the soldiers to meet them, but the prisoners here are the first to fall. Every one of you will die that moment."

This was fearful news, indeed, and bore the strongest air of probability for two reasons ; the first, that Castlecomer was only about the same distance from the town as Killcomney (about nine miles from whence we were threatened in the morning), and the second and weightiest by far was, that the collieries were always remarkable for being stocked with most turbulent, desperate fighting-men, who could scarcely ever assemble at any public place or fair or market without fighting with each other, with or without cause, as if it was only to keep their hands in practice ; in short, the very name of the colliers was terrific.

These reasons made it appear highly probable, nay, almost certain, the town would be attacked, and we lay down with the most dreadful apprehensions of what would probably follow. Sleep, of course, kept far away from us and we listened with the most intense anxiety to try if we could hear any noise or shouting or drums beating to arms. After being a considerable time in this state of anxious suspense, we heard a large party of horsemen on the pavement coming up to the jail door and as the night was so very still, the noise seemed uncommonly great and to us most alarming.

They were halted just at the door, which greatly increased our terror, as we could not at all conjecture what their business could be, except they came for our execution; but, after a very considerable, and to us painful delay, they were marched on and when we were weary with watching and whispering our fears to each other, we were at length overpowered with sleep and got no further alarm till morning. Our conjectures of the colliers joining the rebels fortunately proved groundless, for they very wisely considered that it was a great deal safer for them to be handling the cudgel at home among each other and be dragging their coats after them in the fair of May to rise a fight, than to come to Carlow, to face powder and ball and bayonets; but, at any rate, as long as the rebels remained there, which was about two or three days and nights, we were kept in continual terror of our lives, while the trials and executions in the barrack-yard were going on with as much fury as ever, so that between both dangers we were every moment expecting destruction.

CHAPTER FOURTEEN

COURT-MARTIAL

To give anything like a regular account of the men that fell in these scenes of blood and terror would be quite out of my power after a lapse of forty-four years, and having nothing to assist me but memory alone, I may certainly be inaccurate in placing them in regular order as they suffered, and numbers of them I cannot think of at all ; but this much I can say, that of any of them I do mention I will relate the truth and nothing but the truth.

When this terrific storm had blown over, Major Dennis paid a second visit to the jail, to inspect and examine the prisoners. He was accompanied as before with Sam Carpenter, the magistrate, and a dragoon. They were all called in rotation from the jailer's list and when it came to my turn I went in, in doubt and uncertainty of what would be my fate, though I was quite certain that anything I said on my first examination could not be contradicted and that my conduct in endeavouring to prevent the outbreak of the people would stand the strictest scrutiny and would be all to my credit and that there could not be a single violent act proved against me ; but, notwithstanding all this, the times were so dreadful that innocence itself did not always protect a man. As soon as the major's eye caught me, I bowed most profoundly and I perceived he did not view me with the same terrific scowl he did on the first day but quite the reverse and there was a considerable degree of softness in his voice but accompanied with great dignity, as he leaned towards me and said, " I have considered your case and I will give you your choice either to enlist with Captain Chestyn as a soldier in the Thirty-second Regiment of foot and go to the West Indies, or stand your trial by court-martial."

It would be hardly possible for words to place me in a more grievous dilemma than this announcement placed me, for from the rigid discipline that was kept up in the army at the time, where the private soldier was under the power and check of every man in power, from the colonel down to the lance-corporal, with the harassing duty of drills, guards and long marches (and this too upon slender nourishment), and worse than all, to be stripped naked for the most trifling fault or even mistake and tied to a post and lashed ten times worse than any one would lash a dog; these reflections, I say, gave me such a horror of the life of a soldier, that I would almost prefer instant death to it at the time, provided it was unaccompanied with torture. On the other hand, I knew it was a compliment from Major Dennis to give me any chance of my life at all, and it would be an offence to him if I refused it and that the triangles would surely be my portion next day if I did; so that between the two evils I was obliged to choose the least, and I replied, " Whatever you wish me to do, Major, I'll do."

"Answer the questions, sir!" said he, in an angry tone; " will you enlist in the Thirty-second Regiment of foot and go as a soldier to the West Indies?"

" I will, sir," was the instant reply.

" Very well," said he; " Mr. Carpenter there will attest you."

These words completely electrified me, for I thought I would be bound down that moment, never to get loose, but Carpenter fortunately interfered and said, " Oh, it's time enough; when we have more, they can be all attested together and you may go out now and send in such a person."

I obeyed his order with joy, though I hardly considered myself safe till I got out of the room, and after sending in the person wanting, I walked down to the yard, where I met some of my acquaintances and told them the agreement I had made. In a few minutes all the prisoners had the news and there was a general consultation on it and the unanimous opinion was that I had got off very well and had made a right good bargain of it and some even went so far as to wish they would be allowed to enlist, too, and when their turn came to be called in, actually applied to the major for his permission. The major who, I suppose, had considered that it was better to send men to the West Indies or Egypt or the Helder to fight, than to be taking their lives unnecessarily at home, very civilly granted their request and no men could be more rejoiced at their good fortune than they were, though to me it seemed only "getting out of the frying pan into the fire."

The recruiting-sergeant, Faulkner of the Thirty-second, now began to visit us. This man had already taken numbers of men away from the dreadful scenes that surrounded them, and as far as I could perceive, was a correct, honest man for his station in life and seemed to have the tenderest sympathy for the misfortunes of the people and his manner was so engaging that in a very short time about twenty-five of the prisoners, most of them young lads, took on with him as recruits and agreed to leave country and friends, probably for ever, and go with him to the West Indies, though in this they were disappointed, for, when all the men were mustered at Chatham, they were drafted into different regiments and some of them sent to the Helder, where about four thousand lay dead on the beach at the landing. But the trials and executions were going on with such fearful rapidity, that people were glad to make any exchange.

Sergeant Faulkner, according as they agreed to enlist, gave every man a shilling and at times sent out for beer to treat them but, for my part, I avoided them as much as I possibly could, my principal excuse being to get into a match of handball when he came. Faulkner took notice of this and one day, when he had beer brought in, he enquired particularly for me and wondered greatly how I kept away and never joined their party and sent one of the men for me. I bid the man tell him I was engaged and could not go, but the sergeant was a man too experienced in the ways of the world and too vigilant to let an inexperienced youngster, as I was, elude him, and he sent me back word that he wanted me on particular business and *should* see me, but that he would only detain me a few minutes and I might go back. There was no room for making farther delay and I was obliged to go on. As soon as I walked into the room, the sergeant received me in the most friendly manner and pressed me to drink with him and after the usual compliments had passed on both sides, " Why, I wonder," said he, " how you make so strange with us and keep away from us, as I understand you are to be one of our party."

" I really don't know how that is," said I.

" Why," said he, " haven't you agreed with Major Dennis to enlist ? "

" I have," said I.

" Oh, then, you are to be one of our party and I may as well give you a shilling."

" Oh, no," said I ; " for I have engaged with Major Dennis to enlist with Captain Chestyn and I cannot enlist with any one else."

" It is all the same," said he, " for I am enlisting for Captain Chestyn and it can make no difference whether you take it from me or from him."

" Oh, but it does," said I, " make a very great difference and you must bring me word from Major Dennis if I am to enlist with you, before I can do it."

" I believe," said he, drily, " I may as well tell him you don't intend to enlist at all."

" Tell him no such thing," said I, " for I don't say it ; but tell him to send me word or write me a note to enlist with you and I'll do it that moment."

Several of the persons present here took my part and said it was only fair that I should pay Major Dennis the compliment and told the sergeant to do as I directed, to which he very reluctantly assented, but he had very little time to do anything about it, for he enlisted men so fast in town that he had as much enlisted as he could well manage at once and was ready to march in half the time I expected.

The day was approaching that Sergeant Faulkner was to march away with his recruits and pretty late in the evening before it, the turnkey walked up to my room. I was after amusing myself with a few games of handball in the yard, at which I was very expert, and happened at the time to be in tolerably good spirits. He walked over to me with a countenance full of gloom, and foreboding something disastrous, and in a whisper asked me if I had heard anything.

"No," said I, starting, "have you?"

"By my word, I have," said he, "and I'm sorry for it; you didn't hear you're to go to Leighlin?"

"To Leighlin?" said I in amaze. "Ah, what would I be doing to Leighlin?"

"To be tried," said he.

"Oh, it's all nonsense!" said I; "sure I was in Leighlin before and there is nothing could be brought against me but what they know already, so there would be no use in a trial."

"They have fresh information against you," said he.

"No matter for that," said I; "all the men living can bring nothing fresh against me but what they know already."

"Well," said he, "I only tell you what I hear, but sure we'll soon know it all, and at any rate you are not to go with Faulkner, that I am certain of."

Here he walked out of the room, leaving me in a sea of trouble and doubts and perplexities and an uneasiness and alarm I could not get rid of. I continued in this state the whole night; and next morning there was considerable bustle with the recruits who were preparing to march, which they did shortly after breakfast, in the greatest spirits and joy at getting rid of such a den of destruction, and left me behind.

About one or two o'clock in the day, the far-famed Cornet Lowther of the Ninth Dragoons and a guard came up to the jail and I was called for. This officer was the chief actor at all the floggings and hangings and shootings in Leighlin

Bridge and was so violent in his temper that his very name was a terror in town and country. He was frequently in our shop before he went to Leighlin, where he dealt pretty largely, and as I always pleased him in the work he got done, he seemed to have a particular liking for me. As soon as I was called for, I walked out and the guard moved on with me. When we got some distance from the jail, Cornet Lowther ordered the guard to fall back and took me on with himself. When we advanced beyond their hearing, "Now, Farrell," said he, "there was never any man given in charge to me I think so bad of having anything to do with as you, but I cannot help it. If you were my brother, I must do my duty."

"Oh, I know that, sir," said I.

"But," he continued, "any indulgence in my power, so far as letting you see your friends before you go, you shall have."

To this offer I made no answer and he went on: "I suppose you'd have a wish to see your father and mother?"

"No, sir, I would not," was the reply.

"What! Not wish to see your father and mother! that is very strange, indeed! Why, I'm astonished! And what is your reason for not wishing to see them?"

"Oh, sir, they are in trouble enough already and I wouldn't wish to make them worse."

"Well, at any rate, sure you might go and see Mr. and Mrs. Fitzgerald."

"No, sir, I have just the same objection to see them; I don't wish to see any one belonging to me."

"Oh, very well," said he; "come on, there is a chaise getting ready and I'll send you on to Leighlin."

We then walked on to the inn, which was next door to my sister's house and as soon as the chaise was ready she walked out and asked permission from Cornet Lowther to go with me, but this request he refused point-blank but, with as much politeness as the case would admit, said it was totally out of his power, and turning to me said, "Come, Farrell, step into the chaise."

He then gave me in charge to a guard of the yeomen cavalry, who set off at a smart travelling pace.

As we travelled along, my mind was filled with a variety of conjectures as to what they might be going to do with me, for the times were so uncertain that men in power might do whatever they pleased and Cornet Lowther did not give me the least hint of what the business was; so that I could not know whether they were going to bring me to instant trial or instant execution or not. As we had but six Irish miles to go, we were soon at our journey's end and I was put into the guard-house, not the one I was in before, but into one next to the bridge.

It was a party of the Wicklow Militia had the guard at the time and as soon as I went in the sergeant, who seemed a man of long experience in military affairs, began to entertain his men with a variety of jokes at my expense. He told them of the variety of executions he attended and how expert he was at slipping the noose round their necks and the different articles of theirs he obtained when they were dead. "And I'll serve you the same way, my young lad, so don't be alarmed or have any ill will to me, for if I didn't do it, somebody else would, and you know it's all the same thing to you who does it; and that's a good hat you have and will answer me very well when I'm not on duty." His companions laughed heartily all the time and helped him on, by claiming whatever they fancied belonging to me. At length one of them took notice of my hair, which was long and tied, and called out, "Oh, Sergeant, look here; you didn't see the long hair he has. Why, he must be some great fellow entirely!"

"Show me," said the sergeant, looking over; "Oh, by the laws, he is. He is a general, I'll engage it, nothing less. Well, I never hung a general yet, but I'll try my hand on him, never fear."

"No, Sergeant," said another, "but I'll tell you what he was; he was a bloody rogue that was deceiving people, for he was a rebel in his heart and wore his hair long to pass for a loyalist."

This stroke of wit gained a shout of applause and they all agreed that he hit the mark exactly. During the whole time, I stood as motionless as a statue, for my mind was so absorbed in trouble and the danger I stood in was so great that their discourse made no more impression on me than if I was a statue and could not hear it. I sighed at times, no doubt, but never spoke a word. When the sergeant saw this, he dropped his jokes and began to ask me some serious questions in rather a compassionate and friendly tone, and told me not to mind what passed, that he was only joking but would be sorry to hurt my feelings. I replied to him in the most feeling respectful manner I could, in order to gain his sympathy and those of the guard, and I soon found I was pretty successful; for from that forward they all showed a kindly disposition to me.

The place now used as a guard-house had been a shop not more than about twelve feet square, with the door cut in the middle, as shop doors generally are, and opposite this door, when night came, I was put to lie down with some other prisoners on some very short and very dirty straw and without any covering, one half of the door being shut and the other open. As the weather was excessively warm, I did not feel much inconvenience from cold till the turn of the night when the dead cold damp did penetrate me considerably. As to sleep, I could not sleep much for when the guard saw the time past when there was any danger of interruption by a visit from officers, they commenced card-playing and then such a scene of cursing, swearing and disgusting obscenity followed as totally prevented prisoners from partaking of that luxury and drove sleep " on her downy pinions " far away to " light on lids unsullied with a tear."

Next morning, my sister was early in Leighlin Bridge, as my trial was to go on that day and as all the principal gentlemen of the county dealt at our shop and had large accounts with us, she had great interest. Accordingly she went to such of them as were in town, most earnestly soliciting them in my favour; but every one of them had this one uniform answer: "I am very sorry, Mrs. Fitzgerald, that it's not in my power to assist you. I can do nothing in it; it all rests with himself; he can save himself if he pleases. Let him give information instantly, as there is nothing else can save his life." Fortunately for me, Lieut. Butler of the Myshall Cavalry happened to be in Leighlin at the time. He was a Protestant gentleman, worth at the time about eight hundred pounds a year, and was a magistrate of the county and was a near relation to my mother, though I believe at the time he did not know it, as she was never in the habit of troubling rich relations and never had any occasion till the present time. When all failed with my sister, she went to Lieut. Butler as the last resource and told him her sad case and begged his assistance. His reply was just the same as the rest, that he could do nothing; that it was in my own power to save myself and if I did not do it I could blame no one. She was now driven to a most painful position, for she was one of the wealthiest women in Carlow and her husband held one of the most respectable establishments; still, it was mortifying to her to be compelled to introduce herself to him under such circumstances, but danger, dreadful danger, approached and all other forms and ceremonies were obliged to give way, and she replied at once, "Well, Mr. Butler, that unfortunate young man is a relation of yours."

"A relation of mine?" said he, staring with astonishment at her.

"Yes, sir, he is and Sergeant Cooke[1] can tell you the particulars, and my mother desired me tell you that, as he is the first of the family from Carlow that ever troubled you, she expects you will show what you can do."

It was but short notice he had to do anything, as my trial was to come on in about a couple of hours; but when a man is really intent on being a friend he may find ways of doing something, even in so short a time, and his subse-

---

[1] Sergeant Cooke was his first cousin and permanent sergeant in the corps with him and knew my mother's relationship to him well, as she frequently spent some time at his father's house in Garrahill, when both of them were very young.

quent conduct showed he made every exertion in his power, for when the members of the court-martial had met and I was ordered to be brought forward to trial, who to my great astonishment came for me but Lieut. Butler himself. Yes, he actually walked from the court-martial room bareheaded through the street and into the guard-house where I was; and instead of demanding a prisoner, he asked politely for Mr. Farrell and when one of the guard was drawing his bayonet to guard me on, he made a motion with his hand to stop him and said, " Put it up, I want no guard; I'll be accountable for him." There was no hesitation on the part of the guard and out we both walked side by side through the street. Yes, though I was under the denomination of a rebel and a Papist, he was not afraid or ashamed to own me publicly and protect me like a man with all the influence he had, which makes a former observation of mine hold good; that no matter what a man's creed or station may be, a good man will be a good man in any case.

As soon as I walked into the court-martial room and bowed to the court, I espied two gentlemen from Carlow, Surgeon Johnson and Mr. Byrne, the attorney, sitting in a window convenient and viewing me very intently, which indeed hurted my feelings considerably, to stand in the position of a rebel before gentlemen that knew me so well, but just at the moment who walked into the room but the far-famed Cornet Lowther with his military coat of the highest scarlet colour and his bloated face an exact match for it, which plainly told of the large potations he had taken of strong wine.

As soon as he walked in, all eyes were turned from me to him and one of the gentlemen of the court-martial called out, " Cornet Lowther, what did Colonel Mahon say to you when he was sending this prisoner here with you? " The Cornet was just going to answer, when another member said, " I think Cornet Lowther should be sworn, gentlemen; it's a serious matter and I think he should be sworn." As I thought the question quite unimportant and as I was quite certain Cornet Lowther was my friend and would speak in my favour, I replied, "Oh, gentlemen, his word is sufficient."

"Not at all, not at all," said another; "he must be sworn."

Accordingly the Book was handed to him; and, being sworn in due form, the same question was put: "Cornet Lowther, what did Colonel Mahon say to you, when he was sending this prisoner here with you?"

"He told me," said he, "to bring him here and have him served as Kelly[1] and the rest of them were served, as he is one of the most hardened fellows he ever met in his life."

Nothing could exceed my astonishment at this dreadful declaration and I shouted out at the very top of my voice, "Oh, gentlemen, I never spoke a word to Colonel Mahon in my life!"

This reply completely confused Lowther and when I got him down I kept him so by repeating it: "I never spoke a word to Colonel Mahon in my life, gentlemen!"

"Well, that's what he said to me. That's all I have to do with it," said he, hanging down his head and sneaking out of the room like a rogue. I don't think I ever saw a fellow in my life more embarrassed and (though bad the part he acted) I actually pitied him.

I am not certain whether the charge on which I was to be tried was read before he entered the room or afterwards; but it certainly was a most dreadful one. It charged me with having joined the Society of United Irishmen with intent to overturn the government and with several other things of so alarming and dangerous a nature (but which I cannot now recollect) that when the preamble was ended and I was called on to plead guilty or not guilty, I imagined if I did the former I would be sent out for immediate execution, without any further trial, and as my giving myself up was an acknowledgement of having joined the United Men I could not or did not want to deny it, and I replied, "Guilty, except to the intention."

Here Colonel Rochfort, who presided, leaned over towards

---

[1] Kelly was hanged and beheaded.

me and in a friendly tone said, " I think it would be better for you to plead guilty generally." Though I did not at all agree with this opinion of Colonel Rochfort's, and though I could not at all see how it could by any possibility be better for me to plead guilty to such dreadful charges, still, as he offered me his advice as a compliment, and as joined to my very youthful appearance it might tend to show my innocence and credulity and how easily I might have been led by designing persons into the predicament in which I then stood, I replied, though very reluctantly, " Well, I do, sir."

The trial then proceeded and Jack Kelly was the first witness called in against me ; a man that would not prosecute me only he was flogged and cut to it at the triangles, and the man who actually denied knowing me at all, the first time I was brought to Leighlin. He was a fine, clever, handsome, young man and a member of our county committee and walked in with a bold unembarrassed air. As soon as he was sworn, he was asked if he knew the prisoner. He replied in the affirmative.

" Did you ever know him to be a United Irishman ? "

" I did."

" Did you ever see him transact any business as a United Irishman ? "

" I did."

" Where ? Let us know where and how."

" I saw him at different meetings on committee."

" Where ? "

" In Carlow."

" Had you any particular house of meeting there ? "

" We had ; we always met at Heydon's."

" Well, and when you met there, what were you generally doing ; was your business very important ? "

" No, indeed, I cannot say it was. The most important part, I think, was electing members to go to Dublin, to form the provincial committee."

"And how was that done ? "

" Oh, quite easy ; there was no difficulty at all in it ; every one of the members was handed a slip of paper and he wrote the man's name on it he thought was fittest to be sent and then they were all put into a hat and drawn out one by one and read, and whoever had most votes was elected as first member and so on for the second and third, for there were only three members sent to Dublin."

" Was the prisoner present at the elections."

" He was."

" Did he make himself very conspicuous and active on such occasions ? "

" He did not; but quite the reverse; he left that to others and did not interfere scarce at all."

" But, then, you saw him write on the slips of paper and put them into the hat ? "

" Oh, yes, we all did that."

" Did any other thing very particular occur at these meetings ? "

" I recollect nothing very particular, except once that we were called on by the provincial committee to send up all the money we could."

" Well, and did you send it ? "

" We did."

" How much might it be ? "

"About seventy pounds."

"And what use was this money applied to ? "

" I don't know; we never could learn what was done with it."

Here the examination of this witness ended and I was asked if I wished to ask him any question, but as he said as little as ever he could against me, I knew that my asking him questions might only make him say more, which would perhaps injure instead of serving me; so I replied in the negative and he was told he might retire.

The next witness that walked in was a farmer and was also a member of our county committee. This man was quite grey-headed and from his appearance could not, I think, want much of sixty and formed a striking contrast to my boyish appearance, for, though I was twenty-six years of age at the time, I might reasonably pass for nineteen or twenty. I knew the man well, as I met him several times on committee and he was the very man that brought forward a case I mentioned before, where an unfortunate man who had committed some error against the laws of the United Irishmen was tried by his neighbours, but the matter coming to a scrutiny, some for putting him to death and others against it, that it was agreed at last to get the opinion of the county committee on it, which should be decisive on the point and in which case my interference saved the man's life. He was a man that piqued himself on his great cunning and worldly wisdom and the profound skill with which he could colour any story by making wrong appear right or right wrong. He was not flogged at the triangles to make him turn informer, but his two sons were prisoners at the time, and as he had the interest of a certain great man it was agreed upon between them that he should give information to save their lives, but as he well knew the danger an informer stood in at the time, it was managed so that no one should be taken on his evidence, but that he should swear against someone that was prisoner beforehand, as it would make less noise in the country and he would have a better chance of escaping the vengeance visited on informers at the time. I forbear mentioning his name, as he had many honest people belonging to him, whose feelings I would not willingly wound; and if time has thrown a veil over his crime, let it remain so, it would do me no good at this time of life to remove it, and I will only add that I was the very person that afterwards saved his life and kept him out of an untimely grave from which all his cunning could not have saved him, but for me.

When this man walked into the room, he was sworn in due form, and on the same questions being put to him as were put to Kelly, he affected great reluctance to give answers and laboured mightily to show how tender he wished to be to me, but I saw (or at least thought I saw) his hypocrisy so plain that I both pitied and despised the fellow. When his evidence closed, I was asked if I had any question to put.

"No, gentlemen," said I, " I have not. What they've sworn is the truth. I have nothing to say."

Someone then called out and said, " Well, what defence can you make ? "

" None, gentlemen, I have none to make."

" None ! " said Colonel Rochfort, starting ; " none ! recollect yourself. You stand in a most dangerous position and whatever you have to say, say it at once. You haven't a moment to lose ; you've heard what was proved against you."

These observations of the Colonel's aroused me and I replied, " I have nothing to say, sir, but what I said before."

" Well, and what is that ? " said he. " Speak it now. Now is your time."

" Why, sir, that I did all in my power to cause arms to be given up when ordered by the government and had also given up myself and had got a protection. Here it is, gentlemen," said I (putting my hand in my pocket and opening it out).

One of the members of the court took it from me and read it aloud as follows :

> William Farrell of the Town of Carlow delivered me one bayonet. I give him protection, being impowered by Colonel Mahon commanding the 9th Dragoons. Wm. Farrell also took the Oath of Allegiance before me, same time, Carlow, May 27th, 1798.
>
> HDR. FITZMAURICE,
1st Lieut. C.K.Cy.

That was my protection from Mr. Fitzmaurice, and it may seem strange that to this very day, after a lapse of forty years, I have the same paper still and in a tolerable state of preservation.

As soon as it was read, it was handed to others who knew Mr. Fitzmaurice's handwriting, to try if it was genuine, and when all were satisfied on this head, one of them called out, " Did you tell Mr. Fitzmaurice how deeply you were implicated, when he gave you this protection ? "

" I did not, sir, he didn't ask me."

"Ah, there it is." said he (shaking his head as if intimating that that made it useless): " and then, as to your saying you caused arms to be given up, we have nothing for that but your own bare word."

" Oh, I declare it to God I did," said I.

"Ah, but we'd want something more than that."

" Why, Rogers can tell it, sir," said I; " he knows it."

" Then you should have brought Rogers here and let him prove it before us."

" I did not know what I was coming here for, sir, but he knows it and I'm sure he won't deny it."

" Besides," said he, " the arms given up were so very trifling, they're not worth speaking of."

" I did my best, sir; they were all I could get and if every one had done as much, there would have been no bloodshed since."

Here Colonel Rochfort motioned me towards him and in a very kind friendly tone said, " Now you see what has been proved against you and the dangerous position you stand in; it is not in our power to do anything for you and I would advise you to write immediately to Colonel Mahon and state your case to him, as he alone can do anything for you. I will order you the use of pen, ink and paper, and you shall have time till his answer comes, so do not lose a moment."

This advice of Colonel Rochfort's was to me most extraordinary, as it was only a few minutes before I informed the Court I had never spoken a word to Colonel Mahon in my life, and I replied, "As I never had the honour of speaking to Colonel Mahon, sir, I would be at a loss how to address him. I could not do it; I wouldn't know what to say to him."

" Well, then, you may write to Major Dennis if you please. His interference with Colonel Mahon might serve you, particularly as you say you agreed with him to enlist."

This advice, though more agreeable than the first, still did not satisfy me and I replied again, " I think, sir, if you would allow me to write to Mr. Fitzmaurice, as it was to him I gave myself up and got his protection, that it would answer me best."

"Well then, write to both of them" said he; "both to Major Dennis and Mr. Fitzmaurice and lose no time; and do you (said he to one of the guard who came in) allow him the use of pen, ink and paper."

I bowed immediately to the court and went off with the guard.

CHAPTER FIFTEEN

THE GALLOWS' STEPS

WHEN I arrived at the guard-house, I had a most formidable task before me, viz. to write a letter on life and death, and the more formidable as I was never in the habit of writing letters and of course knew little or nothing about it. However, I got pen, ink and paper; but how to begin or put anything in the shape of a letter I could not think, if I got the universe for it. Twenty times I took up the pen and laid it down again, without being able to do anything, until at last I was actually going to give it up as impossible; but the dread of death and the hope of life urged me on, for the sentence of death was not formally pronounced on me, yet it was clearly enough intimated to me. I took the pen up again and the plan occurred to me to write down every suitable idea as it arose in my mind and afterwards to arrange them in the best way I could in the form of a letter. This plan gave me the greatest relief; for, when I once began to write, a deal of the difficulty vanished, and after long struggling and perseverance I formed the following letter:

Guard room, Leighlin Bridge,

June, 1798.

Lieutenant Fitzmaurice.

SIR,—My unhappy situation, I hope, will excuse me for again troubling you for your interference in my favour. My trial came on this day at Leighlin Bridge. The charges against me were having joined the United Irishmen with intent to overturn the Constitution. I pleaded guilty except to the intention, the real design not having been made known to me. I then made known to the Court how I had acted; that I had done all in my power to cause arms to be given up, when ordered by Government and had also given up myself and had got a protection, which I produced. The Court, however, did not think me entitled to its benefit, as I did not make a full acknowledgement of my crime at the time I received it (a thing you did not require, and indeed, so great was my confusion at the time, I would scarcely have had it in my power to make it known to you) but humanely advised me to write to you that you might speak to Colonel Mahon and that a letter from him would be requisite against tomorrow, as on his answer my fate would chiefly depend. And now, Lieut., if you are so kind as to interfere for me, I shall be entirely at your disposal, to send me to any part of the world you think proper, and shall acknowledge myself indebted for your goodness to me while I live.

I am, &c.,

W. F.

As soon as I had this laborious task performed (and many a pang it cost me) I had to write another to Major Dennis which I cannot now recollect, but it was comparatively easy, compared with the first, and was nearly the same, with a few alterations, and as soon as both were completed, I sent them in all haste to the post, with many a doubt and many a fear for their success.

As soon as Mr. Fitzmaurice received my letter and read it over, he got into a violent passion with Colonel Rochfort because, as he commanded his troop of cavalry and was President of my court-martial, he said he should have honoured his protection and have acquitted me. He then went to every gentleman of his acquaintance and told them the story and showed them my letter, which he praised to the skies as being one of the best he ever saw. He even showed it to Mr. Arundel Best, who, though he was one of the most violent men against rebels at the time, read it over and praised it as much as Mr. Fitzmaurice himself and concluded with a great oath : " By the ——, it would be a pity to hang him." But it seems he could make no impression at all on Colonel Mahon, from whom he derived his authority to give protections to do anything for me, and he declared openly that, if they pushed the law to its rigour against me, he would never draw a sword as an officer or act as a magistrate again. He then wrote a letter to Major Cornwall, requesting in the most earnest manner that he would support his honour, by assisting me in every way he could, and enclosed my letter in it. He did this through resentment to Colonel Rochfort, though he commanded his own troop, for not assisting and honouring his protection in the first instance. Major Cornwall, at the time, was a man in great power and in ordinary cases might have gone to the guard-house and turned out any prisoner he pleased with perfect impunity, but in this case he had two great obstacles to prevent him, viz. Colonel Rochfort, who had the chief command in Leighlin Bridge, and Colonel Mahon who had the chief command in Carlow, so that it was too critical a case for him to touch. My sister was the bearer of the letter to him and as soon as he read it and mine, which it enclosed, " My dear Mrs. Fitzgerald," said he, " this is a case I could not at all meddle in and I am surprised how Mr. Fitzmaurice would call on me to do it. He should have called on Colonel Mahon or Colonel Rochfort, who have the power, but for my part I have not, and I think this letter of your brother's, that he praises so much, will be more injury to him than service; for it is quite plain to anyone that sees it that he is not the very simple innocent person we took him to be, but a man of intelligence, that knew well what he was doing, and my advice to you is to get him to give information at once and save himself, as I know of no other way to do it."

In the meantime, as soon as ever my trial was over, my friend, Lieutenant Butler, went in all haste to my sister, to tell her the news.

" My dear Mrs. Fitzgerald," said he, " your brother's trial is over and has all gone against him, but I'll tell you what you must do; General Asgill is to be in Borris to-day, and you must take a chaise and drive off there like lightning, and I will take my horse and I'll be there as soon as you, and I'll try what I can do with the General. There is nothing else to save his life, so don't delay a moment."

In the shortest possible time, my sister was ready and set off as directed, and Lieut. Butler was as good as his word; he was in Borris to the minute with her, but to the sad disappointment of both of them, General Asgill was not there. As soon as Lieutenant Butler found that: " Now, my dear Mrs. Fitzgerald," said he, " I can go no farther with you. You must go on to Kilkenny and see General Asgill yourself and give him a memorial of your case, as it is the only hope you have."

Away she flew, as fast as she possibly could, and when she got to Kilkenny she got a friend to go with her to the General's lodgings, but it was Lady Asgill she met there, as he was not within, himself. This disappointment, however, proved a providential one, for Lady Asgill received her with the greatest possible kindness, and on hearing her lamentable story, became so interested for her that she promised to use all her influence to serve her. In the course of some time the General returned and Lady Asgill herself opened the case to him in the most moving manner she possibly could, but he positively refused to interfere in it and said it was a case that did not come at all within his power, and that he could not on any account meddle with it and that the law should take its course. Lady Asgill, however, would not be put off, and continued to importune him in the most earnest manner, while he continued inflexible to all her entreaties and would not give way in the least, till at length she exclaimed, "Ah, General Asgill, you must not be too inexorable, particularly in the case of a boy, a young lad, quite a young lad, and you may recollect very well, when you were a young lad yourself, you were just in the very same predicament in America, and that it was a lady there saved your life, and upon my honour I'll save his life and you must do it."

I forgot to mention that, before my sister set off in quest of General Asgill, she called on me at the guard-house to let me know all about it. She also brought me a prayer-book and opening the page headed " Preparation for Death," desired to make the best use I could of it till she came back, and to think of nothing else.

This was indeed a gloomy and an awful day. There were eight or nine prisoners in the guard-house at the time. One of them was an old sailor of the name of Mathias Lannan, who was shot through the hand at Castlecomer, and he protested most solemnly he was not engaged in the battle but was shot by accident; he was given to understand there was no hope at all of his life. All the rest were in the most dreadful apprehension of what would happen in the evening and everyone endeavouring to make the best preparation he could. How swiftly do the minutes fly, as Death approaches. How awful to the young man in the prime of life to look into an untimely grave, particularly if it is opened for himself. But who can depict the horror of the alarmed soul that must fly far beyond the grave, when it is forced unprepared into a boundless region, perhaps of never-ending misery. Ah, it would be well for the world if those legislators whose laws force their fellow-men to the grave and eternity, often for trivial crimes, could stand a few hours in our situation and feel the consequences of them. Those jurors, too, who are so flippant at finding a verdict of " guilty," and those judges who as flippantly pass sentence of death would be greatly benefitted by it and saved from the horrible remorse of finding a man guilty and condemning him to death one day, and the day after his execution finding out that he was perfectly innocent of the crime, a thing that has happened over and over in Carlow and other places these forty years.

The friends of the prisoners during the day were coming with whatever assistance or consolation they could, Lannan's friends in particular, one of whom I think was his wife. He had them all employed abroad in striving to make interest for him, but they all failed; time was wanting, but time he would not get. When he found this, he began to settle his affairs as fast as possible, which took a considerable share of time, as he had a great deal of directions to give them and the evening was advancing fast by the time he had done. The military were in and out, the whole time, and bringing various stories of the executions that were to take place in the evening. Sometimes five were to die, sometimes four, sometimes three, but who they were to be they could not tell; they only knew of one to a certainty and that one was Lannan; but as these reports were calculated to alarm everyone else, we all went on our knees to make the best preparation we could, for no clergyman would be allowed to assist us. The time drew nigher and nigher and there was great apprehension on my account, as there was no sign at all of my sister returning; but just at the critical moment, as the drum was beating to arms to collect the soldiers, the chaise came rolling like thunder over the bridge and one of the men who was next the window cried out, "That's your sister!"

We continued still our prayers, uncertain of what news she brought, when in a few minutes afterwards Mr. John Whelan, the attorney and a Protestant gentleman, stepped lightly up the stairs and beckoned to me and when I went over to him, he said in a very low whisper, "Your sister is after coming. Your life is saved; don't mention my name. Keep it to yourself." He then disappeared in an instant and I went over and kneeled down again with the rest to return God thanks, and carefully concealed the news I heard from them, lest it should add to their affliction.

In a very short time the soldiers were all assembled at the market-square and, as soon as they were, there was a guard sent down to us and, when they walked in, one of them called for Lannan and, as soon as he answered, "Now," said his comrade, "march on."

"Oh no," said he, "I want another."

"You do not," said the comrade, "you were only bid to bring one."

"But I say I do," said he: "I know my orders."

"Well, and who do you want?" said the comrade.

"I'll soon tell you," said he, looking at a paper, "William Farrell I want; that's the man I want."

Here an altercation ensued between them, one insisting I was to go and the other insisting I was not, until at last the one that was for it carried the point and I was walked out along with Lannan. As soon as we came to the market-place, I observed that the soldiers formed a hollow oblong, with a triangle near one end and about ten or a dozen officers in a group near the other. Lannan and I were marched up quite close to the triangle. As soon as we came up, there was no delay made but Cornet Lowther came smartly to us and pulling out a large piece of paper read sentence of death with awful solemnity on Lannan. As soon as he concluded, Lannan was commencing to make something like a defence but Cornet Lowther cut him short in an instant, saying "Rebels like you, caught in open arms, are allowed no defence; tie him up."

"Well," said Lannan, as they put the noose on his neck, "the Lord have mercy on my soul."

They then helped him up on a high stool that was at hand and pitched him off in an instant. Cornet Lowther then called me by name and read sentence of death on me in the same awful manner as he had done before. As soon as he did so, I clapped my hat up to my eyes, that I should not witness the convulsive struggles of the man that was dying before me and endeavoured to pray as well as I could, but in a little time some one came behind me and called me by name. I turned round and perceived it was Mr. Robert Rochfort, brother to the Colonel. "Now, Farrell," said he, "you have only a few minutes to live and I would recommend it to you to give whatever information is in your power in order to put a stop to this unfortunate rebellion you were engaged in; it is the only atonement you can make to your country for all the blood that has been spilled and you should do it to the utmost extent in your power, as it may be a means of stopping it altogether, preventing more bloodshed and restoring peace."

"I wish it was in my power to stop it, sir," said I; "when I was at liberty I done my best to stop it and would do it again if I could, but I could give no information now that would be of the least use."

"That is very strange," said he, turning away. I immediately turned round and resumed my position as before and in a minute or two he came back and called me again. "Now, Farrell," said he, "from the deep manner you were implicated in this business, you must of course, have a very extensive knowledge of men concerned in it, and the gentlemen have taken your case into consideration and wish to show you all the lenity they can and they have now commissioned me to tell you that if you give information against these men, so as they may be brought to justice, you shall have your life. Don't be led away with the foolish notion that it would be any discredit to you to give information against them; it would be the very reverse. You would serve your country by helping to restore peace and you would serve the wretched people themselves because the sooner the rebellion was put down the sooner bloodshed would cease; and if you were apprehensive of any danger from them you should be protected at the Castle or sent abroad to any place you wished."

"It is not in my power, sir," said I, "to give information against anyone."

"Impossible," said he, staring at me.

"Not at all, sir,"

"How so?"

"Why, sir, there has been ten men put to death for the one I ever knew in it; I never made any acquaintance with them except the men I met on committee and they are every one gone."

He returned to the officers with this information, but came back immediately to let me know that if I gave information only against one, against one responsible man, I would be liberated; but he received the same answer and when all efforts failed, Cornet Lowther came forward again and called me. As soon as I turned round to him, he opened up a large paper and read aloud the charges against me for which I was tried and sentenced to death—"but, your case having been laid before General Asgill," said he, "he has thought proper to change the sentence of death that stood against you to transportation for fourteen years." Here I bowed respectfully to him and everyone present expressed their approbation. "But," he continued, "you are so hardened a villain that I will go myself to General Asgill and make him withdraw his respite from you and I'll send you to hell to-morrow evening." The guard was then ordered to take me back to the guard-house and thus ended that evening's tragedy.

CHAPTER SIXTEEN

DISCORDS OF LIBERTY

IT will no doubt seem strange to any person living in the present 'times how any prisoner could be treated in the manner I was; I underwent four most extraordinary changes in one day. I was under sentence of death in the morning; I received General Asgill's respite from death in the evening and afterwards was brought to the place of execution, where sentence of death was again passed on me; and after standing in that perilous state as long as they pleased, was respited again. If a man was under sentence of death for murder or robbery and obtained a respite, he would not be treated in the manner I was. He would not be brought out before the public to be exposed and tortured as I was, it would be handed to him compassionately in his cell. But it was a Ninety-Eight transaction, where such wholesale scenes of blood and torture were performed as I hope will never disgrace any part of the world again. But the whole aim of it was to compel me to give information; to compel me to degrade myself first and then they would give me my life when it would be no use to me. But if they even did succeed in compelling me, I would gladly know what use it could be to them. Nothing that I know of, except the malignant gratification of sowing spite and malice and revenge among as many families of the Irish race as they possibly could; spilling their blood first and making them spill each other's blood after.

It may require some explanation, as blame might seem to attach to Colonel Rochfort, who was chief in command in Leighlin Bridge and to whom, of course, my sister delivered General Asgill's respite, to know why, after having received it, he allowed the transaction to take place at all.

I shall endeavour to give it. It was the custom in the barrack-yard of Carlow, when any victim was torturing at the triangle who had fortitude enough while his blood was streaming under the cat-o'-nine-tails to hold out firmly against being an informer, it was customary in such moments for some powerful overgrown savage to come with a rough-rider's cutting whip in his hand and cut the wretched victim with all his force; and if he succeeded by excessive torture to force from him what the more lenient cat-o'-nine-tails could not do, it was considered a very high point of honour he had attained and he was considered a doubly loyal man, and no one present dare attempt to stop the brute under penalty of being considered a disloyal man himself and running a chance of being disgraced or punished. Cornet Lowther was head hangman in Leighlin Bridge at the time and his name went far and near as a paragon of loyalty, and I suppose he considered that if he could compel me to give information, after receiving General Asgill's respite, it would add a more glorious laurel to his brow than adorned it before, and that as he was such a noted fiery ruffian, Colonel Rochfort did not think it prudent or safe to thwart him or stop him. But the Colonel himself was not cruel and he used his utmost endeavours to stop that curse of Ireland, the United Irish system (as he ought to do), still he was a good kind landlord and a father to the people in his neighbourhood, whom he advised for their good, but who (unfortunately for themselves) did not take his advice, and in my first examination before him he never used as much as a harsh word to me nor ever even hinted that I should give information, so that I put the whole transaction to Lowther's account, who shortly after died miserable.

After I was sent back to the guard-house, my sister met Major Cornwall, who treated her with the greatest courtesy and cordiality. "My dear Mrs. Fitzgerald," said he, shaking both her hands, "I wish you joy of your brother's escape. He got off better than I expected and as to his going away for fourteen years, it will not be much. He will be a young man when it is over, and it may be all for the better. It may be the best thing ever happened him, as he is a lad of some abilities. He will be sent to Duncannon immediately and I will give him a letter to the Governor of the Fort, who is a friend of mine, to whom I will recommend him in the strongest manner I possibly can, and he may come to be a prosperous man yet. You will want to get him some check shirts, but you need not give him any money except barely what he may want for refreshment on the road and you must also take his watch from him, as any property of that kind, no matter how much or how valuable, would be all taken from him the instant he went inside the Fort."

She returned him all the thanks in her power and when she brought me the information I was highly pleased with it. In short if I had been made a present of fifty pounds, it would not have pleased me as much as the news of transportation, as I was fairly tired of the country; for, if ever there was hell upon earth it was in Ireland at the time, particularly in Carlow, which I wished never again to see, but I kept this carefully to myself, for fear if it was known I considered it a favour it would not be granted me. I remained in this state of suspense for some days, wishing every hour to be sent off, when to my utmost horror I was told I should go back again to Carlow and remain there in jail till more prisoners were ready to go with me. There was no use in unavailing complaints or murmurs and I did not do either. I submitted in silence, and while I was pondering on the matter, Cornet Lowther sent a message to inform me he was waiting for me at the market-place. I stepped out quickly and went to him and found he had a guard ready mounted of Dragoons and Yeomen Cavalry. The moment he saw me, his countenance blazed with indignation and turning to the guard he said, with venom in his voice, "Here, guard, what way have you to take this fellow with you?"

"I don't know, sir, except he walks it," was the reply.

"Oh," said another, "that would never do. It would delay us too long if he walked."

Another called out, "There is a chaise from Carlow gone to the Royal Oak and will be back immediately; we can put him in that."

"A chaise!" said Lowther (ready to burst with passion); "a chaise, indeed, for such a rebel, such a scoundrel as that! He shall get no chaise, and if it was here now I wouldn't let him in it. Let the fellow walk; or, there, throw him up behind one of you on the horse, it is too good for him."

The plan seemed really laid beforehand and a completer plan to break a man's neck could hardly be devised. The very tallest horse (I believe) in the regiment was ready with an uncommon high pack, behind the dragoon that rode him, and up on this pack I was lifted by someone. When I got on the pack, I had no way whatever of keeping a firm seat as I would in a saddle, but, though very high I was and unsteady, I did not feel much apprehension of danger, as I did not expect there was any foul play going to be used, but that the dragoon would move on at the usual steady regular pace; but I was very quickly undeceived, for the word was no sooner given to go on than he suddenly reined up the horse and stuck the spurs in him with such force that he leaped and plunged and kicked so violently that it was wonderful how he could keep his feet on the large slippery pavement or how I could keep my seat on the pack. And I suppose I could not, only I slipped my hand in his waist belt and held him fast, for he actually raised the horse as high as if he was going over leaps.

When the villain saw this and that he could not throw me, he stopped the horse and called out to me to let go the belt. I did let him go, thinking it was a kind of truce he was making and that he would not persist any farther and would go on quietly, but the instant I let him go he dashed on the horse (if possible) more violent than at first, until at last he was pitched out of his seat off the saddle and I was pitched off the pack into his place, so that he was in danger of falling only I laid hold of him and kept him up, proving myself a better horseman than he was, for I was well accustomed to riding before this and it was very lucky for myself; otherwise, I suppose, he would have gratified Cornet Lowther by giving me a fall, perhaps killing me on the pavement of Leighlin Bridge.

When we both had adjusted ourselves in our respective seats, he dashed on again but not with near the violence he did at first, for he seemed to have got completely ashamed of his performance and at last he stopped the horse, when he found he could not throw me, and called out, " Get off, I'll carry you no further." As we were a considerable distance before the rest, I would not comply and though he shouted again and again, I would not; for it occurred to me that, if I did get down, he or somebody else might give out I was running away, and make it a pretence for shooting me dead on the spot; and if this happened the story would be good and there would be no more about it than if it was a sparrow was shot.

One of the Wicklow Militia now came running up and when he heard the dragoon ordering me to get down, " Come," said he, " I'll lift you down."

" Oh, no, thank you," said I, " I can get down myself "; for I was afraid to trust him, lest he was an enemy; he might, in pretending to lift me down, throw me under the horse's feet and have me trampled on, so I loosed myself as well as I could on the pack and then, laying both my hands on it, I made a spring (for I was uncommonly active at the time) and though high up I was, I came down safely on my feet and a good way out of the range of the horse. This showed evidently that the villain did not intend to carry me at all from the beginning but to knock my brains out if he could, for the horse would have carried me quietly if he'd let him.

By this time the whole guard was up about me and had a general consultation to know how they would bring me on. At length, one of Sir Richard Butler's Cavalry volunteered to carry me, and I was put behind him on a good strong-looking horse, but he would not carry double but went backward till he nearly backed in to the door of a house and the rider had to shout out in great alarm to me to get off; this, however, was no trouble to me, for I was off in a twinkling. They then held another consultation and another man of the same corps offered his service, and I was put up behind him and we moved on at a regular travelling gait.

When we got on about a mile some of them espied a boy a good distance off riding a horse towards a house in the fields and immediately shouted out they would go on and press the horse. This was done out of sheer wickedness for they didn't want the horse at all, as the one I was on was going very well and the man that owned him was making no complaint and we had only about five miles to travel. The moment the shout was raised, four or five of them set off in full gallop and were not long capturing the boy and horse, whom they brought back in triumph. When they came up with the miserable old *gearran*, I was ordered to change places, which I did very reluctantly, as I saw plainly it was only a plan to annoy and ill-treat me; but there was no help for it, but silence. A murmur, or the sign of a murmur, would only make the matter worse, by gratifying their malice. I therefore never spoke a word, but mounted the poor horse according to their directions, and the boy was put up behind me. When all was ready, one of them shouted out that they should set off in all haste to Carlow, as there was some most important reason for it, and in an instant away we all set in full gallop. This was no trouble at all to me, as I was well accustomed to riding and would just as soon be in a gallop as a walk, were it not that two of the dragoons kept quite close to me, striking the poor horse with the flats of their swords to make him go fast, until after a long run it occurred to me that perhaps the ruffians might, instead of giving the horse the flat, give myself a touch of the edge and pretend it was a mistake, and in a moment I steered him suddenly to the other side of the road and left them there.

We did not go much farther, when some one in the rere shouted and hallooed us to halt, and to my surprise they did slacken their pace and when he came nearer to us he proved to be a man of the name of Curran, a private in Colonel Rochfort's Cavalry. When he came more within hearing, " What sort of usage is this," said he, in a loud angry tone, " to give a prisoner ? I say he is no man nor no soldier that would do it. If a man is a prisoner, let him be used like a prisoner. And," said he, raising his voice to the very highest pitch, " by the —— " (swearing a great oath), " I won't allow any man to do it."

I thought immediately that some of the burning loyal Orangemen present would have taken up his challenge or have made him prisoner for his audacity, but I was never more surprised than to see every one of the sneaking rascals (even the loyal Orange Dragoons) hang their heads and quail before him. There was no more talk of any hurry to Carlow and we went on as quiet as possible ; and besides that, when the old horse cooled after the heat of galloping we had, he grew so stiff that he was hardly able to lift a leg, and I had neither whip nor switch to drive him but was obliged to keep working him with the bridle every step of the road, endeavouring to keep him up to a walk, which with the heavy cold I was labouring under fatigued me most dreadfully. This, to be sure, was bad enough but to be hawked through the town in this manner was like death and daggers to me.

However, done it should be and accordingly they brought me through Burrin Street at the same snail's pace, to be gaped at and stared at by everyone, then through the public market-place and on through Tullow Street. When we got about the middle of this street, I saw Colonel Mahon and Captain Beevor waiting to see us pass, and when we came up, I took off my hat and gave a low salute to Colonel Mahon, which he returned most kindly, but Beevor called out in a loud voice, " Take him to the barrack and hang him up ! " This was an unncesssary insult, as I was under the rule of transportation, but the times were so dreadful and such sport made of men's lives that I could not be certain but his order would be put in execution, till I was landed in the jail.

When I got there, it was, as usual, one scene of terror and mourning, and as my acquaintances were all anxious to know my adventures, they watched every opportunity to come to me and with fearful whispers and mournful looks to make their enquiries. I gratified them as well as I could and in return received the most horrible accounts of the butcheries and cutting-up of human flesh that took place in my absence, so that I grieved over and over again that I had not the good fortune to be transported at once from Leighlin Bridge.

In this manner I continued grieving and wishing to be sent away from this second hell, for if there was a second hell on earth it was Carlow at the time, for though great were the numbers that were sacrificed, the executions still continued; though I cannot at present recollect the one-half of them, still, there was one so very striking that it is quite fresh in my memory.

The victim was a man of the name of Donahoe, who worked as a labouring man for Mr. Kinsella of Tathrush or Ratoath, I am not certain which. He was an active able-looking man, about five feet ten inches high, and was taken to the barrack-yard and cut up in the usual way. When he was coming back, there were but two armed men guarding him and they were quite sufficient, as it was certain death if a man attempted to escape; for, if the shots of the guard missed him, the first Orangeman he met might stab or shoot him without any ceremony, and no relative or friend dare shelter him, on pain of being used the same way. I happened to be peeping through an end window at the time and observed them advancing at a regular pace and I also observed a rough-rider of the 9th Dragoons named Hall, with a heavy cutting whip, such as rough-riders use, in his hand; and a respectable townsman walking close after them. From their manner of walking it struck me as if something extraordinary was likely to happen, and I kept my eye closely on them as, from the position I was in (being a side view from an end window), they could not see me. Just as unfortunate Donahoe raised his foot on the high step of the door going in, Hall stepped forward and drew the cutting whip and struck him with all his force on the face.

The instant I saw it, I drew in my head and hid, for fear I should be seen, but honest Supple, the turnkey, rebuked him severely for the scandalous action. In the course of a little time, I walked down carelessly to the yard, as if I knew nothing of it, to try what state the unfortunate man was in, as I supposed he should be in the deepest agony from the blow he received; but what was my astonishment when I saw him talking to Supple and the prisoners, as coolly as if he did not get it at all or did not feel it, though he was cut from his ear to his mouth.

"Did you see that?" said Supple to me.

"See what?" said I.

"What that vagabond, Hall, the rough-rider, did to this unfortunate man. But I told him it was a rascally action and that he ought to be ashamed of it. What a pity it was there was not some good fellow coming by that would have knocked the scoundrel down; and only I daren't do it, I'd give it to him, though he may report me for what I said, but he may go to the ——, himself and his report. Now, I think worse of that one blow than all he got on his back."

Poor Donahoe stood by the whole time without making the least complaint, just as if he had been stupid or insensible.

It is now nearly time to close this afflicting narration and I should do so with the trials of Mr. McDonald and the Rev. Mr. Travers.

Mr. McDonald, as I said before, was one of the wealthiest men in town. He kept an extensive brewery and every one that had a dealing with him prospered, for he took a pleasure in promoting their interest in every way he could, while to the poor his charities were boundless. He was a very large, full man, not less (I suppose) than eighteen stone weight, and at the time should (I think) be about fifty years of age. He was a man of most extensive information, deep solid judgment, and the happiest manner of expressing himself on any subject, being kind, cheerful and good-humoured, so much so that everyone was happy in his company. When the United test was proposed to him, he objected to the part of it that mentioned something about the representation of the people in parliament (which I forget at present)—and a most fortunate objection it was for himself—and only took the part that related to forming a brotherhood of affection with Irishmen of all religious persuasions, as he said it was his wish to see all mankind united and happy. The Rev. Mr. Travers, as I have mentioned, was famed for his hospitality to everyone, particularly to soldiers and their families, when passing the way, and they were both brought together to the Barrack to be tried.

On Mr. McDonald's trial it was the very man that importuned him to join the United business (I will not mention his name) that meanly came forward to prosecute him. Mr. McDonald did not deny the charge but questioned him sharply on the great number of times he importuned him before he would consent to join it at all, also on his only taking part of the oath that had nothing criminal in it and of his decided objection to the part that had, and appealing to the court said, " Gentlemen, if my life is to be taken for that, God's will be done ; I am resigned to the will of God."

On being questioned about giving money to the support of rebels, he denied it and said, " Gentlemen, my hand and my purse were always open to any fellow creature in distress and I never made any distinction about creed between Catholic and Protestant and never asked them what they meant to do with any relief I gave them."

While the trial was thus going on, two honest Protestants went into the barrack to plead for the good man ; one was the Widow Murrow, who kept a public house in Barrack Street and was well known to all the officers. Her husband was smith and farrier to some regiment of horse, and when he died, left her and a family of small children unprovided for. Mr. McDonald came to hear of it and immediately took them under his protection by taking a house for them and stocking it with every requisite for carrying on business, which enabled the widow to live and rear her family decently. This honest woman went straight to Major Dennis, and throwing herself on her knees, related the whole story to him and most earnestly entreated and supplicated him to shew mercy to the good man that showed so much goodness and kindness to her and her family. The other was a poor man of the name of Bob Johnson who earned his bread for many years by hard labour, as a porter in the Meat Market but who, when he became old and feeble, was befriended by Mr. McDonald. This man, though poor, had a high independent spirit and a greater gift of speech than usually falls to men in his station. He also went into the barrack and spoke loudly and boldly in his behalf to the officers but, notwithstanding all this, and the trivial crime against him, the trial lasted till late in the evening. The Rev. Mr. Travers was prosecuted by an unfortunate man whom the sole dread of the horrible tortures that were inflicted at the time turned into an informer. This miserable man (I will not mention his name either) proved that Mr. Travers was sent as delegate from the United Irishmen to Dublin; that he was to proceed from Dublin to Belfast and from Belfast to France. When he came to this point, Mr. Travers burst out into a loud fit of laughter (as there was not the least probability of truth in it) but Major Dennis checked instantly for it and said, " I'm surprised, Mr. Travers, how you could behave with such levity on such an awful occasion and your very life at stake." " I couldn't help it, Major Dennis, for in all conscience it was far enough to send me to Dublin, or even to Belfast, but to send me all the way to France goes beyond the bounds of all probability."

Various were the rumours flying during these trials, sometimes favourable, sometimes unfavourable to the prisoners, but the last of all very late in the evening was that Mr. McDonald was surely to die and it was uncertain whether Mr. Travers was to die or not. In consequence of this report, a considerable number of the townspeople went up to the barrack and crowded about the court-martial room in full expectation of seeing the execution. In some time afterwards, the door opened and the prisoners and all the officers came out. As soon as we saw it, we went on our knees to pray for our fellow-sufferers but, to our surprise, the crowd remained near the door. This, we thought, was only while preparations were making for the sad tragedy.

At length they began to move and came at a quick pace down the middle of the yard and we watched the gate closely, as we were sure that would be the place of execution, as we had no expectation of their lives being spared but to our surprise and joy the gate opened and they came forward to the jail. When they came upstairs, they were greatly excited and proceeded to tell the whole story of the trial and sentence. "I am to leave the country," said Mr. McDonald, "but I got a choice of the place out of these dominions and I go to America, but I have got leave to dispose of my property to the best advantage I can. I barely escaped with my life, but, glory be to God, I was resigned to His Holy and Divine Will in any case. I had the prayers and good wishes of the poor and Mrs. Murrow and poor Bob Johnson pleaded nobly for me. Why, its consoling to a man to see such gratitude displayed on such an occasion." Mr. Travers was also to be sent out of the country, but as he did not know to what place he was destined he was not very communicative.

Mr. McDonald began at once to make his arrangements for disposing of his property, and Mr. Greene of Killkey was the purchaser. Mr. Greene behaved very honourably, for he took no advantage of Mr. McDonald's situation to cheapen things down too much below their value, but allowed him a reasonable value for everything and Mr. McDonald, on his part, gave him all the instructions and information in his power for conducting the business of the brewery in the most advantageous manner, so that both parties were mutually satisfied. The settling of so weighty a business took a considerable time, I may say ten or twelve days, but all being ready Mr. McDonald made no delay, but quitted his native country, taking with him, it was supposed, about three thousand pounds which, with his wife and two children, he brought safe to New York, accompanied with the prayers and blessings and regrets of everyone that knew him, both rich and poor.

I was all this time expecting the order in for sending me away, as there was nothing I longed for more, as I was completely disgusted with the country and tired of being in it. But, glory be to God, I was like one born to be always disappointed in any thing I wished for in this world. I made different enquiries about it and was informed the government were only waiting for a certain number to send together, that it was nearly complete, and that I might expect the order every day.

Just at this very time, General Henniker came to the country and took a house about a mile from the town. He was a kind good gentleman and set about pacifying the country as fast as he could. He also gave protections to everyone that applied for them, so as they were not guilty of the crimes of murder or house-burning. The whole country was cheered and delighted with him and his fame went far and wide. In the midst of all this joy, my good friend Mr. Harry Rudkin, a Protestant gentleman and a magistrate, went to my sister and told her all the good things General Henniker was doing and told her he thought it would be very well done to have a memorial drawn up and sent to him in my favour, and if it did succeed, I might probably be liberated.

"Do you think, sir," said she, " we would have any chance ? "

" Let us try it," said he, " let us try it ; sure, worse than lose we can't, and if you choose, I will draw the memorial and sign it myself and get as many as I can to sign it with me, so as you go with it and present it to the General yourself."

This proposal was joyfully accepted by my poor sister and as soon as everything was ready, she lost no time but went at once to the general and with the most humble entreaties presented it. General Henneker behaved with that kindness and courtesy for which he was so famed but told her, as it was an important case, he should take time to consider it, but would in a few days let her have an answer.

In the meantime every nerve was strained by my friends (and I had many of them at the time and not one enemy), who from the good character I bore, with the exception of having joined that unfortunate business, and even from the way I behaved, while connected with it, in endeavouring to prevail on the people to accept the terms offered them to give up the sort of things called arms which they had and so save themselves from destruction, that General Henniker to my great mortification ordered me to be instantly set at liberty.

It may seem strange that one confined so long in a prison as I was, amidst such scenes of bloodshed, death and destruction, and that had so many hair-breadth escapes of his life, should regret being restored to his liberty, but it really and truly was the case. I was young and active at the time and was full of the hope that if I was transported to some distant colony I might have a chance of lighting on some good fortune that I never could expect at home, as the name of rebel precluded me from every expectation of receiving support in any business from men in power, as long as a man having the name of a loyalist could be had to oppose me. Besides, the majority of my friends and acquaintances were either put to death or obliged to fly with their lives. The town was drugged with Orange soldiery and militia, who could treat supposed rebels or Papists with every scorn and contempt they pleased, so that, of course, it could not but be extremely painful, and dangerous too, for one of my character to live in such a town.

While everything for my liberation was arranged (which was bail of five hundred pounds that I should remain in the town for twelve months) my poor sister, Mrs. Fitzgerald, quite rejoiced and full of heart and spirits came for me to the jail. She little knew the state of my mind for I never gave her the least idea of it—it would have been quite useless—and I walked along with her through the town quite grave and thoughtful, bearing the appearance (as really was the case) of one more sorry than glad of his liberation. Everything seemed gloomy and dull too. There were no people to be seen as usual in the streets, with their pleasant joke and hearty laugh, but all had the appearance of gloom and terror and only very few had the hardihood to peep out of their doors as I passed.

When I came to the public market-place, it was just the same way quite deserted to what it used to be and out of the scanty number that remained there was only one man to notice me, and that was Mr. McCormack, the victualler, who walked over boldly and shook hands with me and in the kindest and friendliest terms expressed his gratification at seeing me liberated. I was rather apprehensive, indeed, that the good honest-hearted man might be marked out and put to trouble for seeming to know me at all, but he was a man of resolution that would not be easily daunted and was quite competent to defend himself if attacked, as he never was implicated in that unfortunate business.

When I came up convenient to our own house, my good friend Mrs. Carey, the lady that saved me from being flogged in Leighlin Bridge, was looking out of the dining-room window and saluted me over and over, and with every expression of kindness welcomed me home. I took off my hat and returned her compliments, bowing most profoundly, and walked in but nothing could remove the gloom that possessed my mind, not that I had any apprehension of poverty or want, as my brother-in-law was one of the wealthiest men in town at the time, with the whole trade of the town and county and great part of the neighbouring counties, and I was considered one of the best workmen for the times we lived in; but it was mortifying to be confined to a town where, whichever way I went, I was certain of meeting enemies who would mark and watch me and wish perhaps for any opportunity or pretence of laying hold of me again. This, I thought, was mortifying enough, and so it was, but I had no idea at the time of seeing our parliament, that great bulwark of our rights and liberties, made prisoner and brought in chains to England, and the countless and enormous robberies that would be perpetrated on the country for want of that guardian, nor the destruction of every kind of trade by the wholesale introduction of English goods in every line of business (particularly my own) until the country, from being industrious and wealthy, presented one appalling scene of idleness (for want of work) and misery and starvation. I had no idea of this, or that I would live to see our own prosperous trade completely gone and my rich friends dead and buried, after living for years without any trade on the wealth they made in other times, and finally myself after seeing all gone and reduced to the want of a shilling in my native town, until my good God, that always protected me in every danger, afforded me shelter from the storms of the world by placing me, in the 64th year of my age, as gate-keeper to the Lunatic Asylum. I had no idea, I say, of all this. If I had, I would have gone as far as a ship could sail or the sun shine, before I would have stood to be a witness of it.

I have been now forty-five melancholy years suffering with my suffering country but, glory be to God Almighty, I have lived to see the time when one single Irishman has given the great robber of the world (shameless, dishonoured, treacherous England) an emetic that will make her disgorge part at least of her enormous plunder of my country and compel her to give back that inestimable treasure, our parliament, again—I say part only, because of the unnumbered thousands she sent to their graves by the pitchcaps, the triangle, the gibbet, those burned to death in houses and worse than all, if possible, the countless thousands she has sent to death by the slow silent process of yearly starvation and the various distempers arising from it; these cannot be given back and must only stand in horrible array against her, till the dreadful day, be it far or near, when the Lord Himself shall visit the hideous, bloated culprit for them.

A new era (thank God) has opened for my long-suffering country. Her great champion, the renowned benefactor of the human race, has been released from prison, where he was incarcerated for his fearless and powerful advocacy of the rights of suffering mankind. He has stripped the shameless, villainous ministry of England naked and exposed them to the scorn and derision of the world, and to the descendants of the kings and princes of Ireland he has given the hope that, from being the poor persecuted hewers of wood and drawers of water, they may be restored to the rights of freemen. They have had a long, long night of the most degrading and miserable slavery, and I cannot say but they richly deserved it; for when they had the whole power and authority of the country in their own hands, they used it badly. They were all blood-relations, for the crown would not be put on the head of any man appointed king until his genealogist first traced his family regularly back to Milesius. They were all one religion, and notwithstanding all this and that they were owners of the finest and most plentiful island in the world, they could not or would not live in peace with each other. The king of Munster should fight with the king of Connaught, until numbers of the finest men in the world were killed on both sides, and in like manner the king of Leinster should fight the king of Ulster, and all perhaps for some trifling dispute that twelve peaceable men could settle amicably over a good dinner and a few dozen of wine. But peaceable men were despised in these fighting times. No matter how kind as a husband or father, or hospitable as a friend, a man might be, all was nothing if he was not a fire-eater. And no matter how many bad qualities the other might have, all were excused, if he was but a fighting-man. The breed of these fighting-men was kept up as carefully as the breed of game-cocks and from their earliest years they were impressed with the notions of supporting their honour by fighting, no matter whether right or wrong; and to such a pitch did these notions carry them, when they came to be men, that if they heard of a man of courage and action within any reasonable distance of them, a man one of them never saw and of course never gave him any provocation, it was considered a most high point of honour to make a long journey purposely to challenge him and try (as it was called) which was the best man. Thus, from the king to the basket-boys, all were fighters. I have read Irish history with as much attention as I could and I could not discover any other public crime to charge them with, and this public crime notwithstanding, all their noble qualities (I have no doubt) was the very crime that brought down the severe chastisement on them they have so many centuries endured. If it was not so, how could the insignificant handful of English that came to invade the country have any chance of subduing so warlike a people? It would have been impossible.

But as I said before, a new era has opened for my long-suffering country. We are to have no more fighters. Our great leader has discovered the grand secret, that moral means alone is capable of effecting a revolution that cannon and bayonets would fail in, and that the descendants of Adam would be much happier in cultivating the mild arts of peace and good-will with their fellow creatures, than in fighting pitched battles and spilling their blood.

I do not mean however to say or to insinuate that wars at times are not just and necessary, although I believe they are very rarely so. But such a war as was carried on by the great Brian Boroimhe, to expel from his country a horde of barbarians and robbers, who had taken possession of it and were inflicting the most revolting persecutions on its inhabitants, such as war for such a purpose deserves all the encomiums that were ever passed on it or ever will be. It is also just and necessary, if a man's house or person be attacked by robbers, to defend both against them by every means in his power.

CHAPTER SEVENTEEN

LAST GLANCES

THERE was another action performed in the year Ninety-Eight which, though it did not happen in this county, and though I did not intend to mention the doings of any other, still, from its peculiar character, it would be a pity to have lost. The action I mean was one performed at a place called Prosperous in the County Kildare, the particulars of which have been carefully suppressed by any writer I have met with on the subject, and even the verbal accounts of it, by persons from that part of the country, were very deficient in that respect, and it was only by mere accident I had them from a man that actually fought in the battle and was brother to the hero that commanded.

It is true the Battle of Prosperous was publicly spoken of with the burning of the barrack which contained a Company of the Cork Militia, a large body of armed yeomen, and all the armed loyalists of the surrounding country, commanded by the celebrated and far-famed Captain Swayne of burning pitch-cap, triangle and gibbet notoriety; but I always imagined that this barrack was some thatched house in the town with other houses attached to it, and that it was by setting them on fire the barrack was destroyed, as I never imagined that a party of countrymen, no matter how great their number, dare attempt so strong a position by any other means. I was quite mistaken. The barrack stood by itself and was a large strong house that had been the residence of some nobleman or gentleman, and this very circumstance of its strength probably aided the enterprise, for it made Swayne so confident of his power that he ravaged the country without mercy, putting pitch-caps on the people's heads and setting them on fire for mere merriment, besides flogging, hanging, burning houses, terrifying or destroying every unfortunate person that came in his way.

But this was not all. His cup was not yet full. He had one step more to take and he took it. He went into the chapel on Sunday, at the very time the Rev. Mr. Higgins, a venerable old gentleman, was celebrating Mass. He no less than walked up on the altar. He made a speech to the people ordering them at their peril to bring in their arms to him in a certain time, and turning to the venerable priest, he said, "And if you don't have it done, I'll pour boiling lead down your throat."

Nothing could show in a clearer or stronger light the degree of terror and alarm the people were under than this shocking transaction. Had it been in other times that such a man was guilty of such profanation, his life probably would have been the forfeit, but on this most grievous occasion not a man dared so much as to murmur a complaint, so much were they in dread of the tortures inflicted by this terrible man. Great, however, as his power and the terror of his name was, he never dreamed or imagined when he went on the altar of God to make a speech and threaten His mild and saintly servant, that it was his own last speech he was making and that he never would see the rising of another morning sun.

The people after prayers dispersed in sullen and silent indignation, whispering their wrongs and insults and breathing vengeance at any hazard. A meeting was called that night, at which Doctor Esmond, who was their Colonel, attended. He made a speech to them and repeated all their wrongs and sufferings, particularly the unpardonable insult that had been inflicted on them that day in the person of their priest and in the House of God, and that it was the duty of every man to come forward and attack their enemies and either die like men or get satisfaction, and that he would be the first man himself in leading them on in any danger that might happen. This was agreed to in a moment but just as he was going to proceed, Captain Farrell stepped forward and cried out, " No, sir, you shall not lead on the men to-night. If anything happened you, we would be all ruined. You would be more loss than us all. But this man here (mentioning the name) and I will lead on the men, for go you shall not."

This being agreed on, the Doctor gave him up the command and Swayne's pass-word, which he had obtained.

Captain Farrell immediately drew out from the people and said, " Now, my friends, it is not numbers I want, but men. Any man here that is willing to fight and die for his country, let him come forward and join me. I want no other and I will have no other. Every one else may go home, I do not want them."

The selection was soon made for very few dared to go on the perilous adventure as it was a game of life or death that was to be played. As soon as he had them ready, he gave Doctor Esmond his advice not to leave the spot he was in till he heard from him, and then marched on, ordering his men to observe the strictest silence.

Captain Swayne, on his part, though he had no apprehension of any attack on his strong post from any party of terrified countrymen with pitch-forks in their hands (for what better were pikes?) still did not neglect the necessary precautions used against an enemy but had sentinels out in the proper directions to give the alarm if any should approach. Captain Farrell and his men, on the other hand, marched on silently and when challenged by the first sentinel gave the pass-word, closed on him, and dispatched him at once and took his arms and ammunition. They did the same to every sentinel they met, till they came to the guard-house, which was convenient to the garrison and in which were confined about twenty prisoners, who were to suffer death next day. They rushed in like a torrent, surprised and killed every man of the guard, took their arms and ammunition also and liberated the prisoners.

They had now a large supply of arms and ammunition, which were carefully and silently distributed to the men best qualified to use them and who were placed in the most advantageous positions, but the important work of all was still to be performed. The garrison itself was still to be attacked. Captain Farrell went boldly up to the door, accompanied by a man about six feet four inches high and one of the strongest men in Ireland. This man was a smith by trade and had an enormous sledge on his shoulder. When they came up to the door, "Now," said he to the Captain in a whisper, " if I don't put in that door the second blow, do you run with your life."

He then wound the sledge round his head and the very first blow he knocked the door in pieces. The noise of the blow was so great that like a warning gun it alarmed the whole town. The soldiers were up in an instant in their shirts and Captain Farrell as promptly rushed in through the breach and ran upstairs into Swayne's room, who was just after jumping out of bed and was in the act of taking down a fusee that was up over the chimney-piece, when Captain Farrell struck him to the ground and left him a lifeless corpse on the floor.

Thus fell the sanguinary tyrant of a hundred murders and a hundred burnings and the audacious profaner of the House of God. As soon as this exploit was performed, the Captain hastily retreated downstairs, and having plenty of straw and help at hand, he set fire to the stairs, which completely cut off the retreat of the soldiers and yeomen who nevertheless continued to fire with the most fierce determination, but which was returned with equal ardour by the assailants. The fire, however, was advancing terrifically to end the combat, until at length they were obliged to leap out of the windows to escape the flames. This, however, was only flying death one way to meet it another, for as fast as they came down, they were met and killed by those below, till out of the whole garrison only about three escaped. While the battle was going on, one of the assailant party, a fellow of the name of Phil Mite (afterwards the notorious informer) got so terrified that he ran away as fast as he could to Doctor Esmond, and told him that Captain Farrell and the whole party were killed and warned him to make his escape as speedily as possible. Doctor Esmond, having no doubt of the story, did retreat into Naas where he was made prisoner and lost his life for his credulity.

When the battle was over, the Captain led his men on to various engagements during the rebellion, in every one of which he uniformly displayed the same skill as a general and the same courage as a soldier, being always victorious. Times at length began to wear a more peaceable aspect and he found means at last to open a correspondence with the General commanding the district, from whom he obtained permission to leave the country. Everything being arranged, he set sail for America, where he arrived safe but did not survive very long.

The various fatigues he went through, I suppose, were instrumental in bringing him to a premature grave, but he had the happiness of laying his bones in the land of liberty. May he rest in peace. Amen.

The people of Prosperous and its vicinity were so overjoyed at the destruction of Swayne and his myrmidons, that they had a song composed in honour of it, which I heard sung by the Captain's brother. I just recollect the first verse, which was as follows :

Air : *The Woods are cutting*
The twenty-fourth of May as Phoebus was adorning,
Our boys got under arms, Prosperous to invade ;
By Captain Farrell's orders, heart and hand we marched
And in the town we halted and set it in a blaze.
Where red-hot balls were flying, groans of soldiers dying,
Flames to the skies were rising and Swayne expired there.
To retreat our Colonel ordered, still we never faltered,
But killed, wounded and slaughtered and won the battle there.

It does not, to be sure, chime very harmoniously, like the measure of first-rate poetry, but with that exception it conveyed the sense of the transaction forcibly and quite to the taste of the enthusiastic people it was intended for.

I did imagine I was done with the horrible affairs of Carlow and that I had related as much of its butcheries as would be sufficient to satiate the most craving appetite for blood and slaughter, but I forgot one case, a pitiable case that should not be forgot and that I shall not let be forgot, as it tends to show the small value set on men's lives in those days of wholesale destruction.

It was the case of Mr. Patrick Hackett of Graigue, Carlow. This man, who was never a United Irishman and who, of course, considered himself safe from any information, was taken on suspicion. He was a man nearly six feet high and apparently of great bodily strength, but like Sterne's Uncle Toby he would not hurt the hair of a fly's head. He was one of the wealthiest men where he lived, being extensive in the grocery and spirit trade, and also kept a porter and punch house and had what is usually called a houseful of children. Wherever he went, to funeral or any other public meeting, he was always "King of the Gregory," for if there was twenty in company he invariably treated them all. In short, he had the esteem of everyone, rich and poor, and a child might play with honest Paddy Hackett, as he was familiarly called.

This man and myself were taken and put into jail on the same day, and at night the place was so thronged with prisoners who had previously occupied all the beds that we and three others had to lie down in our clothes on a shakedown of straw that was laid on the boards for us and covered with some pieces of old blankets to cover us, which done well enough, as we had something else to think of besides an easy bed. In the course of a few days, Hackett's friends, who were using all their interest for him, prevailed so far as to cause Major Dennis to come to the jail to investigate the matter, as they loudly proclaimed his innocence and the great hardship of keeping a man confined from his business and family who had committed no crime, and if anything was alleged against him, either to have it brought forward and tried at once or have him liberated. At this interview, Major Dennis questioned Hackett with the most searching scrutiny as to whether he had any connection with the United system, which he positively denied and said he was ready then or would be ready at any time to stand his trial if any crime of the kind could be brought against him, because he was certain there could not. At length Major

Dennis brought the matter to a conclusion in his usual awful manner with the following words: "Now, tell me the truth and nothing else, for if I find you out in anything, I'll show you no mercy," Hackett replied promptly and firmly, "And if you do, I'll ask no mercy from you." Upon the whole of the matter, as there was no information whatever against the man, he was liberated and sent home to his family.

He had been at home only about a week, when a trial came on in the barrack at which some unfortunate man, who had been flogged and cut to it, mentioned that a meeting was held in Hackett's house. The instant it was mentioned, Major Dennis fastened on it but as a company of people going in to drink punch or porter could not bring guilt on Hackett, he was asked if Hackett was the person who attended and brought them drink and if he took any part in their proceedings. He replied that he did bring them drink but did not sit down in the company, but stood and spoke to them and heard their conversation while he stayed. He was then asked if he was not considered a United Irishman would he be allowed to stand and hear their conversation. He said he thought not and for his part he had no doubt of his being one. This was considered sufficient and a guard was instantly ordered to go and bring him prisoner. There was no difficulty at all in finding him, for though he had time enough to make an escape if he was conscious of guilt, still he never left the neighbourhood and of course was made prisoner without delay and brought to the barrack where, on that shadow of evidence (for I never could hear anything more), he was in the course of about one hour hanged up in the barrack-yard.

He was about forty years of age, in the full strength of manhood at the time and, were it not for that disaster might probably be a living man at the present time, 1844, in the eighty-fifth year of his age, with his children and grandchildren settled respectably and comfortably in the world; but his death brought ruin on them all. His wife struggled on for a few years, but as one misfortune never comes alone, the business, for want of his superintendence, declined from bad to worse, until at length the whole property being nearly gone, she died and left the children to struggle through a cold uncertain world as well as they could.

This was only one case out of thousands where destruction was wreaked on families living and families unborn, but bad as it was, it wasn't the worst case, for though honest Hackett lost his life, he left no stain or disgrace on his family, and his children to this day are respected on his account, but in cases where men were compelled by dint of most excruciating tortures to inform against others, it left an indelible stain on their families and caused the bitterest hate and animosity of the families of those informed against; so much so that an informer was watched and killed with nearly as little scruple as a mad dog. This was the most bitter ingredient, I believe, in the whole persecution and this was the chief reason why I have carefully abstained from mentioning the names of any unfortunate men that failed in the dreadful trial, that I should not add an additional pang to the sufferings of my bleeding country. Even of the men that swore against myself, I have mentioned the name of but one of them, and that same I would not do (for he was by far less to blame than the other) only his name was so public as an informer that himself or family could receive no additional harm from my mentioning it, though his blood was spilled at the triangles before he failed. But the other was a low mercenary schemer, who never got a lash, but who being under the wing of a man in power, nearly as mean a schemer as himself, got his life for swearing against one single person, which person I was. But this was not the worst of it, for after he had sworn against me on my trial, for which I was condemned to death, he had the unparalleled effrontery to go through the country and give out that it was I swore against him, and being a man of some property, and treating people copiously to drink, he succeeded for some time in staving off his fate. But the matter was closely sifted to the bottom and all his low cunning and dexterity would have been useless were it not for my interference to save him.

There were certain men in the country at the time who made a regular trade of shooting informers and these men actually came to town to buy powder to shoot him. A friend of mine happened to meet with them, to whom they told their business. As soon as he heard it, he came to me and told me the story. I was instantly struck with horror at the recital and begged and entreated him to stop it. He told me it was not in his power; that the men were so determined they would not be stopped by any man, for do it they would. I renewed my entreaties and told him it could do me no service; that I would not for the world wish such a thing should be done on my account and that it would be horrible to send an unfortunate man into his grave, perhaps in the midst of his sins. In short, I never begged so hard for my own life as I begged for his. But at all events I succeeded (thank God) in preventing his blood being spilled and the thought of it to this day is a gratification to me, for I could never have ease or peace if I had any concern, directly or indirectly, in such an affair. His own torture of mind and the grief of his family on his account were surely sufficient punishment for his crime without my interfering to steep them in additional tears and publish what they so much dreaded to the world.

I will just give one instance of the horror people had of any disgrace coming on their families in that way.

There was a respectable farmer's son made prisoner and brought into the barrack-yard. He was put to the torture but failed under the fiery trial and gave information. Notwithstanding this, they found some flaw against him and hanged him. His mother was in town the same day, and ran into a friend's house of mine like one frantic and asked for something to wet her mouth. As soon as she got it and recovered a little, " Oh," said she, " sure it is not the loss of my son I regret, but that it should be said he did anything dishonourable or brought any disgrace on me or my family."

In the persecution of Elizabeth, whom Englishmen are not ashamed to call their Queen, notwithstanding the horror of her birth, and whose like no nation under heaven ever had for a queen before and never will again, whom the shameless pack of scoundrels have the audacity to dignify with the title of " virgin," though they endeavour to lessen and degrade the Virgin Mother of God and swear (as I have been told) she has no more power in Heaven than any other saint (though they never tell us who brought them the news) ; in her horrible and cursed reign, which surpassed in malignity and cruelty any persecution ever set on foot by heathens against Christians, when the green corn was cut down to prevent Christians of having food, when their priests were hunted like wolves and the same price set on their heads, when there was such a sanguinary slaughter of a Christian people by Englishmen, when no ceremony need be used where an Irishman or Papist (as they designated Roman Catholics) was met but kill him as he was a mad dog or bird of prey, till they were obliged to fly with their lives into the woods and caverns, when the soldiers were brought up and divided into parties and ordered to scour the woods and not leave one of them alive ; in all this horrible barbarity of Christians upon Christians still, like the persecution of the heathen emperors, it was all open undisguised murder on one side and all unresisting suffering on the other. All the odium was on the remorseless murderers, all the pity for the innocent and unoffending sufferers. But in this horrible persecution, the odium, by a process of modern ingenuity quite unknown to the barbarians of antiquity, was dexterously thrown on the shoulders of the sufferers, because, forsooth, they had the unparalleled ingratitude to turn like the trampled worm upon the ancient and insatiable robbers of their country and to arm themselves (poor fools) with pitch-forks or pikes, which were nearly alike against the horse, foot and artillery of haughty and powerful England. Because they did this at the instigation of the knaves or fools that planned the system that brought such destruction on a simple unthinking people, Englishmen with their polished hypocrisy pretended the state was in mighty danger from such formidable assailants, though they were in possession of their plans all along and could have stopped them at any time with as much ease as the coachman can stop the horses when the bits are in their mouths and the reins in his hands.

They pretended, I say, that the state was in mighty danger and that they were compelled to make war upon them (though they actually forced them out to fight) thus throwing the whole blame on them and striving to clear themselves of any blame, and after destroying them as described, by throwing in the hellish ingredient of torturing them into informers against each other, left the country in such a state, for many years after, of murder, disgrace of families, broils and heart-breaks, as tore the peace of the people in pieces and set them persecuting each other after their enemies were glutted with it.

Elizabeth, the mercenary Englishmen's great idol, never knew how to act in this manner. She was a plain, bold, undisguised tyrant. She slaughtered openly and by wholesale, regardless of what the world would say. She did not want the world to call her merciful. She made no pretensions at all to it like that sneaking scoundrel, Pitt, who after deluging a peaceable country in blood and robbing it of everything valuable he could lay hold of, artfully threw the blame on the people and said it was all their own fault. Just as fairly might the midnight house-robber lay the blame on the unsuspecting inmates whom he had destroyed.

Elizabeth, in another respect, showed herself a great burglar; she cut down the green corn for the purpose of creating a famine and destroyed the people by starvation, but by so doing the corn was lost to everybody. Your modern murderers take quite a different course. They allow the corn to come to perfection; it is let to be reaped, stacked, threshed, cleaned and brought to the scales and then taken away in shiploads out of the country, leaving scarcely as much behind as is wanting for seed the ensuing year. But this is not all; the beef, mutton, pork, butter, aye, the very eggs and potatoes are drawn off as well as the corn until, as might be expected, a regular yearly famine ensues, by which more thousands of the hapless human race are starved, aye, actually starved to death, than ever there were in Elizabeth's awful time, but with this difference, that in Elizabeth's time they were starved publicly and by her orders and those of her ministry, and they bore the blame of it; but by the modern mode they are made to starve in thousands in silence and retirement and there is no blame laid to any one.

Verily, England, you have a most appalling account to settle on the score of murder and robbery, when you are called on; and called on you will be. The time is approaching rapidly, and all the statesmen you have, with all their dexterity, are not able to stop it.

Starvation in every country that had the misfortune of getting under your grip was the powerful and deadly engine you used. You compelled the people of India to purchase the food of their own country from you (that was only an intruder and a robber) with all the wealth they had; and when all their wealth was exhausted, you left them to die miserably of hunger in their own country. Yes, one of your own historians (I forget his name) has recorded it that there was the enormous number of three millions of human beings starved actually to death in one single year in India, after giving up all the gold and jewels and diamonds they possessed to save their lives. This was brought home in shiploads, to fill the boundless maw of England, while its unfortunate owners were lying in their graves. But did all this enormous wealth fill the maw of England? No, nor if the mines of Golconda were added to it, all would fail; England would swallow all and want more. Her pride and luxury were so boundless she seemed to think the whole world and its wealth were made solely for her use and certainly she spared neither force or fraud to grasp it.

But her race is run; her star is set; her sun is going down. Her trade, that she prided in so much, is gone, never to return, and the deadly doses of famine with which she drenched other countries have returned back with all their horror on herself, and her over-fed bloated population, who were almost surfeited with roast beef and plum pudding, are compelled by dire necessity to resort to the brewery yard to assuage the cravings of hunger by eating the very draff and grains. What is to follow, God only knows. As for my part, though I have been suffering under her penal laws from my cradle to the present hour, still I would not wish for her total destruction. Our merciful Lord Himself says He wills not the death of the sinner but rather that he should be converted and live; and why should I, who am a miserable transgressor, say anything else. I would indeed rejoice at England's conversion, but if she should unfortunately resist and not be converted, I would wish most earnestly she should lose the power of doing mischief. Farther than this I would not go, but leave the whole matter in the hands of the Almighty, beseeching Him to temper His justice with His mercy.

I have now done. What I began in May, 1832, I finish in February, 1845, being a space of nearly thirteen years, during which time I have been tossed round and round in the storms of this tempestuous and uncertain world and cast away on the dreary shores of poverty and distress and left almost as naked in the world as when I came into it. My sufferings and afflictions during the time have been great, until at last my bountiful, my merciful Creator was pleased in His boundless goodness to afford me a nook to rest in, where from time to time I have endeavoured to narrate the foregoing account. I have not written it through any intention of obtaining any empty fame this world might bestow, as it shall not be made public while I live, and after that it will be of little consequence to me what the world will say either of praise or censure.

I know very well I have not been able to dress it up in the style of modern writers, but if anyone after me shall choose to give it to the public in a more fashionable dress, he is heartily welcome and has my free leave and liberty to do so; and with the most sincere wishes for the happiness of the whole human race, particularly for that of my own long-suffering country, and in the seventy-third year of my age and on the 25th day of February, 1845, I lay down my pen.

Also available from
WOLFHOUND PRESS

Women & Irish History

Edited by
**Maryann Gialanella Valiulis
& Mary O'Dowd**

Written by leading researchers in the field, *Women & Irish History* examines the public role of women from the eighteenth through to the twentieth century. Many of the articles raise serious questions about the traditional historical assumption that women were passive agents in the political narrative. From philanthropic work in the 1700s to campaigning against de Valera's Constitution in 1937, Irish women have a long history of public action. Concentrating on women challenges historians to explore new definitions of State, nation, citizenship and power — issues that have been central to the debate on Irish history.

Moreover, this volume also examines the writing of women's history and suggests innovative ways in which it can contribute to a reinterpretation of Irish history. *Women & Irish History* demonstrates how our understanding of Irish historical experience changes with the inclusion of women.

This is a collection of essays in honour of Dr Margaret MacCurtain — feminist, historian, pioneer of women's history in Ireland, and a member of the Dominican order.

ISBN 0-86327-579-6

The Wolfhound Guide to Dublin Monuments

ELIZABETH HEALY

A tour of the memorials, statues, sculptures and corporate art that adorn the streets, squares and gardens of Ireland's capital. The perfect accessory for both visitor and native.

ISBN 0-86327 637 7

The Wolfhound Guide to The River Gods

ELIZABETH HEALY

Long celebrated in story and song, Ireland's rivers, together with the Atlantic Ocean, have also been immortalised in stone, and decorate the arches of James Gandon's Custom House in Dublin.

ISBN 0-86327-642-3

The Wolfhound Guide to the Irish Wolfhound

MURIEL MONSELL BREMNER

A treasure trove of all the things you ever wanted to know about this great dog's close identity with Ireland's history — along with lots of interesting things you never thought to ask.

ISBN 0-86327-636-9

The Wolfhound Guide to the Irish Harp Emblem

SÉAMUS Ó BRÓGÁIN

The story of one of the oldest and most distinctive national emblems in the world — now the familiar badge of the Irish state — is told here for the first time.

ISBN 0-86327-635-0

The Fenians in Context
Irish Politics & Society 1848–82
R.V. COMERFORD

'Comerford's book can be heartily recommended as by far the best one-volume analysis of the rise and progress of the Fenian movement in Ireland.'

Linen Hall Press

'Comerford has a snappy and informative style of writing. We are provided with much valuable social history. The Fenians are seen in the context of their time. No serious scholar of the period can ignore the book.'

The Irish Post

R.V. Comerford restores fenianism to its original context and explains it as a product of its own time. He examines Irish politics and society over a period that is often covered very unevenly, and provides the first sustained interpretation of many major political and social developments in the years 1848 to 1882.

The result is a new perspective not just on fenianism, but on the whole political and social history of mid-Victorian Ireland.

ISBN 0-86327-627-X

Irish Rebellions 1798–1916
An Illustrated History
HELEN LITTON

Using newspaper reports, speeches, eyewitness accounts and a mass of photographs and illustrative material, Helen Litton turns her accessible style to the major events of 1798, 1803, 1848, 1867 and 1916. She introduces us to the people involved — Wolfe Tone, Robert Emmet, Anne Devlin, Thomas Davis, James Stephens, Patrick Pearse.
She discusses the United Irishmen, the Young Irelanders, the Fenian Brotherhood, and the Easter Rising.

Irish Rebellions 1798–1916: An Illustrated History is a clear and informative survey of the most well-known rebellions of Irish history, from the United Irishmen of 1798 to the Irish Volunteers of 1916.

ISBN 0-86327-634-2

Also by Helen Litton:

The Irish Famine: An Illustrated History
'As a short intelligent overview of 1845–50, it will be hard to surpass.'
RTÉ Guide

The Irish Civil War: An Illustrated History
'The illustrations are many and fascinating, the text ... lucid and informative in its own right.'
The Irish Times

The Celts: An Illustrated History
'A small book on a big subject, which manages ... to pack in a huge amount of information.'
Sunday Tribune

Available from:
WOLFHOUND PRESS
68 Mountjoy Square
Dublin 1
Tel: (01) 874 0354
Fax: (01) 872 0207